MARCO POLO

SINGAPORE

www.marco-polo.com

THE TOURING APP

**shows you the way...
including routes and offline maps!**

FREE!

GET MORE OUT OF YOUR MARCO POLO GUIDE

IT'S AS SIMPLE AS THIS

1 go.marco-polo.com/sin

2 download and discover

GO!

WORKS OFFLINE!

6 INSIDER TIPS
Our top 15 Insider Tips

8 BEST OF...
- 🟢 Great places for free
- 🔵 Only in Singapore
- 🟠 And if it rains?
- 🟣 Relax and chill out

12 INTRODUCTION
Discover Singapore!

18 WHAT'S HOT
There are lots of new things to discover in Singapore

20 IN A NUTSHELL
Background information on Singapore

26 SIGHTSEEING
30 Colonial Quarter 39 Marina Bay 44 Chinatown & Singapore River 49 Little India/Arab Street/Kampong Glam 53 Harbourfront & Sentosa 58 In other districts 60 Further afield

62 FOOD & DRINK
Top culinary tips

SYMBOLS

INSIDER TIP	Insider Tip
★	Highlight
🟢🔵🟠🟣	Best of...
📷	Scenic view
🌿	Responsible travel: fair trade and ecology
(*)	Telephone numbers that are not toll-free

PRICE CATEGORIES HOTELS

Expensive	over 175 S$
Moderate	95–175 S$
Budget	under 95 S$

The prices are for two in a double room per night without breakfast

PRICE CATEGORIES RESTAURANTS

Expensive	over 48 S$
Moderate	24–48 S$
Budget	under 24 S$

The prices are for a starter, main course and non-alcoholic drink

4 On the cover: The amazing Marina Bay p. 39, 75 | A Michelin star food stall p. 66

CONTENTS

72 SHOPPING
For a fun-filled shopping spree!

82 ENTERTAINMENT
Where to go?

90 WHERE TO STAY
From low budget to luxury

98 DISCOVERY TOURS
98 Singapore at a glance
102 Katong – through time and cultures 105 Romantic Singapore 107 The Southern Ridges – city in a garden
110 Tiong Bahru – dip into the melting pot

114 TRAVEL WITH KIDS
Best things to do with kids

116 FESTIVALS & EVENTS
All dates at a glance

118 LINKS, BLOGS, APPS & MORE
Plan ahead and use on the go

120 TRAVEL TIPS
From A to Z

126 STREET ATLAS & INDEX

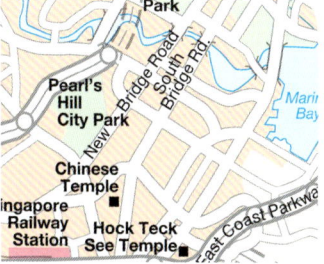

146 INDEX & CREDITS

148 DOS AND DON'TS!

DID YOU KNOW?
Time to chill → p. 46
Fit in the city → p. 55
Spotlight on sports → p. 61
Favourite eateries → p. 66
Local specialities → p. 70
For bookworms &
film buffs → p. 86
More than a good
night's sleep → p. 94
National holidays → p. 117

MAPS IN THE GUIDEBOOK
(128 A1) Page numbers and coordinates refer to the street atlas
(0) Site/address located off the map. Coordinates are also given for places that are not marked on the street atlas.

(*A–B 2–3*) Refers to the removable pull-out map
(*a–b 2–3*) Refers to the additional map on the removable pull-out map

INSIDE FRONT COVER:
The best Highlights

INSIDE BACK COVER:
Public transportation map

5

The best MARCO POLO Insider Tips

Our top 15 Insider Tips

INSIDER TIP Souvenirs with something to say
In *Naiise*, Singapore designers leave their literal mark on T-shirts and cushions → p. 81

INSIDER TIP Magic spirals
The wooden *Henderson Waves*, Singapore's highest pedestrian bridge, winds at treetop height through a jungle park → p. 57

INSIDER TIP Rock 'n' roll on the waterfront
Singaporean bands give free concerts when night falls at the weekend on the open-air stage in front of the *Esplanade Culture Centre* → p. 106

INSIDER TIP Occupied Singapore
Former *Old Ford Factory*: where cars once left the production line, you will gain deep insight into life in the city state during the time of the Japanese occupation
→ p. 60

INSIDER TIP Be amused with the drag queen
Kumar, Singapore's top drag queen, makes fun of everything her countrymen hold sacred. (S)he is definitely the only one who can get away with it → p. 89

INSIDER TIP Tasty Laksa
Singapore's traditional dish is much more than just noodle soup – and it tastes best at the *328 Katong Laksa* snack bar (photo right)
→ p. 71

INSIDER TIP Chinatown's best strip
Keong Saik Road is one of the most colourful streets in Asia. During the day, in the evening, but particularly at night! → p. 46

INSIDER TIP Bales of material
If you love fabrics, the thrill of the hunt, and haggling to your heart's content, make sure to visit the Chinese stores in *People's Park* (photo above) → p. 80

INSIDER TIP ▶ **Spinning round in circles**

A top-class Chinese restaurant, the *Prima Tower*, revolves above an old flour mill. The establishment's famous Peking duck tastes all the better in the 1960s ambience and with the spectacular view → **p. 66**

INSIDER TIP ▶ **Bargaining a must!**

Paradise for shopaholics: the traders at the *Queensway Shopping Centre* offer sports shoes and eyewear at special prices in their typically jam-packed Asian shops. Goods are original products by popular sports brands, 20 percent below city-centre prices → **p. 77**

INSIDER TIP ▶ **See and be seen**

Guaranteed to cause a stir! Send the folks back home your favourite photo of Singapore – as a *postage stamp*. But let the recipient in on the secret: make sure the little gem on your holiday greetings doesn't end up unnoticed in the waste paper basket → **p. 123**

INSIDER TIP ▶ **Putting your feet first**

There's nothing wrong with luxury spas. But sometimes you find the most invaluable experts behind no-frills façades. *Health Step* is a simple but absolutely wonderful place for authentic foot reflex zone massage → **p. 46**

INSIDER TIP ▶ **Peace at last**

Stuff a few black leaves in the pot, pour some boiling water on top and away you go? How uncivilised! The tea ceremony at *Tea Chapter* offers you so much more than a hot drink → **p. 64**

INSIDER TIP ▶ **Mosque with a lean**

Hajjah Fatimah Mosque was built by a woman. Pretty and pretty skew → **p. 51**

INSIDER TIP ▶ **Hippest lane**

Hip, hipper, *Haji Lane*: it's small, it's fine and a mecca for anyone looking for hot clothes, spicy food and short nights → **p. 51**

BEST OF...

GREAT PLACES FOR FREE
Discover new places and save money

FOR FREE

● *Free Friday*
On Friday between 6pm and 9pm you do not have to buy a ticket to go to the revered *Singapore Art Museum*. You can start the weekend by admiring the art of South-East Asia and the special exhibitions free of charge → **p. 37**

● *Refreshing water*
Each restaurant in sweltering Singapore can turn out to be a real oasis; since you can generally get free *iced water* to drink. Just ask for it if it is not offered automatically. Your glass will be refilled as often as you like during the meal → **p. 71**

● *Waterside panorama*
At weekends, Chinese residents *fly their kites* on the roof of the Marina Barrage. With good reason: from here, you get a fabulous view of the skyscrapers, the new Botanic Gardens and the sea → **p. 42**

● *Playtime*
Many attractions for children have to be paid for in expensive Singapore. But the younger generation can romp around for free in the old Botanic Gardens: *Jacob Ballas Children's Garden* provides climbing frames, a water playground and a delightful café next door → **p. 114**

● *Free titbits*
You can sample the local specialities such as biscuits, grilled pork and mooncakes (photo) at the stands set up in the special area in the basement of the *Takashimaya* department store on the days before important Chinese festivals → **p. 76**

● *Work up a sweat for free*
Are you fit and not put off by a little heat? Then you should give some of Singapore's sports a try – from dragon-boat racing to a so-called 'Prosperity Run', which is supposed to make you wealthy! The *Singapore Sports Hub* offers free two-hour sessions, mostly on Saturday mornings, when you can have a go at these and more besides → **p. 55**

●●●●● Dots in guidebook refer to 'Best of...' tips

ONLY IN SINGAPORE
Unique experiences

● *Eat like the locals*
Forget all about the gourmet restaurants and eat seated on a plastic stool in one of the countless food courts or 'hawker centres'. Do not worry about the quality: taxes and rent are very low, so that makes it possible for the stall owners to serve high-class traditional food for a couple of dollars. One of the best hawker centres in the city is *Makansutra Gluttons Bay* directly next to the Esplanade → p. 65

● *Black delights*
It is true; they do look like they were dipped into axle grease. Put on an old, dark shirt (to hide the spots), mingle with the Singaporeans and sink your teeth into the *Black Pepper Crabs* at the *East Coast Seafood Centre* → p. 69

● *Speed along the coast*
If you want to find out what Singapore is really like, pedal along the surfaced promenade of the *East Coast*. Just take a taxi as far as Marine Cove where you can rent bikes and inline skates every few hundred yards; all the rental facilities are equally good → p. 55

● *Shop until you drop*
The Singaporeans love shopping – the real spending variety or just window shopping. Do not only stroll through the main malls, visit the small merchants on Pagoda Street in *Chinatown* or in the side streets of Serangoon Road in *Little India* → p. 44, 49

● *Gamble like the Chinese*
The Chinese love to gamble. Spend an evening with the locals and join in the fun. The best place is in the *Marina Bay Sands complex* where the charm of Las Vegas goes hand in hand with the compulsive gambling of the Chinese → p. 25, 43

● *Floral glory*
Singapore's national flower is the orchid (photo). Prominent visitors to the city state are often honoured with a new variety named after them. One recent addition you will be able to admire in the beautiful *Orchid Garden in the old Botanic Gardens* is the *Vanda William Catherine*. The Duke and Duchess of Cambridge were one of the first to inhale the perfume of its purple and white-coloured blossoms in 2012 → p. 58

BEST OF...

AND IF IT RAINS?
Activities to brighten your day

● *Feel at home*
There are fully grown trees from good old Europe in the cool glasshouses in the *Gardens by the Bay*. The flora is fascinatingly displayed, and it is well worth spending a rainy day here sheltered by the glass → **p. 41**

● *In the jungle*
Of course, you will get wet here, so put on your flip-flops, shorts and a light top. You will also need an umbrella to protect you from the monsoon rain. Wandering through the old rainforest in the *Botanic Gardens* becomes a very special tropical experience → **p. 58**

● *Dry shopping*
No matter how heavy the monsoon rain is, you will be able to walk for miles through the shopping centres without your feet getting wet. Most of the *malls on Orchard Road* are connected with each other underground. Start at *Wheelock Place* and make your way to the *Ion* with its gallery of luxury shops (photo) → **p. 72, 75**

● *Art-itecture*
The *National Gallery* has widened Singapore's art horizon immensely. The collection of South-East Asian painting is of course stunning. But it's worth a visit for the architecture alone, and the rooftop terrace affords one of the prettiest views of Marina Bay Sands → **p. 34**

● *Sweet comforter*
Bad weather – bad mood? Take a taxi to the *PS. Café*. Nowhere but in Australia will you find bigger slices of cake, but here you can sit under tropical trees and listen to the falling raindrops → **p. 64**

● *A try-out for life*
Your son wants to be a fireman and your daughter a doctor? No problem: in *Kidzania* your little ones can try out their dream job come rain or shine → **p. 114**

RAIN

RELAX AND CHILL OUT
Take it easy and spoil yourself

● *Born again*
Too long on the plane? Have you 'shopped till you dropped'? Let yourself be pampered at the *Beauty Emporium at House*. They sell some interesting care products, too → p. 46

● *Sightseeing light*
No matter whether you choose to set sail in an old wooden boat from *River Cruise* or a bumpy, amphibian vehicle from *Duck & Hippo*, it is always a wonderful experience to be taken on a cruise of Singapore's waterways and marvel at the breathtaking views of the city from the water (photo) → p. 115, 125

● *Silent observer*
The fragrance of joss sticks and the rapt devotion of the faithful in the *Thian Hock Keng Temple* in the middle of the hustle and bustle of the metropolis will help you get your feet back on the ground. Here, nobody minds onlookers → p. 49

● *Romantic sundowner*
The sun sinks into the sea behind the tropical trees, the birds' twittering heralds the coming evening and the waiters in the outdoor lounge of *The Knolls* at the luxurious *Capella Hotel* on Sentosa know exactly what their guests want without having to ask → p. 67

● *Hollywood reclining*
The only place where it is more pleasant to watch a film than in the *Golden Village* in the *Vivo City* shopping centre is at home on your sofa: you can make yourself comfy in the reclining chairs and even order dinner → p. 57

● *Cycle deluxe*
Of course, it is easy to get around in Singapore by underground, bus or taxi, but it is much more fun and very comfortable to be driven around town in a *rickshaw*. All of your senses can focus on the life going on around you; you will not have to walk far and avoid all the pushing and shoving. Furthermore, find out which tales the drivers can tell you about old Singapore → p. 125

CHILL OUT

11

INTRODUCTION

DISCOVER SINGAPORE!

Asia for beginners? A *city of sterile buildings* with no character, without any soul? Few other places in South-East Asia are laden down with as many clichés as the five-million metropolis of Singapore. Everybody thinks they know the small *tropical island* – 42 km (26 mi) long and a maximum of 23 km (14 mi) wide – at the south-eastern tip of the Asian continent: most visitors immediately think of marathon shopping sprees on Orchard Road. Or maybe about the famous *Singapore Sling* cocktail, a wonderfully refreshing mix from times long past when the city was a British crown colony. And there is hardly a visitor who does not joke about the ban on chewing gum and the *'fine city'*, the wonderful town with all its penalties for wrongdoing. You're quite right – with almost everything. Singapore offers the chance to *shop around the clock*, the cocktails under tropical trees are really tempting, and, yes, the city state is governed very strictly. The city actually is *'Asia light'* because it does all it can to make Europeans feel at home in no time. Nowhere else is it as easy to get to know Asia, practically without any risk. The Singaporeans are waiting or you! Singapore has *metamorphosed* time and again. The scruffy harbour island that transformed itself with iron discipline into a colonial metropolis and then rose to become the

Photo: Gardens by the Bay

centre of South-East Asia has blossomed into a *global, cosmopolitan city*. You are immediately immersed in another world on the journey from the airport into the city: palm trees! The sparkling sea to the left! And every bridge planted with bougainvilleas. Singapore keeps on coming up with something new: the racing cars roar in the Formula 1 night race. Two casinos await, offering you exciting evenings in a classy atmosphere. There are breathtaking museums, world-class restaurants and *secret street food treasures*, and the Universal Studios theme park will leave everyone in awe, not only children.

> **Everyday life is determined by traditions from China, India and Malaysia**

You can easily explore Singapore on your own. *Everyone speaks English*, and everyone is eager to be friendly to tourists. It's therefore no surprise that some 16 million visitors come to this tropical paradise every year, a great many of them from English-speaking countries. They enjoy the courteous service in the hotels, relish the *colonial flair* and make the most of the hypermodern luxury the city has to offer: you can hear the cash registers in the shopping malls ringing from ten in the morning until ten at night, seven days a week. And it's not only shopaholics who get their fix. There are *luxury goods from all over the world*, but also surprises from Asia, in all the markets – prepare to leave with more than you came with.

Singapore shows it is also a truly Asian metropolis in districts such as Chinatown

INTRODUCTION

And Singapore has much more to offer. The *multicultural city* – 74 percent of the population is Chinese, 13 percent Malay, and nine percent Indian – is a genuine Asian metropolis. Buddhists, Muslims, Christians and Hindus live alongside each other *in harmony*. *Two public holidays* were selected from *each religion*, and they apply everywhere on the island. That is one reason for Hindus celebrating Christmas, Christians Chinese New Year, and Muslims the Hindu Deepavali festival – the other reason is that it boosts sales figures.

> **All Singaporeans share a love of fine food**

While exploring districts such as *Chinatown* or *Little India*, visitors will be able to get a glimpse of life behind the modern, Western façades of the metropolis that, at first glance, seems to characterise Singapore. Everyday life is still determined by the traditions of the Singaporeans' home countries. Take the plunge into the hustle and bustle of Chinatown's markets and the oppressive humidity of Little India – there's so much to discover! Women go shopping in Little India in dazzlingly *colourful saris*, while in Chinatown you will mainly see elderly ladies going about their business in comfortable Chinese clothing. Some still wear the *colourfully patterned polyester suits* that look like pyjamas. The Malay children look absolutely adorable on their way to the mosque dressed up in their finest clothes.

The *temples* of almost all religions are also open to you. The smells, the bells, the singing of the priests – you'll soon be immersed in a completely different world. On your stroll through Chinatown, you will not only inhale the fragrance of *joss sticks* in the Chinese temples but also on many corners in the district: the perfume essence is stuck into colourful fruit on little altars.

Are you hungry after your first recce of the city? Pensioners in fine-rib singlets and businesswomen in their elegant suits meet at the same *hawker stall*, in the food markets, on the corner at lunchtime – the space in-between could be yours: everybody is united in their love of good food – young and old, rich and poor, Chinese, Malays and Indians. Your neighbours on the next table will be happy to explain the dishes, some of which may seem quite exotic: the Indian curries, the burning *hot chilli crab*, or Laksa, an orange-red *noodle*

15

soup, which, thanks to the coconut milk, tastes of the tropics. No one needs to feel any caution in Singapore: everything is clean here and monitored by the authorities.

> **The city state's aim is to develop into the 'control tower' of Asia**

But even the glittering city can only afford what it has first earned. Singapore is an international financial and commercial centre and is completely justified in seeing itself as the *hub of the entire region*, the city everything revolves around, not only to the benefit of its immediate neighbours Indonesia and Malaysia, but all of South-East Asia. Nowhere else in the world do so many millionaires and billionaires live on such a small area – no wonder the motors of Ferraris and Lamborghinis roar through the high-rise urban canyons. More than two-thirds of all the goods shipped from Europe to South-East Asia pass through Singapore's *impressive container terminal* on their way to their final destination in other countries in the area. Singapore has only achieved this by instilling a *stable order*. Guests to the city also profit from this. It's the reason you can still go for a walk in the cooler tropical air late in the evening – no danger lurks around the corner, no threat of being mugged. The People's Action Party (PAP), assisted by media aligned to the state, remains *benevolent* as long as nobody questions their opinion. The party of the autocratic, but charismatic, founder of the state, Lee Kuan Yew, whose image you will come across time and again in the city, makes life for opposition parties difficult.

However, meanwhile a surprising *opening process* has started: Singapore is to grow into a centre for Asia, where the managers of the international concerns are to have their offices. It is to be the location of research and development centres, and where top universities mould students of the region. In spite of the noticeable opening, there is *not the same freedom* that one sees in Europe: the trade unions have been transformed into instruments of the government, the media are censored, there is no freedom of assembly. However, the majority of the population is satisfied with their government, even though there is an *increasing gap between the rich and poor*. Guests to the city quickly recognise what makes Singapore so attractive to the citizens of surrounding countries, too: hospitals offer their services to anyone – you, too, should you have a mishap. The neighbouring countries are envious of the island state's *excellent health system*. There is a low crime rate and the construction of social housing gives citizens security.

But the past of oh-so modern Singapore is also fascinating and full of anecdotes – it is as thrilling as a whodunnit and as colourful as a fairytale from 'Arabian Nights': Singa Pura, *Lion City*, was the name chosen by the discoverer of this coastal village, the Indian Prince Nila Utama, in the 13th century after he had seen an awe-inspiring creature that he thought was a lion in the dense tropical forest. 'Singa' is the Sanskrit word for lion. When he landed there in January 1819, the British colonial administrator *Sir Thomas Stamford Raffles* immediately recognised the strategic importance of the village on the Straits of Malacca. Raffles acquired the island for the *East India Company*. In the following 50 years, Indian prisoners cleared the malaria-infested

INTRODUCTION

Half lion, half fish and completely white, the Merlion majestically spurts water into Marina Bay

jungle, built streets and canals. Chinese coolies carried ivory and spices, tea, silk, precious timber and opium, and later tin and rubber, from the ships to the warehouses. By 1911, Singapore's population had increased to around 250,000 and included *48 ethnic groups*. Most came from South China; many others from Indonesia, Malaysia and India.

The conquerors came by bicycle

For the British colonial powers, Singapore was an extremely important and perfectly *fortified base* – *impregnable* from the sea. However, as part of their *campaign to subjugate* Asia, the Japanese cleverly resorted to – bicycles! They pedalled down the Malay Peninsula and conquered Singapore, which was unprotected from that side, on 15 February 1942. *Japanese forces* ruled the island with extreme brutality for three and a half years until their capitulation on 21 August 1945. That is when the British returned, and Singapore became a *crown colony*.

The mythical beast that Prince Nila Utama saw was chosen to be the city's symbol: *Merlion* has the head of a lion and body of a fish. His statues welcome visitors to Sentosa, *Marina Bay* and the souvenir shops. Take one home with you – as a memento of this fantastic metropolis, the melting pot of Asian cultures.

WHAT'S HOT

1 Say cheese

Conquered by Camembert & Co. High-end shops are opening cheese rooms. Restaurants organise cheese degustations. And cheese connoisseurs, like the Frenchman Gérard Poulard, are regular guests to the city. Bringing cheese to Singapore was as difficult as importing the stinky durian to Paris, he says. But: 'Today Singaporeans are much more adventurous and their taste buds have developed.' *Goreng pisang*, fried bananas, are now served with cheese. And the Singaporean tea company *Liho* makes cheese-flavoured teas. At the weekend a whole cold store is opened up for a cheese buffet in the Italian restaurant *Basilico (1 Cuscaden Road | #2 | The Regent Singapore)* and *Jones The Grocer (BLK 9 Dempsey Road | #01–12 | Dempsey Hill)* offers cheese to his customers every day.

On your bike

2

Cycling is hip Singaporeans are starting to get on their bikes. At first it was only the elderly who would struggle against the flow of traffic in Chinatown. Then the Australians, New Zealanders and the Dutch started to race through the city on their bikes from 5 o'clock on Sunday mornings. Now racing bikes are the new Ferraris. Bike paths are popping up everywhere. Companies are even installing changing rooms. *Obike*, *Ofo* and *Mobike* have been making a business out of the trend since 2017 with their rental bikes. The bikes wait on the side of the road to be picked up and are unlocked easily via an app. Half an hour costs between 50 cents and one dollar. It's a shame they are so small, though. You run the risk of banging your chin with your knees... And the traffic in Singapore isn't exactly the safest. So you'd be better off riding on the pavement, albeit with the pedestrians in mind.

There are lots of new things to discover in Singapore. A few of the most interesting are listed below

Soldering instead of studying

I want to be a start-up! At every family party for Chinese New Year the children used to declare they wanted to be doctors or pilots, a Chinese woman told us. That's changed. 'Now they all want to be entrepreneurs.' The young enterprisers debunk the rumour that Asians only study hard and aren't creative. More and more new spaces are being created for them in the container buildings of *Future Hubs (JTC Launch Pad@One North | 73a Ayer Rajah Crescent)*. For some, setting up a business is easy because daddy has already made some money. Others see the potential in the huge Asian market to change their lives by creating an app. Now there are handicraft lessons at school – Singapore's youth should not only learn programming, but also woodwork and soldering.

We are somebodies!

Self-confidence à la Singapore This wasn't always the case. *The little red dot* on the map used to feel a little bit ashamed of itself. It felt lost. But all that is forgotten: the new Singapore really enjoys itself. And shows it: hip designers, young authors, theatre makers, local fashion brands, funny souvenirs. Some profit from state funding for creatives, others push at the boundaries set by the censors. But all of them change the image of the boring city of prohibition to a creative location that lends the tropics some glamour, e.g. in *Good Company* in the department store *Tangs (310 Orchard Road) (photo)* or *Gnossem (66 Kampong Bugis | #04–01)*.

19

IN A NUTSHELL

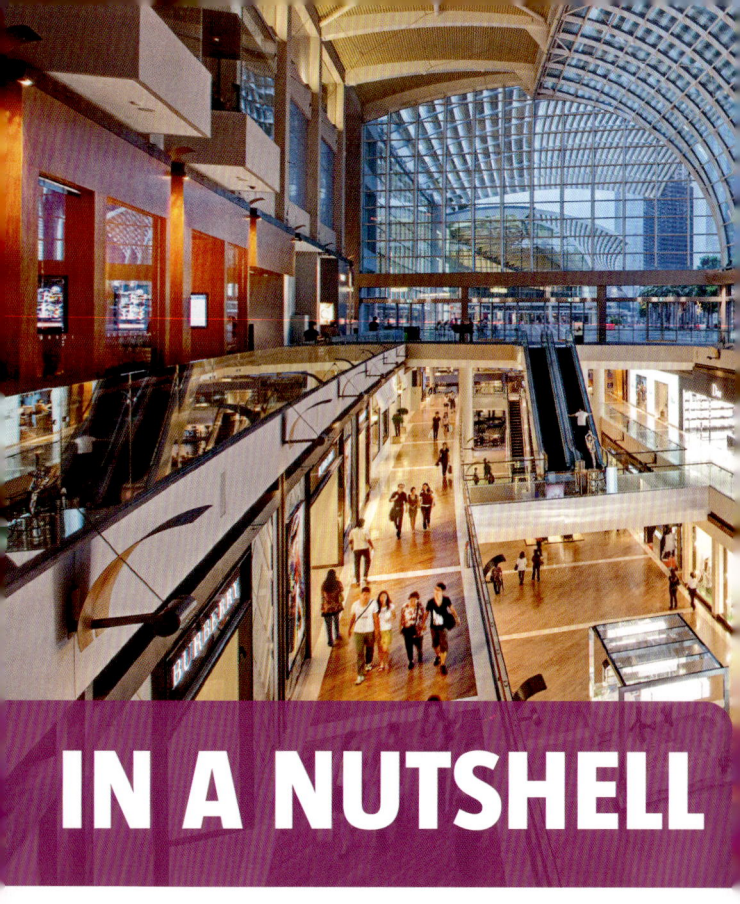

SHORTHAND

Travel into the city with the MRT from the HDB instead of being caught in a traffic jam on the blocked PIE and then having to pay at the ERP? If that sounds Greek to you, you need a crash course in Singapore speak because it is simply teeming with these kinds of abbreviations. New ones are added to the list by the day. The solution: MRT is the Mass Rapid Transit Authority, the underground and suburban trains. HDB stands for the Housing Development Board, which sells state flats. It is also used as a synonym for the high-rise towers in the satellite towns. PIE is the Pan Island Expressway, one of Singapore's motorways. And ERP means Electronic Road Pricing – a toll system in which fees for road use and many multi-storey car parks are read from a chip card in the car. It is impossible not to notice the bridges with the scanners such as those over Orchard Road.

THE GREATEST LOVE

No guest has ever left this city without waxing lyrical about its food. The adage is get out there and eat, whether in Chinatown, in the shopping centres on Orchard Road or in Little India. There is something to satisfy all tastes and all budgets, from the hawkers – the cook-

From feng shui, kiasu and a passion for malls to the five Cs, the Singlish language and life in a fully air-conditioned wonderland

shops, in the food markets – to the five-star chefs in the Marina Bay Sands Casino Complex. And the quality? Professor Tommy Koh, formerly a Singaporean ambassador, boasts: 'I consider that our Char Kway Teow (a popular dish of rice noodles, sausages coated with wax and fish paste) and our Laksa (noodle soup) are better than any other noodle dishes in the world. I do not know of any Western salad that can compete with our Rojak (fruit and vegetable salad). And I am sure that, when they are warm and fluffy and eaten with Chicken Curry, our Roti Prata (Indian pancakes) easily beat any pizza I have ever tasted.' He could be right!

POSITIVE INFLUENCE

It's all about feeling, sensing: feng shui (translated, it means 'wind and

21

water') is the Chinese art of geomantics, recognising those positive and negative influences of a house that influence health and commercial success. Harmony is the magic word, and the direction a building faces, the position of its windows and doors is precisely determined. Believe it or not: if the feng shui is wrong, a shop will stay empty. Until the master comes and rearranges it, by having the door moved for example. Then the buzz returns – and no one in Singapore bats an eyelid. Feng shui walks are offered by several agencies, e.g. by the Singapore Tourism Board *(short.travel/sin12)*.

Singaporeans to do business and make money – to turn Singapore into what it is today. The other side of the coin is that human relations suffer when attention is focused on one's bank account and personal success defined by the five Cs that are the driving force behind everyone in Singapore: *Career*, *Credit Card*, *Condo* (complete with swimming pool), *Club* (with membership fees of several thousand dollars; the more exclusive the better) and *Car* (import duty make cars far more expensive than they are in Europe).

As green as it gets: Singapore's lovely old Botanic Gardens now have a younger counterpart

THE FIVE CS

Although he was clearly proud of Singapore's achievements, the state's founding father, Lee Kuan Yew, was also sometimes concerned about his people. He was the man who encouraged the

GARDEN CITY

If you look down on the city, from a bar in one of the high-rises for example, you'll immediately recognise how green Singapore is. The streets run like green veins through a sea of buildings. And spotted here and there are parks and nature reserves. Singapore is, without

IN A NUTSHELL

doubt, the greenest city in Asia. You can really breathe here and find shade under the trees. One wonderful old Botanic Garden wasn't enough for Singaporeans – they needed a second one, which was built on land reclaimed from the sea. Since the government of the financial centre on the equator is not only rich but also very clever, it has spent around 1 bn S$ on the project. It has long been common knowledge here that green areas increase the price of properties around them considerably. But because it's always hot here, some things work the other way round to what you might expect: they don't need tropical greenhouses here. Instead, two huge cool houses in the *Gardens by the Bay* make it possible to present Singaporeans with pines or oak trees. The Gardens by the Bay spread over an area of 100 hectares (250 acres) – half the size of Monaco – and it would take a whole day to explore every corner of this botanical paradise. The city state's aim is to develop from being a 'garden city' to a 'city in a garden'. In the past 25 years, the green areas in Singapore have increased from around one third to half of the city's surface area. The city covers skyscrapers vertically with plants. You might not see salads or cauliflowers sprouting here yet. But even that should change: the city wants to cultivate as many vegetables as possible on the walls of the high-rises, in order to become more independent from imports – there isn't much farmland here, after all. According to the government, by the end of 2030 some 80 percent of all buildings in the city will be 'green'.

LITTLE DICTIONARY OF COFFEE

Learn your coffee ABC's in Singapore: coffee here is known as kopi and is served with milk. Kopi-O is black, with sugar. Kopi-C combines sugar and milk; kopi-peng comes with milk, sugar and ice.

WE LOVE CAMPAIGNS

Nothing works without a government campaign in Singapore. The cleanliness activities of the 1970s are legendary; at the time, a person took up a position next to every public toilet and asked the users if they had flushed properly. Posters in the city and large newspaper articles often refer to the newest campaign. It might request that rubbish not be thrown out of high-rise windows. Or that citizens should make space for others on the bus.

THE PULSE OF ART

Art, whereever you look: no, it doesn't always have to be Venice. Singapore has grown into a centre of art, whose influence reaches far beyond Asia. The *Biennale* has developed into a permanent prominent event in the arts calendar. Many foreign artists take part and often bring a breath of fresh air into even out-of-the-way areas of the city with their sculptures and installations. The *Art Stage* art fair opens its doors every year in January: in a mere three days, this offshoot of Art Basel shows everything Asia has to offer in the way of art. The motto in the wonderfully restored *Gillman Barracks* is art not guns. The city has located a gallery quarter here. The Saturday openings, when exhibitions change, are really good fun. But you can also discover Salvador Dalí, Henry Moore, Roy Lichtenstein and Fernando Botero on the side of the road: Singapore has a lot of pubic art. You can easily spot Dalí's *Homage to Newton* and Botero's *Bird* on a stroll along Singapore River; Botero's stout sculpture perches imposingly on Boat Quay. You will also find bronze figures here, such as *First Generation*, a

23

group of children jumping into the river, by the famous Singaporean artist Chong Fah Cheong. His work reflects on the old and the new life in the city. Roy Lichtenstein's gigantic *Six Brushstrokes* brightens up a high-rise in the Suntec City business quarter. This is also home to the *Fountain of Wealth*, reportedly the biggest fountain in the world, created by Calvin Tsao and Zack McKown.

MALL MANIA

The Singaporeans love their shopping malls. The city state has hardly any hinterland and therefore the possibilities for leisure-time activities are limited. Of course, there are sports arenas, nature parks and countless possibilities to use one's free time sensibly — but all appeals have so far been in vain: most Singaporeans spend their spare time in shopping centres. They are open every day and usually from 10am to 10pm. It can even be rather difficult to walk along Orchard Road at the weekend. During the week, you see school children doing their homework in the halls and — even more popular — fast-food restaurants. It is pleasantly cool there and many of the HDB flats are not equipped with air conditioning.

NEW GROUND

Even the banks here are built on sand: Singapore is small. That's why it has to grow. But that's only possible if it raises more land from the sea. So far an area of around 120 km^2 (46 square miles) has been reclaimed: the city state once measured 580 km^2 (224 square miles) and it plans to grow to 760 km^2 (293 square miles) in the long term. Singapore's modern airport Changi, for example, is built on reclaimed land. The island Tekong in the north east is currently being expanded. The banking district is also built on reclaimed land, as is the new business city currently being built around the harbour. The land is reclaimed by depositing sand — sand that the island state must buy from Indonesia at great cost. The original coastline ran along Beach Road. But that is very hard to imagine nowadays.

NEW MONEY

Sometimes you won't believe your eyes. At the traffic lights there's a Lamborghini on the left, a Rolls-Royce on the right. By 2020, a good 180,000 of Singapore's population of around 5.5 million people will be millionaires — one in 30 people on the island will then be in the Ferrari-owning class. Many have become wealthy because real-estate prices have increased steadily over the past decades. However, not everybody is rich: there are still old people in Chinatown or Little India who collect paper in order to survive. The taxi drivers are often as old as Methuselah, too, as they could not afford to live in the millionaire's metropolis without working.

SHOPHOUSES

Some of the traditional shophouses still exist in Little India, in Chinatown, on Arab Street and Boat Quay. The government came to its senses shortly before the last of these houses, which once belonged to the early immigrants, were demolished. Today, most of the shophouses provide space for small stores and pubs. However, there are still families who live the way they did in days gone by. The ground floor is used for storage or as a salesroom and the family lives on the top floor.

SINGLISH

Almost all Singaporeans speak two — and many three or four — languages. It is compulsory to learn the

IN A NUTSHELL

lingua franca, English, at school and the youngsters speak their parents' language – Mandarin, Tamil or Malay – at home. A genuine Singaporean usually also speaks a dialect made up of a mixture of English with scraps of Chinese: Singlish. The added syllable *lah*, as in okay-lah, is famous. *Kiasu* is important. The word from Hokkien Chinese means 'fear of losing' – a quality the Singaporeans attribute to themselves. This is what leads to pushing and shoving at sales and also impedes their courage to risk something new. That is why official Singapore is trying to get the Singaporeans to do away with *kiasu*.

GAMBLING

The Chinese are not the only people who like to gamble but they are especially fond of it. Gambling for money used to be forbidden in Singapore but now the city state has had a complete change of heart. There are two new casinos: the Marina Bay Sands and one at the Resort World Sentosa. Foreigners get in free, but in an attempt to curb their compulsive gambling, Singaporeans have to pay 100 S$. Revenue from gambling in both casino complexes, rather shamefully referred to as 'integrated resorts', lies at around 6 bn S$ – almost as high as in Las Vegas. However, dyed-in-the-wool Singaporeans are not at all pleased about the new gambling dens. They are afraid that this will lead to prostitution and criminality.

The love of gambling and search for profit goes so far that the 'Singapore Straits Times' reported that employers sometimes give their workers thousands of dollars and send them to the casinos during working hours to play – and hopefully win – for them. The workers are all in favour: they can spend the day in air-conditioned comfort instead of in the tropical heat and get a cut of ten percent of any winnings. The downside: they can lose their month's wages if the losses are too great.

Shop downstairs, home upstairs: this is the charming Chinese version of a 'department store'

SIGHTSEEING

> **WHERE TO START?**
> **Raffles Monument (136 B2)**
> (*J4*): Start at the memorial to Sir Stamford Raffles in the old Colonial Quarter. The North-South and East-West underground lines stop here. If you look across at the banking district, the Asian Civilisations Museum lies in front of you and the Fullerton Hotel is on the right. Chinatown awaits you and just a few steps downriver, you reach Marina Bay with Singapore's new symbol, the Marina Bay Sands complex.

No matter whether you decide to walk between the skyscrapers in the Central Business District, past the small shophouses in Chinatown and Little India or explore the city's many parks and gardens, there is one rule you should bear in mind: do not rush, walk slowly.

On no account should you make your personal sightseeing programme too full. Even a short stroll can be strenuous in the humid, sticky climate of this tropical city state where the temperature seldom sinks below 30°C (86°F). You will be able to deal better with the high humidity if you take regular breaks and drink a lot of mineral water.

Photo: Hindu Sri Mariamman temple

Traditional rhythms dominate the lifestyle in Chinatown and Little India – while just a few streets away, the metropolis races

Sneakers or hiking sandals are the best mode of transport in Singapore. The city is perfectly suited to being explored on foot. Sir Stamford Raffles, the founding father of Singapore, established the Chinatown, Little India and Arab Street districts; he thought it would be a good idea to keep the ethnic groups separated from each other. Today, Singapore's multicultural society would be amused at such notions – there are as many Chinese businessmen in Little India as there are Indian tailors in Chinatown. But you'll still be fascinated by the bright and colourful Indian saris, the smells from the street kitchens in Chinatown, the haggling in Tamil at the market in Little India and the chatter in the Chinese dialect Hokkien in front of the shops by the Buddha Tooth Relic Temple when you

DISTRICT MAP

LITTLE INDIA/ARAB STREET/KAMPONG GLAM PAGE → 49

COLONIAL QUARTER PAGE → 30

CHINATOWN & SINGAPORE RIVER PAGE → 44

MARINA BAY PAGE → 39

HARBOURFRONT & SENTOSA PAGE → 53

The map shows the location of the most interesting districts. There is a detailed map of each district on which each of the sights described is numbered.

wander through these quarters. Take your time and immerse yourself in the various cultures: with a leisurely walk around *Serangoon Road*, where friendly merchants sell their necklaces of fresh jasmine blossom. In the Thian Hock Keng Temple in Chinatown, where soothsayers tell the future with fortune sticks. With a walk along the river to its mouth at Fullerton Hotel, where you will experience the flair of the metropolis' former colonial splendour. Only to discover the modern Singapore on Orchard Road, in the Central Business District and in the newly developed Marina Bay area straight after. Singapore is simply relentless: every second, every street corner tempts you with the unknown. The real highlight, however, is the new Botanic Gardens by the Bay and the Marina Bay Sands complex (MBS).

The rapid building boom is conspicuous, well-known international and local architects are creating the modern urban landscape – from the National Museum and the National Gallery to new hotel and shopping complexes. Two highly modern casinos offer fun and entertainment at their gambling tables, and the Universal Studios theme park on the island of Sentosa is an adventure, not only for children. But the city is much more than just its centre: the spotlessly clean, cool MRT underground trains take you to the satellite towns. There, among the endless rows of skyscrapers in Pasir Ris, Sembawang and Boon Lay, you will be able to explore Singapore's heartland, as the

SIGHTSEEING

island dwellers call this area far away from the inner city. Covered footpaths lead into the high-rise complexes that are mostly surrounded by small shops. The floors of the markets for vegetables, fish and meat in the basements are kept washed down and this has led to them being known as 'wet markets'.

Distances are short in Singapore. And yet different areas are worlds apart. The city attempts to create a link between Asian and Western culture that appeals to all ethnic groups.

The Singaporeans are all descendants of immigrants from countries of a very different culture and they often find it difficult to fully appreciate each other's cultural assets and achievements. While performances of Indian dance and Peking opera have little appeal for other groups, street-theatre groups – now permitted on Orchard Road – attract a mixed audience. In spite of the goal of developing an intrinsic Singaporean cultural identity, it is important for the multinational state to preserve the artistic heritage of its Chinese, Malay and Indian peoples; you will find information on all activities under *www.yoursingapore.com*.

Art is still a relatively new chapter in the history of the city but the government has recognised that it needs to catch up in this area. The world's largest museum for South-East Asian art, the National Gallery Singapore, opened its doors in 2015. The former Supreme Court and City Hall were gutted and merged together for this purpose. The former Gillman Barracks were transformed into a gallery district. Art fairs and auctions complete the picture. The *Esplanade Theatres on the Bay* stage concerts, plays and changing exhibitions. The delightfully

MARCO POLO HIGHLIGHTS

★ **Asian Civilisations Museum**
The entire region on show for all to see
→ p. 32

★ **National Gallery Singapore**
The world's largest museum for modern South-East Asian art
→ p. 34

★ **Orchard Road**
Superlative shopping boulevard → p. 35

★ **Raffles Hotel**
The institution among the hotels in Singapore
→ p. 36

★ **Botanic Gardens**
Two fantastic gardens – one old and one new
→ p. 41, 58

★ **Marina Bay Sands**
Almost blinding luxury → p. 43

★ **Chinatown**
Renovated shophouses and Clarke Quay for night owls
→ p. 44

★ **Sri Mariamman Temple**
A colourful Hindu house of worship
→ p. 48

★ **Thian Hock Keng Temple**
A glittering gem
→ p. 49

★ **Little India**
Between gods and spices → p. 49

★ **Resort World Sentosa**
A real must for kids: the Universal Studios amusement park → p. 55

★ **Singapore Zoo, Night Safari & River Safari**
Animals by day and night in large enclosures → p. 61

COLONIAL QUARTER

renovated Victoria Theatre and its concert hall are worthy additions to the cultural scene.

There are around 140 large churches, mosques and temples in Singapore, plus hundreds of smaller places of worship. They are all open to the public. You must take off your shoes before entering a mosque or temple and, especially in Muslim houses of worship, women should be appropriately dressed. The main prayer halls of the mosques are reserved for men. Follow the locals' lead in the temples; buy joss sticks and light them at the altar, join the faithful as they walk around (always to the left!). Leave a small donation; the churches, temples and mosques depend on them. *The houses of worship are usually open all day.*

COLONIAL QUARTER

Here, the colonial period comes alive. The magnificent, lovingly restored buildings and old parks in Singapore's city centre will take you a century back in time. The heart of the city developed along its earlier lifeline, the Singapore River. The most beautiful restored colonial buildings can be seen on its banks: where Sir Stamford Raffles landed in 1819, where tradition meets modernity, where art and culture blossom, and from where the city is governed.

The city's most beautiful museums, the large hotels and most exquisite shops are all located in the Colonial Quarter between Chinatown, Little India and the Central Business Districts. The city fathers, however, have shown courage in combining the new with the old: the old City Hall, in which the Japanese signed the declaration of surrender in 1945, and the Supreme Court behind it now form an outstanding museum for South-East Asian art. The new building is graced by a cupola by star architect Sir Norman Foster. The city has also set a sign for its future in its very centre: Singapore has established the green campus of its Management University (SMU) here. The impressive building of the Art University SOTA with its hanging gardens is located directly opposite.

Well done! City founder, Sir Stamford Raffles

◼ ARMENIAN CHURCH
(136 B1) (*J4*)

A double treasure: of all his buildings in Singapore, this church from 1835 is

SIGHTSEEING

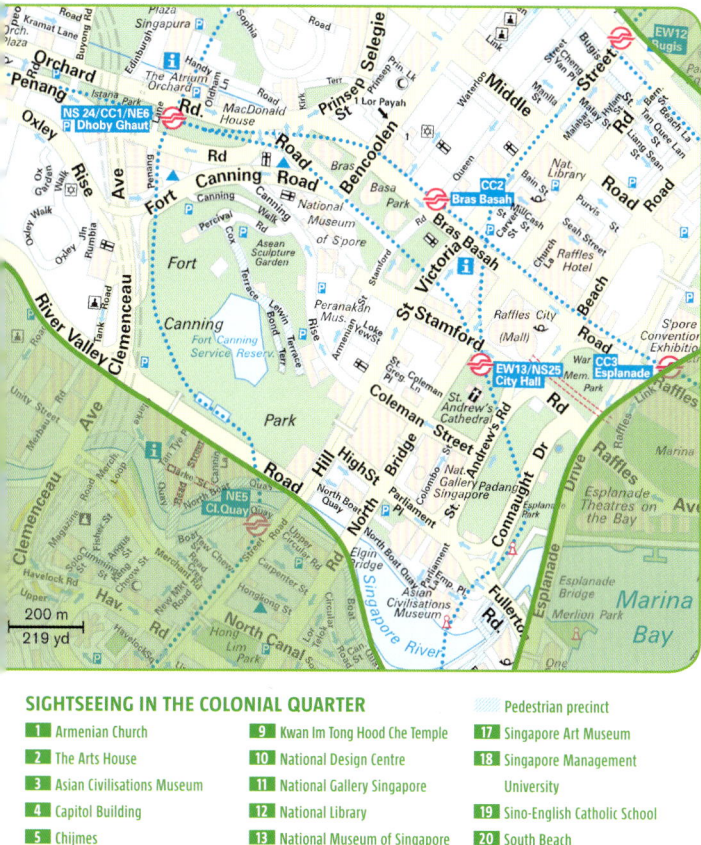

SIGHTSEEING IN THE COLONIAL QUARTER

1. Armenian Church
2. The Arts House
3. Asian Civilisations Museum
4. Capitol Building
5. Chijmes
6. Fort Canning Park
7. Fullerton Hotel
8. Istana
9. Kwan Im Tong Hood Che Temple
10. National Design Centre
11. National Gallery Singapore
12. National Library
13. National Museum of Singapore
14. Orchard Road
15. Raffles Hotel
16. Raffles Place
17. Singapore Art Museum
18. Singapore Management University
19. Sino-English Catholic School
20. South Beach
21. Sri Krishnan Temple
22. St Andrew's Cathedral
23. Victoria Theatre and Concert

Pedestrian precinct

architect Georg Coleman's masterpiece. But the real asset is in the cemetery behind it: the grave of Agnes Joaquim, who discovered Singapore's national orchid *Vanda Miss Joaquim*, which blossoms next to her gravestone. The church and cemetery have now been proclaimed national monuments. *60 Hill Street | MRT EW 13, NS 25 City Hall | MRT CC 2 Bras Basah, then bus 197*

2 THE ARTS HOUSE
(136 B2) (*J4*)

Chilling in front of colonial walls. The white building in the heart of the city on the Singapore River has a chequered history: built in 1829 by Irish architect George Coleman as a merchant's residence, it was later re-designated a law court. Then parliament moved in. But because Singapore wants to trans-

31

COLONIAL QUARTER

form itself into a cultural metropolis, the former Old Parliament House was renamed *The Arts House* and re-opened as a gallery and event centre with restaurant and live music. Parliament had previously moved a few hundred yards up river to a new building. *1 Old Parliament Lane/corner of High Street | MRT EW 13, NS 25 City Hall | www.theartshouse.com.sg*

3 ASIAN CIVILISATIONS MUSEUM ★
(136 B2–3) (*J4*)

Lovers of Asian art and culture must pay a visit! The departments of this museum are contained in two buildings. The main building opposite the Boat Quay concentrates on the cultures of South-East Asia, China, South Asia and Islam. The 135-year-old building is an eye-opener itself and was once the seat of government. At the *Peranakan Museum* (136 B1) (*J3*) *(daily 10am–7pm, Fri until 9pm | admission 6 S$ | 39 Armenian Street | MRT EW 13, NS 25 City Hall | www.peranakanmuseum.org.sg)*, in the second house on Armenian Street, visitors can discover the world of the descendants of the early Chinese immigrants from Malaysia and Singapore. The settlers married women from Malaya (the former name of Malaysia) and took on some of the customs of the British colonial masters to create the totally unique and new mixed culture of the *Peranakan*. The extensive exhibition in the building that was constructed as a schoolhouse in 1910 will stimulate all the senses. *Daily 10am–7pm, Fri until 9pm, daily guided tours | free admission | 1 Empress Place | opposite Fullerton Hotel | MRT EW 14, NS 26 Raffles Place | www.acm.org.sg*

4 CAPITOL BUILDING
(136 B1) (*J3*)

The tearful goodbye was followed by a commercial new beginning. Great care was taken in transforming Singapore's beloved old cinema into an event centre with sunken seating. The splendid former auditorium was preserved. It forms an ensemble together with the colonial *Stamford House*, which is now the five-star hotel Patina, with a connected luxury shopping mall and restaurants. *Stamford Road/North Bridge Road | www.capitolsingapore.com | MRT EW 13, NS 25 City Hall*

5 CHIJMES (136 C1) (*J3*)

The 'j' makes the name of this former convent appear a little unusual but it is simply pronounced *chimes*. The full name was the 'Convent of the Sisters of the Holy Infant Jesus' or CHIJ for short; that explains the 'j'. The buildings themselves are the actual attraction and have been

LOW BUDGET

Dare to step out onto the *Skybridge (daily 9am–9pm)* on the 50th floor of the *Pinnacle@Duxton* (135 E–F5) (*H6*), a flagship social housing complex in the heart of Chinatown. From up here you get a fabulous view of the city for 5 S$ on your Ez-link Card. Admission info: *www.pinnacleduxton.com.sg*

Enjoy the skyline of the Colonial Quarter from the roof of the new *National Gallery*, with or without a drink. The view stretches from Padang to the three MBS towers and the Straits of Malacca. Simply take the elevator up to the terrace and marvel at the view for free – or visit one of the rooftop bars.

SIGHTSEEING

restored to house galleries, restaurants, cafés and boutiques. The mood gets festive in the evening. *Daily 8am–midnight (shops daily 11am–10pm) | free admission | 30 Victoria Street/Bras Basah Road | MRT CC 2 Bras Basah, MRT EW 13, NS 25 City Hall*

6 FORT CANNING PARK
(136 A–B 1–2) (*H–J 3–4*)
You will be able to get a breath of fresh air here, only five minutes away from Orchard Road. Delightful Fort Canning Hill provides tranquillity in tropical greenery and a good overview of Singapore's history and modern culture. It doesn't get much more romantic than watching the annual *Ballet under the Stars* here. It also hosts the *Womad* music festival. The *Ancient History Walking Trail (www.nparks.gov.sg)* provides interesting insights into Singapore's early history. The hill is the oldest royal residence on the island: this is the site of the *Keramat* where it is said that Sultan Iskandar Shah was buried. The founder of Singapore, Sir Stamford Raffles, built his first residence on the hill. There are also some graves of early settlers up here. All of your senses are engaged as part of the grounds were once the enchanting spice garden of the first Botanic Garden, which smells of nutmeg, cinnamon and lemongrass. The *Hotel Fort Canning* with the adjacent *The Legends Fort Canning Park* are on the other side of the hill. *The Legends* is a private club in a building from 1926 with some restaurants open to the public. A few metres further is *The Battle Box (daily 9.30am–5.30pm | admission 18 S$ | 2 Cox Terrace | www.battlebox.com.sg)*, a bunker buried in a hill. Now it's an interesting museum on the fall of Singapore. *MRT CC 1, NE 6, NS 24 Dhoby Ghaut, then approx. 10 min walk*

Sultans and settlers found their last resting place under the old trees in Fort Canning Park

COLONIAL QUARTER

7 FULLERTON HOTEL
(136 C3) (*m* J5)

The Fullerton Building was erected in 1928 as the main post office and is now a grand hotel that makes no secret of the fact that £310 million (400 million US$) were spent on its renovation. Singaporeans and tourists alike love to sit on the terrace and look down at the river. A fortress was built at this strategically favourable location in 1829 and named after the first governor, Sir Robert Fullerton. *1 Fullerton Square | MRT EW 14, NS 26 Raffles Place*

8 ISTANA
(130 A4) (*m* H1)

The Istana – Malay for palace – was once the residence of the representative of the British crown and is now the official address of the President of Singapore. You have to be lucky to see the inside of the palace: the magnificent building, located in the centre of an enormous park (the entrance is on Orchard Road), only opens its gates five times a year: on 1st January and 1st May, as well as Chinese New Year, *Hari Raya Puasa* and *Deepavali*. *Orchard Road | MRT CC 1, NE 6, NS 24 Dhoby Ghaut*

9 INSIDER TIP KWAN IM TONG HOOD CHE TEMPLE (131 D5) (*m* J2)

The interior decoration of this modern Buddhist temple might not be spectacular, but if you want to see local colour, you've come to the right place. The faithful quickly put down their shopping bags and take up bundles of joss sticks that they then reverently hold in their hands. They kneel or sit in prayer in front of the statues of Buddha. Many of them use so-called 'fortune-telling sticks' in their attempts to get an idea of what the future holds in store for them. It is strictly forbidden to take photos inside the temple. *178 Waterloo Street | MRT EW 12 Bugis*

10 NATIONAL DESIGN CENTRE
(131 D6) (*m* J3)

The place for young creatives is in an art-deco building. As well as visiting changing design exhibitions you can also buy work by Singaporean designers, from jewellery to chocolate, from the design collective *Keepers*. *Kapok* also sells Singaporean and international lifestyle products in its shop with an affiliated café. *Daily 9am–9pm | 111 Middle Road | MRT CC 2 Bras Basah*

11 NATIONAL GALLERY SINGAPORE ★ ● (136 B2) (*m* J4)

A further highlight of the transformation of colonial buildings into modern architecture: at a cost of over half a billion dollars, the city state gutted its former City Hall and Supreme Court buildings. Now joined together, they offer over 645,000 historical square feet showcasing around 800 works of the overall 8000 pieces of South-East Asian art. The most fascinating aspect is that the historic chambers and offices have been preserved. The golden canopy over the entrance extends upwards to the roof terrace. *Sun–Thu 10am–7pm, Fri/Sat 10am–10pm | admission 20 S$ | 1 Saint Andrew's Road | www.nationalgallery.sg | MRT EW 13, NS 25 City Hall*

12 INSIDER TIP NATIONAL LIBRARY
(131 D6) (*m* J–K3)

The new building of the National Library is much more than just a tower full of books. A great number of Singaporeans – more than 1.9 million – are members of the library, which has a stock of around three million books in Chinese, Malay, Tamil and English. Both the building itself and the ☼ views over the city from the upper floors are interesting, as are the many different kinds of events held here. *Daily 10am–9pm, except public holidays |*

SIGHTSEEING

Superlative shopping: the shops and malls on Orchard Road are spectacular

100 Victoria Street | www.nl.sg | MRT EW 12 Bugis, then bus 851

13 NATIONAL MUSEUM OF SINGAPORE (130 C6) (*m J3*)

Singapore's oldest and largest museum is easy to make out by its architectural highlight, the 24 m (79 ft)-wide glass dome, which is also illuminated at night. The building hosts touring exhibitions of an international standard and provides an overview of specific aspects of Singaporean history, such as fashion and food in the city, on almost 20,000 m² (215,000 square feet) of ultra-modern exhibition space behind its impressive colonial façade. *Daily 10am–7pm | admission 15 S$ | 93 Stamford Road | www.nationalmuseum.sg | MRT CC 2 Bras Basah | MRT CC 1, NE 6, NS 24 Dhoby Ghaut*

14 ORCHARD ROAD ★
(129 D–F 4–5) (*m E–H 1–3*)

Singapore's 'Champs Élysées' can now satisfy the most demanding wishes: the shopping street Orchard Road sells everything the world has to offer. You will soon regret not bringing an empty suitcase with you – but you can buy them here, too. Occasionally on Saturday evenings Orchard Road is closed to traffic – and is then packed with hundreds of thousands of people. The consumers' paradise also includes *Tanglin Road*, which enters into Orchard Road, and *Scotts Road*, which crosses the main shopping street. There are some expensive antiques shops in the *Tanglin Shopping Centre*, the second oldest in the city. The highlight of Orchard Road is the *ION Orchard* at the junction with Scotts Road.

35

COLONIAL QUARTER

There are 335 shops on the 59,000 m² (635,000 square feet) of floor space. Shoppers can choose between Adidas and Yves Saint Laurent, between Italian ice cream and Ice Kachang – frozen water with syrup. *Ngee Ann City,* with the Japanese *Takashimaya* department store, offers regular bargain markets in the basement. On the other side of the road you will find many luxury brands such as Burberry or Miu Miu at *The Paragon*, but also cheap shoes and clothes at Metro or Marks & Spencer. The new Bermuda triangle for teenagers – with South East Asia's first Apple flagship store, H&M and Victoria's Secret – is on the *corner of Grange Road*.

The Singaporeans are particularly fond of *313@Somerset* with eight floors of shops such as Zara and Uniqlo. There are also excellent *food courts* on the top floor. *Orchard Central* and *Orchard Gateway* together make up the huge shopping complex. Young people are magically drawn to the trendy *The Cathay* at the bottom of Orchard Road. The renovated *The Heeren* is home to a branch of the traditional Robinsons department store. The large shopping malls are open from 10am to 10pm. *MRT NS 22 Orchard, NS 23 Somerset*

15 RAFFLES HOTEL ★
(136 C1) *(ꝳ K3)*

The 'Grand Old Lady of the East' is unique in its white colonial splendour, a legend just as alive as it ever was. It began in 1887 when the three Armenian Sarkies brothers founded the hotel directly on what was then the beach promenade and named it after Sir Stamford Raffles. They made the Raffles the top address in town. Emperors, kings and presidents, heads of state and stars have all lived at the Raffles. Writers and journalists from all over the world used to meet in the *Writers Bar* and to sip in the *Long Bar* the *Singapore Sling* – a cocktail of gin and exotic fruit juices that really packs a punch. The hotel still retains its colonial flair, even after its refurbishment, which was completed in 2018.

Walk up the gravel driveway to the elaborate wrought-iron portico, have a look inside the enormous hotel hall, see if you can still find traces of Somerset Maugham, Hermann Hesse and Noel Coward in the Long Bar. You can relax in style in the attractive inner courtyards, in the tropical garden and the restaurants. Afterwards, several dozen high-class boutiques and the choice souvenir shop await your custom. *Sandals, shorts and sleeveless shirts are not deemed appropriate in the hotel | 1 Beach Road | MRT CC 2 Bras Basah*

16 RAFFLES PLACE (136 B3) *(ꝳ J5)*

You can feel the heartbeat of the financial metropolis around Raffles Place. At lunchtime the suited white-collar workers stream out of their super-cooled offices to eat here. The core of Singapore's Central Business District is surrounded by a ring of high-rise towers belonging to the banks. If you take Exit B out of the underground station, you will see Caltex House on your left with the Bank of China, built in a classical modern style, further to the left. Today, its 18 storeys seem rather insignificant, and it is almost overpowered by the gigantic Maybank Building on the right. The two towers housing the offices of the United Overseas Bank next to the sweeping Standard Chartered Bank Building resemble a stack of coins on top of each other. *MRT EW 14, NS 26 Raffles Place*

17 SINGAPORE ART MUSEUM ●
(130 C6) *(ꝳ J3)*

Art goes back to school: the building, which once housed St Joseph's Institution, the first Catholic school in Singa-

36

SIGHTSEEING

Where banks soar skywards: Raffles Place financial centre

pore, has been lavishly renovated and now serves as the National Gallery. The permanent collection is made up of 5500 exhibits focusing on contemporary South-East Asian art. The museum shop is run by the Singaporean brand *Supermama*, which produced the porcelain series *Singapore Icons*. Very unusual souvenirs! *Daily 10am–7pm, Fri to 9pm | admission 10 S$, Fri from 6pm free admission | 71 Bras Basah Road | MRT CC 2 Bras Basah*

18 SINGAPORE MANAGEMENT UNIVERSITY (130 C6) (*J3*)

This building is not a university but a declaration – a declaration of the city's desire to be an academic centre, and that is one of the reasons that the SMU Building was erected between historical buildings in the very heart of the city. The third university in the five-million metropolis is closely modelled on American institutions of this kind and attracts students from all over the world. Anybody who wants to experience the feeling of young Singapore and its desire to learn should not hesitate to visit the open campus or the passages in the basement. *81 Victoria Street | www.smu.edu.sg | MRT CC 2 Bras Basah*

19 SINO-ENGLISH CATHOLIC SCHOOL (130 C6) (*J3*)

Murals await just one corner on. You will find small shops and restaurants in the former school, built in 1935. That alone might not make a visit worthwhile, but seeing the original mural on its side certainly will. It shows typical scenes of Singapore from the years 1930 to 1960. These are pictures of things like the old National Library, loved by Singaporeans, but demolished. The door to a long lost world opens a crack... *51 Waterloo Street | MRT CC 2 Bras Basah*

COLONIAL QUARTER

20 SOUTH BEACH
(136 C1) (*m* K3)

A trend project on military grounds. At first look up: two futuristic towers jut up above four listed buildings. Here, star architect Sir Norman Foster has built a mixed-use complex composed of a classy 634-bed hotel, luxury apartments, office space, shops and restaurants. Foster's towers mark the edge of the Colonial Quarter like a wall. The *JW Marriott*, furnished by French designer Philippe Starck, is to be found in one of them. Take a breath in the covered *South Beach Avenue*: trendy restaurants, bars and shops entice you to step out. The officers' houses and the officers' club of the former military headquarters were restored and integrated into the site. What an ensemble, if you include the Raffles Hotel opposite! *Beach Road/Bras Basah Road | MRT EW 13, NS 25 City Hall | MRT CC 3 Esplanade*

21 INSIDER TIP SRI KRISHNAN TEMPLE
(131 D5) (*m* J2)

The vibrant colours are the most fascinating attribute of this Hindu temple. Ceremonies are held in the midst of the hustle and bustle of everyday life; quite often accompanied by music. The various gods – Shiva, Vishnu and Brahma representing the past, present and future – are decorated with fresh flowers. Curiously Buddhists from the neighbouring *Kwan Im Tong Hood Che Temple* often drop in to pay their respects to the Hindu deities. *152 Waterloo Street | MRT EW 12 Bugis*

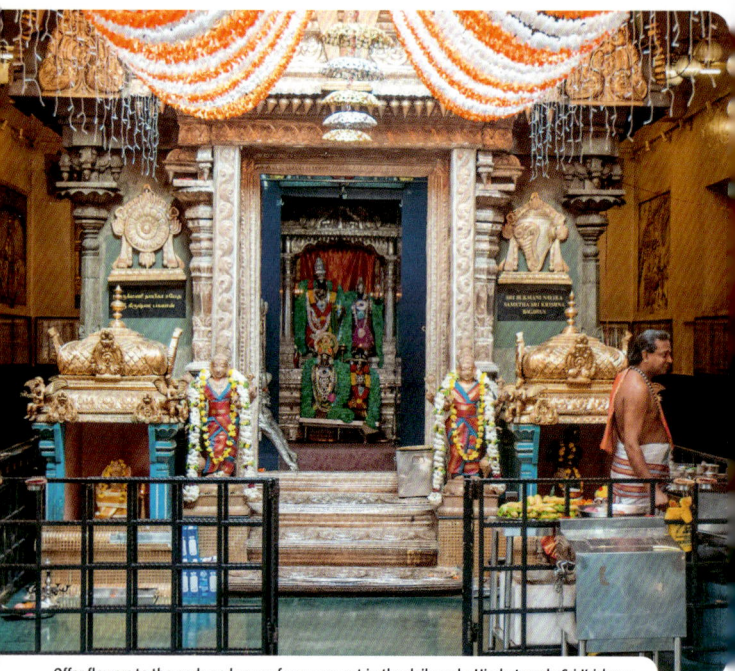

Offer flowers to the gods and pause for a moment in the daily rush: Hindu temple Sri Krishnan

SIGHTSEEING

22 ST ANDREW'S CATHEDRAL
(136 B–C1) (*J4*)

All in white: this neo-Gothic Anglican church was built by Indian prisoners in 1862. The dazzling white of the façade and tower are the result of a unique mixture known as Madras Churam, which was used for the plastering: shells, egg white and coconut fibres were stirred into it. *11 St Andrew's Road | MRT EW 13, NS 25 City Hall*

23 INSIDER TIP VICTORIA THEATRE AND CONCERT HALL
(136 B2) (*J4*)

A huge amount of time and money was invested into renovating Singapore's traditional *Victoria Concert Hall* in 2014. The façades remained intact, while the interior was given state-of-the-art acoustics. The clock mechanism in the bell tower was restored by the same British company which had built it at the beginning of the 20th century. The old chairs were used to create the ceiling of the bar; elements of the armrests provide sound insulation. Both halls serve as prime examples of Singapore's new approach to preserving the old and harmonising with the new. *Daily 10am–9pm | 11 Empress Place | www.vtvch.com | MRT EW 13, NS 25 City Hall*

MARINA BAY

Singapore is continually reinventing itself. The government feels that this is the only way the tiny city state, The Little Red Dot, will be able to remain 'relevant'. The district around Marina Bay is the latest symbol of this rebirth.

Marina Bay is the city's newly created quarter that offers tourists an almost unbelievable number of attractions in a very small area: the new emblem of the city, a museum, a theatre, a new Botanic Garden, the Merlion, luxury hotels, restaurants, bars and hawkers, the skyline of the CBD, the quays for cruise ships, a Ferris wheel and of course the bay itself.

This was once the mouth of the Singapore River but now the artificial bay is the largest fresh-water reservoir in the city, and Singapore is no longer dependent on being supplied with water from its neighbouring country Malaysia. The lake is also a paradise for water sports enthusiasts – this is where motorboat races and sailing regattas are held; there are fountains and ship parades. Marina Bay is only a stone's throw away from the Business District, the streets around Shenton Way and the Boat Quay promenade. The bay is also only a short walk away from the Colonial Quarter. The *Suntec City* commercial centre is also part of this district. This shopping area, which was designed as a city within the city, is flanked by the towers of five office buildings in the form of a hand, in the centre is the huge *Fountain of Wealth*. Marina Bay is dominated by the three gigantic towers of the *Marina Bay Sands Hotel*, MBS for short. An enormous rooftop terrace spans the trio of towers at a height of 200 m (656 ft) above the ground; its top is open to visitors. The panoramic view from here reaches as far as the Indonesian island of Sumatra and to Malaysia. In the meantime, the MBS has become the most photographed building in Singapore and probably in all of South-East Asia.

The chic casino, the 'Louis Vuitton Island', as well as congress centres and restaurants are located beneath the towers. Right next door is the newly created Botanic Gardens, the *Gardens by the Bay* and, opposite, there is the popular *Singapore Flyer* – a giant observation wheel. This new city district was established on new land wrested from the sea.

39

MARINA BAY

1 ART SCIENCE MUSEUM
(137 D3) (*K5*)

From the outside, this futuristic construction looks like a gigantic lotus blossom while the architecture creates fascinating spaces in the interior. Some of the world's best exhibitions are shown here – from a show about the sinking of the Titanic to a futuristic vision of human life in a completely technological world. *Daily 10am–7pm | admission 17 S$, combined ticket for all exhibitions 38 S$, families 46 S$ for 2 adults and 2 children, Fri family day: 2 children get in free on an adult ticket | 10 Bayfront Av. | ticket hotline tel. 66 88 88 26 | www.marinabaysands.com | MRT CE 2, NS 27 Marina Bay | MRT CC 4 Promenade | MRT CE 1 DT Bayfront*

2 ESPLANADE
(136 C2) (*K4*)

Of course this place is all about the sound. But even the sight of the Esplanade, which includes a 2000-seat theatre, a concert hall for an audience of 1600 and a shopping centre, is polarising: while the building's fans are wild about its appearance, those less enamoured lambaste the design of the glass roof with its spiky protective construction. This has led to the nickname of the two domes: they are known as *durians* because they look like the prickly skin of the South-East Asians' favourite fruit. It is really delicious but the smell is so pungent that it is forbidden to eat it on buses and trains. *1 Raffles Av. | www.esplanade.com | MRT EW 14, NS 26*

One of the new symbols of Marina Bay: the lotus blossom of the Art Science Museum

SIGHTSEEING

SIGHTSEEING IN MARINA BAY

1. Art Science Museum
2. Esplanade
3. Gardens by the Bay
4. Marina Bay Cruise Centre, South Pier & Maritime Gallery
5. Marina Bay Sands
6. Merlion Park & Fullerton H.
7. Red Dot Design Museum
8. Singapore Flyer & Formula 1

Pedestrian precinct

Raffles Place, MRT EW 13, NS 25 City Hall | MRT CC 3 Esplanade

3 GARDENS BY THE BAY ⭐ 🌿
(137 E–F 2–4) (*m* L–M 4–6)

Super trees and domes – these are the eye-catchers of Singapore's new, second Botanic Garden. It is enormous, just like everything else created here. The Gardens by the Bay cover an area of around 100 hectares (250 acres), making them half the size of Monaco. Further gardens are spread over three strips of land around Marina Bay. *Bay South* – actually the new botanic garden – covers an area of 54 hectares (133 acres) itself. Visitors can satisfy their hunger in 13 restaurants, one of which, the *Pollen* in the Flower Dome, is run by London star chef Jason Atherton. Nothing is too exclusive for these gardens. The architects, for instance, paid 30,000 S$ for a 500-year-old camellia that they found in China.

The botanical splendour hides the latest environmental technology. The two domed buildings, *Flower Dome* and *Cloud Forest*, are home to 🟠 greenhouses. They cool instead of warming. In this way even

41

MARINA BAY

Pools with wow factor: the Skypark on the three towers of the Marina Bay Sands Hotel

trees from the Alps can survive on the equator. The special glass was developed by German scientists. And the lofty artificial tropical trees made of steel are useful attractions: they serve as exhaust ducts for the air-conditioning, which is fuelled with green waste. The restaurant *Supertree by Indochine* is in the highest of these *super trees*. The main building of the *Marina Barrage (Sun–Mon 9am–9pm | free admission | 8 Marina Gardens Drive | www.pub.gov.sg | MRT CE 2 Marina Bay, then bus 400)*, a barrier to a gigantic fresh-water reservoir, is on the sea side. Climb onto its roof – from the 🌿 rooftop terrace you can even see Sumatra. At weekends Chinese fly their 🟢 kites from the terrace. *Daily 9am–9pm | admission 28 S$ | 18 Marina Gardens Drive | www.gardensbythebay.com | MRT DT 16, CE 1 Bayfront | MRT NS 27 Marina Bay*

4 MARINA BAY CRUISE CENTRE, MARINA SOUTH PIER & SINGAPORE MARITIME GALLERY
(137 E6) (K–L 8–7)

Is it a cruise ship? Or a harbour building? You will spot the striking *Cruise Centre (61 Marina Coastal Drive)*, where the imposing ocean giants dock, from far off. If you don't really want to set sail for good, but have had enough of the big island, then visit the little ones, from *Marina South Pier (31 Marina Coastal Drive)*: day trips to *Kusu Island* and *St. John's Island* will take you to another world, despite being just a few kilometres away. Kusu offers a Chinese temple and three Malaysian shrines, which are visited by many worshippers.

St. John's Island has simple places to stay the night. There are peaceful sandy beaches on both islands *(www.islandcruise.com.sg)*. Even if you aren't sea-

SIGHTSEEING

worthy, you can become a captain on the pier. On Level 2 of the South Pier building is the INSIDER TIP *Singapore Maritime Gallery* (*Tue–Sun 9am–6pm | free admission*), where you can sail your own ship – in a simulator.

5 MARINA BAY SANDS ★
(137 D3–4) (*K–L5*)

Who needs to go to the city centre anymore, now there's the MBS? This gigantic complex is actually a city in its own right with a hotel, 50 restaurants, the ● casino, a musical theatre and a skating rink made of plastic. Above the ground, it is dominated by the *MBS Hotel* with its 2560 rooms *(www.marinabaysands.com)* and the congress centre opposite it.

There is even a 146-m (160-yd)-long pool on the roof, which is unfortunately reserved for hotel guests. The express lift whisks visitors up to the *Skypark* on the rooftop terrace *(Mon–Thu 9.30am–10pm, Fri–Sun 9.30am–11pm | 23 S$, tickets at the site, at tel. 66 88 88 26 | www.marinabaysands.com)* in a mere 19 seconds.

Underground, you will be amazed by the sheer extent of the shopping area, which is full of luxury boutiques and has a very good *food court* at the end. In the cellar, Indonesian gondoliers will row you along a canal that ends underneath an enormous water funnel. Rain gushes into the funnel during tropical downpours and produces a magnificent spectacle that is intended to symbolise a shower of money. It (sometimes) rains real money right next door in Singapore's largest casino: it offers more than 650 gaming tables and one-arm bandits. Foreigners do not have to pay an admission fee.

It is also well worth making a visit to the flagship store of the luxury luggage brand, Louis Vuitton, which is located on an island in the bay. During the day walk a few metres further to the escalator that leads to *Marina Bay Link Mall*. Here there are some bakeries and lovely delis such as *Ichiban Boshi* (#B2–14/15) or *Salad Stop* (#B2–77/78). In the evening, the MBS waterfront becomes the projection surface for a magical display of lights *(15-minute laser show Wonder Full Sun–Thu 8 and 9.30pm, Fri/Sat 8, 9.30 and 11pm). MRT CE 1 DT 16 Bayfront*

6 MERLION PARK & FULLERTON HERITAGE (136 C3–4) (*J–K 4–5*)

A mythical creature as heraldic animal: Prince Nila Utama named the small piece of land he discovered in the late 13th century *Singa Pura* after a mythical beast – half fish and half lion – the prince is said to have spotted in the dense rainforest. Singapore has taken on the Merlion as its symbol. The 8.6-m (28-ft)-high statue at the end of the *One Fullerton* restaurant complex spouts water into the sea. Try not to get mixed up with all the 'Fullertons' here: not only the impressive hotel in the Colonial Quarter is named after him, the entire region has Robert Fullerton, the first governor of the *Straits Settlements*, the British crown colony consisting of Penang, Malacca and Singapore, to thank for its name.

The *Fullerton Waterboat House* is behind One Fullerton; if you walk along the water, you will soon reach the new restaurant district around the *Fullerton Bay Hotel (www.fullertonbayhotel.com)*. But if you're hungry, stop for a bite first: the *Clifford* restaurant, in the delightfully restored arrivals hall of *Clifford Pier*, serves up Singaporean specialities. Fullerton Bay Hotel is expensive – it is one of the top luxury hotels in the city and it is also very romantic. Its rooftop terrace *The Lantern* is ideal for chilling in the evening. Those who prefer it a little less

CHINATOWN & SINGAPORE RIVER

A leisurely revolution: Singapore Flyer

8 SINGAPORE FLYER & FORMULA 1 (137 E2) (*L4*)

Leaving the Marina Bay Sands complex via the Helix Bridge (137 D2–3) (*L4–5*), you soon reach the *Singapore Flyer*, an observation wheel. In spite of some turmoil concerning its financing, it turns quite happily. Even though it may not seem like it, the Singapore Flyer revolves twenty-four hours a day – but very slowly. Behind the observation wheel is the building with the box stops for the *Formula 1* races. The Singapore Grand Prix, held every autumn, is the first ever night-time event in Formula 1 racing. *Singapore Flyer daily 8.30am–10.30pm | 30-minute ride 33 S$, many special prices | 30 Raffles Av. | www.singaporeflyer.com | MRT CC 4 Promenade*

swanky go one door down to the *Customs House*. Its *Kinki Roof Top Bar* offers the same view for less. *MRT EW 14, NS 26 Raffles Place*

7 RED DOT DESIGN MUSEUM (136 C4) (*K6*)

An extraordinary museum in a unusual building: the glass palace, once the info centre for Marina Bay, is now home to the Design Museum. It has more than 1000 exhibits from the fields of product and communication design. *Mon–Thu 10am–8pm, Fri–Sun 10am–11pm | 11 Marina Blvd. | www.museum.red-dot.sg | MRT CE1, DT16 Bayfront*

CHINATOWN & SINGAPORE RIVER

Anybody who just thinks of ★ Chinatown as another tourist attraction will miss out on all its enigmatic aspects. Make sure that you have enough time to explore the hidden lanes in this area.

Four quarters, and none is like the other: Chinatown (135 E–F 2–5) (*H–J 4–6*) is divided into four quarters on both sides of the main axis South Bridge Road. Each has its own character. The big prayer houses, the street markets and the souvenir shops are on Temple and ● Pagoda Street – it's usually very busy here. Your first destination are of course the temples, with their exotic smells and the sounds of the conch shell horns. The diversity and tolerance is astonishing: Hindu temple, mosque and Chinese prayer house all stand peacefully next to each other on

44

SIGHTSEEING

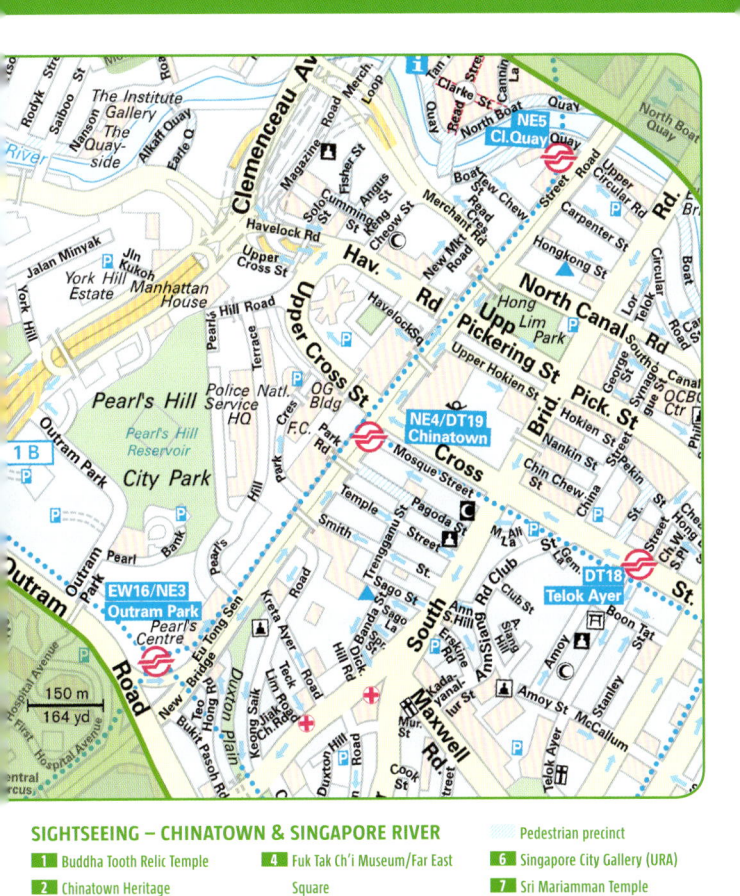

SIGHTSEEING – CHINATOWN & SINGAPORE RIVER

1. Buddha Tooth Relic Temple
2. Chinatown Heritage Centre
3. Chinatown Visitor Centre
4. Fuk Tak Ch'i Museum/Far East Square
5. Singapore Chinese Cultural Centre (SCCC)

- Pedestrian precinct
6. Singapore City Gallery (URA)
7. Sri Mariamman Temple
8. Tan Si Chong Su Temple
9. Thian Hock Keng Temple

one street. The district is particularly interesting at Chinese New Year in January or February. Weeks before the event, the entire district is transformed into a market with hawkers and lanterns, glowing everywhere in the evening, and animals made of wire and silk that represent the new year in the Chinese calendar.

You can also eat well here, although the prices are not always reasonable. Chinatown is a good place to buy souvenirs. You can have a merchant weigh out tea for you to take home, for instance, or inhale the aroma of dried seahorses and lizards in a traditional chemist's shop.

The area on the other side of the road offers bars, restaurants and shops in Club Street and Ann Siang Road, which are also frequented by bankers from the bordering CBD. Telok Ayer Street is quieter than South Bridge Road, but just as pretty. It's not rare for the odd Champagne bottle to

45

CHINATOWN & SINGAPORE RIVER

be cracked open around Duxton and Tanjong Pagar Road. It is also starting to get hipper on the other side, around **INSIDER TIP** *Keong Saik Road*, where more and more bars are opening. But there are still some gems: the trendy chefs haven't driven out all the old-school street kitchens yet.

Chinatown was the birthplace of Singapore as an important trading centre. Here the street scene is defined by business people and labourers. This is still reflected in the architecture. The original houses in Chinatown are a reminder of the luxury merchants once lived in and the power of the Chinese clans. The architecture is a mixture of Chinese elements and Doric and Corinthian columns with a dash of Classicism from Italy; the final result is now known as 'Chinese Baroque'.

If you are looking for something more relaxed and need a fresh breeze, stroll across to the *Singapore River*. One side exudes a romantic atmosphere. In the early evening, people walk past the magnificently restored colonial buildings in the shade of the old trees. On the other side and along the upper reaches of the river, you will find the best pubs and bars in town. The nightlife here on Clarke Quay is boisterous, loud and fun, it is the perfect place to see and be seen. In short: party animals are welcome! *MRT NE 4, DT 19 Chinatown*

1 BUDDHA TOOTH RELIC TEMPLE
(136 A4) (H5)

No matter whether the revered tooth is real or false – the newly built temple is definitely worth a visit. Here you can find the Buddha that fits to your year of birth, hear monks praying, see a huge prayer drum on the roof garden and a bistro serving simple food in the cellar. *288 South Bridge Road | www.btrts.org.sg | MRT EW 15 Tanjong Pagar*

2 CHINATOWN HERITAGE CENTRE
(136 A3) (H5)

Films, music and computer screens help the younger generation to understand the old Singapore. This museum depicts the often hard but also colourful life of the Chinese immigrants in Singapore, presented in painstakingly renovated, former shophouses. At the same time

TIME TO CHILL

Singapore is perfect if you want to pamper yourself – the possibilities are enormous. Painted nails are a must, especially if you decide to wear flip-flops. The specialists at *Snails Beauty* **(129 D4)** *(F2)*, centrally located with a view of Orchard Road, work quickly and professionally – you could hardly ask for more *(501 Orchard Road, #03-01 Wheelock Place | tel. 6738 01 00 | MRT NS 22 Orchard)*. Enjoy deep relaxation with an authentic foot reflex zone massage without all the pretence at **INSIDER TIP** *Health Step (daily 1am–7.30pm | 4a Lorong Mambong | tel. 6468 26 55 | www.healthstepfootreflexology.com | MRT CC 21 Holland Village)*. The ● *Beauty Emporium at House (8d Dempsey Road)* **(0)** *(B2)* offers everything to do with beauty. Its own *Spa Esprit (daily 10am–10pm | #02–01 | tel. 6475 73 75 | www.spa-esprit.com)* rates as one of the best in the city.

SIGHTSEEING

Typical Chinatown: colourful mix of shophouses, modern architecture and old symbols

it explains the history of the Chinese exiles, the formation of the clans and also Chinatown's most recent developments. Highly recommendable tours through the quarter begin here, also by trishaw. *Daily 9am–8pm, closed 1st Mon in month | admission 15 S$ | 48 Pagoda Street | www.chinatownheritagecentre.com.sg | MRT NE 4 Chinatown*

3 CHINATOWN VISITOR CENTRE
(135 E4) (*ω H5*)

You can get tips on shops, restaurants and tours through Chinatown as well as tickets for many of the city's attractions here. Inside, an exhibition provides information about Chinatown and its history. There are also many wacky souvenirs for sale. A board outside displays before-and-after photos of Chinatown's historically interesting houses, which have now been renovated. *Mon–Fri 9am–9pm, Sat/Sun 9am–10pm | 2 Banda Street | at Kreta Ayer Square, next to the Buddha Tooth Relic Temple | MRT NE 4 Chinatown*

4 INSIDER TIP FUK TAK CH'I MUSEUM/FAR EAST SQUARE
(136 B4) (*ω J5*)

Some things here make it seem like a toy shop – the small figures, the junk, the Chinese Opera. And yet Singapore's oldest temple, *Fuk Tak Ch'i*, with its dioramas, gives an insight into the everyday life of the first Chinese immigrants. The small museum is part of *Far East Square*, a former residential district between Telok Ayer, Pekin, China and Cross Streets. Part of the area was restored at the end of the 1990s and covered with a glass roof. *Daily 10am–10pm | free admission | 76 Telok Ayer Street/Far East Square | MRT NE 4 Chinatown*

5 INSIDER TIP SINGAPORE CHINESE CULTURAL CENTRE (SCCC)
(136 B5) (*ω J6*)

Symbol of the new identity of Chinese Singapore: the fantastic cuboid building in red, grey and gold is the modern translation of Chinese tradition. The centre for

47

CHINATOWN & SINGAPORE RIVER

art and culture, which has only recently opened, reflects the city's new identity. Singapore has strong mainland-Chinese roots, but has developed its own character over the years. Art exhibitions, music, dance and theatre as well as discussion forums provide evidence of this. The cultural centre forms a strong unit with the *Singapore Chinese Orchestra* building next door. Its architects are among the country's most renowned. You feel that nowhere better than on the planted roofgarden, which also offers a wonderful view. *Mon–Fri 9am–6 pm | free admission | 1 Straits Blvd. | www.singaporeccc.org.sg | MRT EW 15 Tanjong Pagar*

6 INSIDER TIP SINGAPORE CITY GALLERY (URA)
(136 A4–5) (*H6*)

This is the place for anybody who is interested in Singapore's city planning and architecture: the Singapore Gallery in the building of the Urban Redevelopment Authority (URA) has two gigantic models of the city with plans for its development over the coming decades. Interactive screens and 3D animations create a visual image of the new Singapore. *Mon–Fri 9am–5pm | free admission | 45 Maxwell Road | www.ura.gov.sg | MRT EW 15 Tanjong Pagar*

7 SRI MARIAMMAN TEMPLE ★
(136 A4) (*H5*)

Without doubt the most colourful and cheerful temple in Chinatown: the photographers' favourite temple is veritably overflowing with elaborate carvings and sculptures. The *Gopuram*, the entrance door, tells a long story in pictures itself. Weddings are held here almost every day; there is traditional music in the evening and fire-walking – barefoot over glowing

Sri Mariamman Temple – a Hindu sanctuary in Chinatown? Completely normal in Singapore

SIGHTSEEING

embers – takes place in the inner courtyard during the Thimi festival. *244 South Bridge Road | MRT EW 15 Tanjong Pagar, MRT NE 4, DT 19 Chinatown*

8 TAN SI CHONG SU TEMPLE
(135 E–F2) (*m* H4)

If you're going to pray, then do it here: this temple, which was completed in 1876, has the best *feng shui* in the city. It is said that prayers said in this temple have a better chance of being heard. Here you will be able to experience many fascinating rituals including the Tao liturgy and telling the future with fortune-telling sticks. *15 Magazine Road | MRT NE 4, DT 19 Chinatown, then bus 51*

9 THIAN HOCK KENG TEMPLE ★ ●
(136 A4) (*m* H5)

Entering this gateway, you immediately feel like you've stepped into deepest China. Chinese seamen had a temple dedicated to their patron saint Mazu erected here on what was once the coastal road in 1842. Today, it is difficult to believe that the goddess once looked straight out to sea – there's now a forest of skyscrapers in front of the temple. Material from all over the world was used in its construction: the statue of the goddess comes from China, the wrought-iron railings from Scotland, the tiles from England and Holland. The walls and columns are decorated with carvings. The faithful light joss sticks in front of the altars and burn slips of paper with their prayers and vows on them. However, the fortune tellers now work with computers! *158 Telok Ayer Street | MRT DT 18 Telok Ayer*

LITTLE INDIA/ ARAB STREET/ KAMPONG GLAM

Colours, sounds, smells – these two districts appeal to all the senses. Little India, with its small side streets, is the most colourful shopping paradise in all of Singapore, while the calls of the muezzin reverberate over the rooftops of textile dealers and shisha cafés in the Arabian-Malay district of Kampong Glam.

You can find everything the subcontinent has to offer in ● ★ *Little India* (130–131 C–E 2–4) (*m* J–K 1–2) – but without any of the local travel risks. Here you'll find the most gold shops, fresh fruit and vegetables in the *Tekka Centre*, henna tattoos and handmade jasmine blossom necklaces. In the meantime, Little India has also become a destination for the new coffeeshop and bar scene. But Indians

49

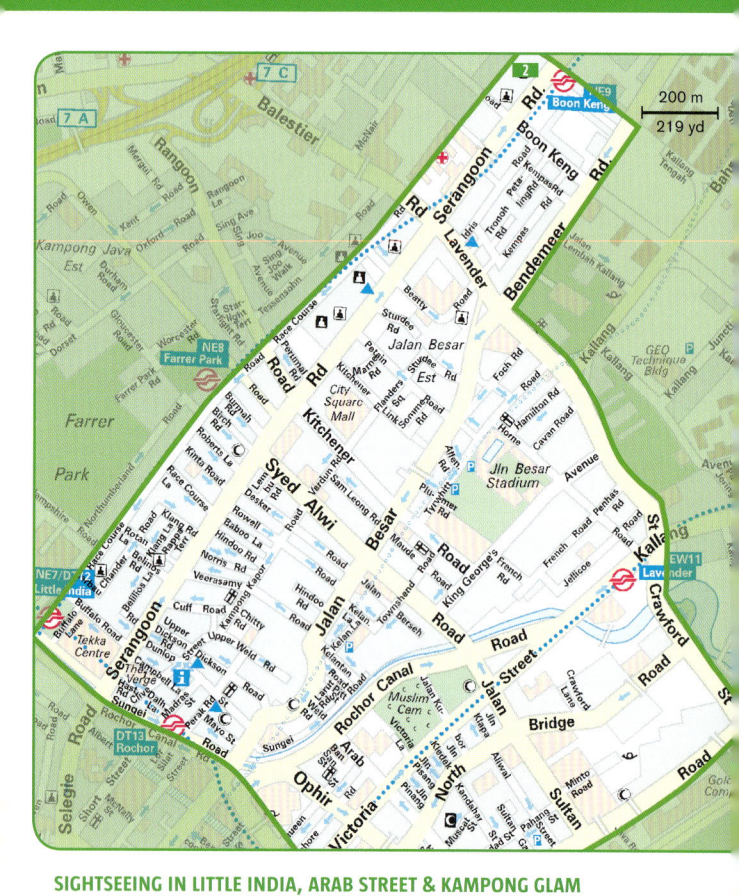

LITTLE INDIA/ARAB STREET/KAMPONG GLAM

SIGHTSEEING IN LITTLE INDIA, ARAB STREET & KAMPONG GLAM

- **1** Arab Street
- **2** Haji Lane
- **3** Hajjah Fatimah Mosque
- **4** Indian Heritage Centre
- **5** Malay Heritage Centre
- **6** Sultan Mosque
- Pedestrian precinct
- **7** Tekka Centre

remain in the majority – women in saris and men in turbans and the traditional lunghi or dhoti trousers. The busiest time here is on Sunday evening, when many immigrant workers get together. The fabric sellers on *Arab Street* in *Kampong Glam* offer Chinese brocade, Thai silk and batiks from Indonesia and Malaysia.

The adjacent Muslim quarter is the place to buy perfume oils; the perfumers can also conjure up your favourite fragrance. The district is dominated by the *Sultan Mosque* with its golden roof. Next to it, you will not only find the best Muslim restaurants in Singapore but also the *Malay Heritage Centre* in a restored sultan's palace. Bars and clubs are shooting up at a dizzying speed. Most of the shops here are closed on Sunday and on Friday afternoon. During the fasting month of Ram-

SIGHTSEEING

adan the pavement restaurants open their doors after sunset and there are usually long queues of people waiting to enjoy all the delicacies. *MRT NE 7 Little India*

1 ARAB STREET (131 D4–E5) (*M K2*)

Here the shops are piled high with rolls of fabric. Please barter – this is exactly what the traders expect. And have fun doing it. You should be able to get ten percent discount. The Arabs were among the first trading partners of old Singapore. Here, in the Malaysian quarter *Kampong Glam*, which is quite clearly influenced by Islam, there are very good restaurants and tea shops, wickerwork and perfume oils. Singapore's increasingly open in-crowd is now discovering the streets and their attractive nightspots. *MRT EW 12, DT 14 Bugis, then bus 2, 7, 32*

2 INSIDER TIP HAJI LANE (131 E5) (*M K2*)

A whole road for shopping and eating for the over 20s. Small hip labels, vintage clothes, bars and restaurants – as fast-paced as the zeitgeist and the rise in rents. *MRT EW 12, DT 14 Bugis*

3 INSIDER TIP HAJJAH FATIMAH MOSQUE (131 F5) (*M L2*)

The oldest mosque in Singapore is architecturally more beautiful than the larger Sultan Mosque. What makes it special is that it was built by a woman, the Malay Hajjah Fatimah. She came into money because she married a rich sultan, whose trading company she managed after his death. *4001 Beach Road | MRT EW 11 Lavender, then bus 100, 961, 980*

4 INSIDER TIP INDIAN HERITAGE CENTRE (130 C4) (*M J2*)

Behind its colourful façade, the Indian Heritage Centre gives a good insight into the lively Indian district. It offers courses such as 'Cooking with the queen of spices' or 'Indian printing techniques'. The population donates old treasures and photos of Little India in days gone by

Everyone shops in colourful Little India: Muslims, Hindus, Buddhists, Christians, tourists

LITTLE INDIA/ARAB STREET/KAMPONG GLAM

for the the permanent exhitibion. *Tue–Thu 10am–7pm, Fri/Sat 10am–8pm, Sun 10am–4pm | admission 6 S$ | 5 Campbell Lane | www.indianheritage.org.sg | MRT NE 7 Little India*

5 MALAY HERITAGE CENTRE (131 E5) (*L2*)

The centre has permanent and temporary exhibitions of Malay art and culture. Situated in a restored sultan's palace, it also offers visitors courses in traditional Malay arts and crafts. Singapore has put a lot of effort into re-appraising the legacy of this ethnic group. *Tue–Sun 10am–6pm, guided tours Tue–Fri 11am | admission 6 S$ | 85 Sultan Gate | www.malayheritage.org.sg | MRT EW 12, DT 14 Bugis, then bus 7*

6 SULTAN MOSQUE (131 E5) (*K2*)

The golden roof dominates the Muslim district. The Sultan Mosque, completed in 1928, is the spiritual centre for Singapore's Muslims and has the largest prayer hall in the city. *No visits during the hours of prayer | 3 Muscat Street | MRT EW 12, DT 14 Bugis*

7 TEKKA CENTRE (130 C4) (*J1–2*)

Sheep carcasses hang from the ceiling, all kinds of sea creatures, fruit, vegetables and of course spices from all around the world are on display. Such a colourful ambiance not only attracts the photographers – everyone likes to dive into this jam-packed world of Indian food. *Daily 6.30am–9pm | Bukit Timah Road/Serangoon Road | MRT N 7 Little India*

Gilded faith: the Sultan Mosque watches over the Muslim quarter

SIGHTSEEING

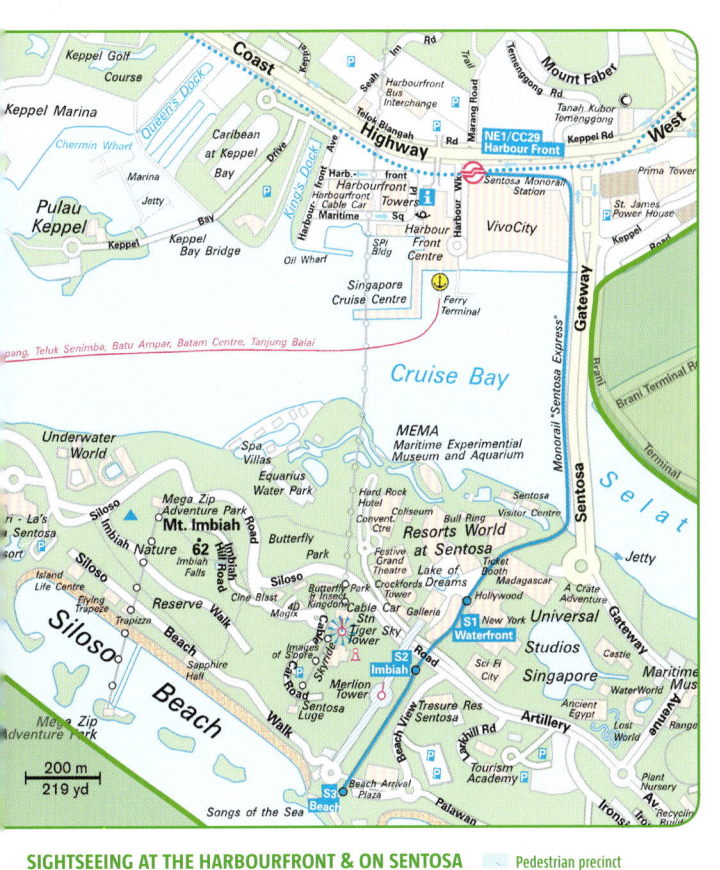

SIGHTSEEING AT THE HARBOURFRONT & ON SENTOSA

- 1 Mount Faber
- 2 Mount Imbiah Lookout
- 3 Resort World Sentosa
- 4 Southern Ridges
- 5 Beaches
- 6 Vivo City
- Pedestrian precinct

HARBOUR-FRONT & SENTOSA

You're never far from the high seas here. But you'd be better off going overboard on land, for the island of Sentosa, self-proclaimed 'state of fun'.

And don't miss out on its surroundings either.

Sure, Sentosa island, with around 250 recreational offerings and many sandy beaches, is the main attraction. But the *Harbourfront* has much to offer too: beautiful parks, hiking on the Southern Ridges, the view from Mount Faber with its funicular to Sentosa, icons of architecture like the Libeskind towers, which seem to sway in the wind, and Vivo City,

53

HARBOURFRONT & SENTOSA

A bit of Disneyland, a touch of Hollywood, right in the heart of Singapore: Resort World Sentosa

the most beautiful shopping centre in the city.

Sentosa island *(sentosa.com.sg)* is a completely unique world. Once upon a time, the one-and-a-half-square mile 'Island of Peace and Tranquillity' was only a fishing village. The British started using it as a military base in 1880 to protect Singapore from an attack from the sea – which actually never took place. That's why there are still many large, colonial military buildings here, which have now been converted into luxury hotels. Today, Sentosa is a paradise for anybody looking for amusement: there are countless attractions around the *Resort World Sentosa* amusement park, high-class restaurants, beaches and the aquarium – you could spend days on Sentosa!

The island is connected to the city by a cable car from Mount Faber (see p. 54), which is now being extended even further by the Sentosa Line. You can reach Sentosa easily by taking the *Sentosa Express (daily 7am–midnight from Vivo City, 3rd floor | admission 4 S$ with Sentosa Pass | MRT CC 29, NE 1 Harbourfront)*, taxi, car or by walking across the new *Sentosa Boardwalk (admission 1 S$, Sat/Sun free)*. There are different prices for taxis and cars ranging from 2–7 S$ per vehicle. The means of transport on Sentosa itself are free; the yellow, red, and blue bus lines and Beach Train head for the various destinations. The island is also ideal for being explored on a 🟢 *Segway tour (daily 10am–8.30pm and night tours | from 17 S$ starting at Beach Station)* or by 🟢 *electric bicycle (daily 10am–8pm | from 15 S$ starting at Siloso Beach)*. More about Sentosa on the informative website *www.sentosa.com.sg*.

1 MOUNT FABER
(138 B–C1) (*P4*)

Many visitors begin their excursion to Sentosa at Mount Faber: a cable car runs from there to Mount Imbiah on Sentosa. But Mount Faber, the second-highest mountain in Singapore, has much more than just a spectacular view over the city to offer – especially in the evening. The cable car leaves from the *Faber Peak Singapore*, which is next to some restaurants with a view and a souvenir shop. *Daily 8.45am–10pm | return ticket 29 S$*

SIGHTSEEING

incl. admission for Sentosa, many special rates | tickets: Faber Peak Singapore, Harbourfront Centre, Harbour Front Tower 2, Sentosa Tour Desk | www.faberpeaksingapore.com | MRT CC 29, NE 1 Harbourfront

2 MOUNT IMBIAH LOOKOUT
(138 B3–4) (*P6*)

Arriving on a funicular, gliding over the sea on the Megazip – all of this is possible at Mount Imbiah. Sentosa's highest elevation is now also the end station of the funicular from Mount Faber. Latch your carabiner on the steel rope and away you go on a breathtaking ride to the offshore island on the *Megazip (39 S$)* – and that's not all. The *Mega Adventure Park (daily 11am–7pm | admission from 15 S$ | 10a Siloso Beach Walk)* also offers the climbing park *MegaClimb*, the climbing wall *MegaWall*, trampolines *MegaBounce* and *MegaJump*, a simulated parachute jump. Next door, luges race down into the valley at *Skyline Luge Sentosa (daily 10am–9.30pm | from 18 S$)*.

And if you have time for a celebrity hunt afterwards, buy a ticket for *Madame Tussauds (Mon–Fri 10am–6pm, Sat/Sun 10am–7.30pm | admission adults 39, children 29 S$ | 40 Imbiah Road)*.

3 RESORT WORLD SENTOSA ★
(138–139 C–D 3–4) (*P–Q6*)

The full program: the huge RWS resort with aquarium, water park, dolphin island, hotels, restaurants, shops, casino and the Universal Studios. The first things visitors see after they have crossed over the *Sentosa Gateway* bridge are the small towers and battlements of the *Universal Studios Singapore (usually daily 10am–7pm | day pass adults 76, children 56 S$)*. Wherever you go, you will meet Shrek, the animal heroes from Madagascar and the dinosaurs from 'Jurassic Park'. Dozens of restaurants, the Hollywood Boulevard with the Walk of Fame and a live show with stuntmen and stuntwomen from California will keep children and their parents entertained for at least a day. But

FIT IN THE CITY

For early birds: blow away the jet lag, shake the sleep from your bones – go for it! Groups meet up for tai-chi, sword and fan dancing and gymnastics from sunrise in the old *Botanic Gardens* **(128 A–B 1–4)** *(C–D1)*. If you prefer to train alone, you can take one of the running trails. Well-trained cyclists peddle around the island along the so-called *Park Connector (Signpost: PCN Park Connector Network)* that links the green areas of the city. Those who do not feel quite so energetic can choose one of the individual sections such as the one along the ● East Coast starting at *East Coast Park* **(0)** *(N–S3)* *(www.nparks.gov.sg | www.lifestyle recreation.com.sg)* heading east. Be warned: at the weekend, it seems as though all of Singapore is here having a good time! You can hire bicycles and inline skates every day at the small booths or so-called PCN pit stops along the route. Those who want to add a bit of diversity to their sporting routine should visit the ● *Sports Hub (2 Stadium Walk)*. It offers lots of free taster courses in Asian sports from Speedminton to dragon boat racing. Register in advance at *short.travel/sin14*

HARBOURFRONT & SENTOSA

things will start to get tough if your little ones want to go on the wildest rollercoaster in South-East Asia. Singapore's second casino is located in the basement of the RWS, as is a *Musical Theatre (tickets from www.sistic.com.sg)*. The *Marine Life Park* offers everything water lovers ever dreamed of: the world's largest *Aquarium S.E.A. (daily 10am–7pm | day pass adults 34, children 24 S$)* also houses the remarkable *Maritime Experiential Museum (Mon–Thu 10am–7pm, Fri–Sun 10am–9pm | admission 5 S$)*, which tells the story of maritime trade. A few yards on, you come to the *Adventure Cove Water Park (daily 10am–6pm | day pass adults 38, children 30 S$)*. Animal lovers will probably head directly for *Dolphin Island (daily 10am–6pm | adults from 58, children from 48 S$)*. If you'd prefer to stroll around at your leisure, send the children to the *Kids Club (daily 10am–10pm | 12 S$ per hour)*. At nightfall, two spectacular, free displays await you at the water's edge: the *Crane Dance (daily 10pm)* sees two huge cranes imitating the touching courtship dance of their feathered namesakes. The *Lake of Dreams (daily 9.30pm)* is a fire, water and light show. The RWS has restaurants in every price segment. If you can't get enough of the fun, book a hotel room directly on the RWS Complex – say, at the *Hard Rock Hotel (Expensive)* or at the *Michael (Expensive)*. 8 Sentosa Gateway | www.rwsentosa.com | MRT NE 1, CC 29 Harbourfront, continue with Sentosa Express SE 1 Waterfront.

4 SOUTHERN RIDGES

(132–133 A–F 3–6) (*A–D 5–7*)
One of the loveliest hiking trails is made unique by spectacular bridges such as the

Siloso Beach – green-belt recreation in the true sense: palm trees, white sand and the city as the backdrop

SIGHTSEEING

wooden INSIDER TIP *Henderson Waves* – the highest pedestrian bridge in Singapore – and elevated paths on stilts at the height of the treetops. The trail begins in Hort Park, covers a distance of 9 km (5.5 mi), passes over three hills and ends at the Vivo City. After all your hard work you can reward yourself with an ice cream and the view of the sea. *www.nparks.gov.sg | MRT CC 27 Labrador Park, then bus 100 to Hort Park*

5 BEACHES
(138–139 A–E 4–6) (Ø O–R 6–8)
Admittedly, the water along the busiest shipping route in the world could be cleaner but the good 3 km (almost 2 mi) of white sandy beaches on Sentosa – Siloso, Palawan and Tanjong – still have a certain amount of charm. The beaches are connected with each other by the Beach Train. This is a great place to chill out when the daytime tropical heat fades away in the evening: the New Year's Eve *Rave Party* is famous. But the *Pizzeria Trapizza* and *Kidzania* also attract families on normal evenings or the party continues in the beach bars *Bora Bora*, *Coastes* and *Tanjong Beach Club*. Water sports fans who are a bit wary of the seawater here can use the *Wave House (Mon–Fri noon–9pm, Sat/Sun 11am–9pm | from 12 S$ | www.wavehousesentosa.com)* at Siloso Beach for surfing on artificial breakers. The southernmost point of the Asian mainland is on a small island just off Sentosa's main beach. From here, you have a view of Singapore's southern islands, such as Kusu Island and St John's Island, of which some can be reached from the Cruise Center with the ferries from *Singapore Island Cruise and Ferry Services (ticket 18 S$ | 31 Marina Coastal Drive | tel. 65 34 93 39 | www.islandcruise.com.sg | MRT NS 28 Marina South Pier).*

6 VIVO CITY
(138 C2) (Ø Q5)
Shopping and feasting without the edge. The shopping centre with a view of the harbour designed by the Japanese architect Toyo Ito reminds one of a spaceship. The white building, without any corners or sharp edges, houses branches of many of the top chains from Aldo to Zara. Singapore's newest shopping paradise is made complete by a number of good restaurants with views of departing and arriving ships. This is also where you will find the city's most modern cinema with reclining seats; food is even served to guests in the auditorium of the ● *Golden Village*. Children (and their parents) can cool down in huge pools with fountains on the roof. *Daily 10am–10pm | 1 Harbourfront Walk/Sentosa Gateway | www.vivocity.com.sg | MRT NE 1 CC 29 Harbourfront*

IN OTHER DISTRICTS

BOTANIC GARDENS ★
(128 A2–4) (*A1*)

Singapore is really proud of this, and rightly so: its old Botanic Garden is now a Unesco World Heritage Site. The mixture of ancient trees, glorious flowerbeds and colonial buildings makes the park into a garden of experience, only a few minutes' walk away from the shopping paradise of Orchard Road. It sounds unbelievable: more than 2000 different plant species grow in the gigantic 52-hectare (128-acre) grounds. There is a ● primary rainforest as well as manicured lawns, waterfalls, lakes, fern and rose gardens. The ● Orchid Garden, with species blooming all year round and more than 60,000 individual plants is famous throughout the world. Cacti, herbs, medicinal and water plants are each to be found in their own gardens; often enchanting and hidden. The extension of the garden to include a piece of jungle that the city bought from its neighbour, the Sultan of Johor, is very new. It has become an absorbing *Learning Forest* with a *Treetop Walk*. Children love the large playground and they will also be fascinated by *Eco Garden*, the copy of a primeval landscape. Originally, the Botanic Gardens – as well as the predecessor laid out by Sir Stamford Raffles – were an experimental site for the commercial use of plants. Raffles concentrated on edible plants and spices and the botanist Henry Ridley started trial plantings of rubber trees, whose seed had been smuggled to Singapore from Brazil, in the middle of the 19th century. He was initially made fun of as 'Mad Riley' but he actually laid the foundations for the production of natural rubber that became one of the most important sectors of Asian economy. *Daily 5am–midnight | free admission | Orchid Garden daily 8.30am–7pm | admission 5 S$ | Jacob Ballas Children's Garden Tue–Sun 8am–7pm | free admission | 1 Cluny Road | entrance, corner of Holland Road | www.sbg.org.sg | MRT CC 19 Botanic Gardens | MRT NS 22 Orchard, then bus 7, 77, 106, 123, 174 from Orchard Boulevard*

GEYLANG SERAI (0) (*d3*)

Malaysian everyday life and brothels – you'll find a colourful mixture of all sorts here. The best restaurants, which also offer specialities like frog's legs and durians, alternate with little workshops and hotels, including some where prostitution is practiced. Wealthy Arabs and Malays had their magnificent villas – many of them built in a gingerbread-house style – erected in this part of the city. In the small shops next door you can find fabrics or spices, like nowhere else in Singapore, for example in the *Joo Chiat Complex (1 Joo Chiat Road)*. Malay culture still characterises life in Geylang, especially on religious holidays. For Muslim holidays such as Hari Raya Puasa, the festive meal that marks the end of Ramadan fasting, Geylang Serai is always splendidly decorated. *MRT CC9, EW 8 Paya Lebar*

HOLLAND VILLAGE (0) (*A1*)

Expat Heaven: the envoys of the banks, multinational companies, medium-size firms and schools like to have their homes near Holland Village. Here, they are close to the city centre but still in a green environment. There are some inexpensive shops that cater to Western tastes in this district – especially in the *Holland Village Shopping Centre*. Tailor shops, shoes and fashion, souvenirs, hair salons, nail studios and a small post office – all under one roof. The Indian newsagents on the

SIGHTSEEING

street corners have a wide selection of international newspapers. On the left of Holland Avenue is the old military housing area *Chip Bee Gardens,* especially on *Jalan Merah Saga* are the especially hip restaurants. On the right are the shopping complexes and the local market with *hawker centre*. It's buzzing here every evening, the streets are closed to traffic and the pubs and restaurants are brimming. *MRT CC 21 Holland Village | bus 7, 77, 106 from MRT NS 22 Orchard/Orchard Boulevard*

for Singapore's smart set. The district lies hidden between Holland Village and the inner city, opposite the Botanic Gardens. The feeling of space, the former military barracks and the tropical trees are what combine to make this district so attractive. Once a nutmeg plantation, new life has since moved in with restaurants, wine shops, antique dealers, boutiques, galleries and spas. It will take you a while if you intend to walk up the hill, but you will be rewarded with many interesting discoveries. These include fashionable meeting places like the *PS. Cafe at Harding*, as well as dealers in old Buddha statues such as *Shang Antique,* the chocolate factory *Anjalichocolat* or the carpet shop *Lotto Carpets*. *MRT NS 22 Orchard/Orchard Boulevard | then bus 7, 77, 106, 123, 174*

Green, tropical, luxuriant and full of pleasant surprises: Botanic Gardens

TANGLIN VILLAGE (DEMPSEY HILL)
(128 A–B 4–5) (*C–D2*)

The number of Ferraris, Maseratis and Porsches parked here will make it clear that Dempsey Hill is the absolute hotspot

59

FURTHER AFIELD

Feathered diversity: Jurong Bird Park

FURTHER AFIELD

EAST COAST PARK (0) (*N–S3*)
BBQing, camping, fishing, cycling, inline skating or just relaxing by the sea – this park, which runs for miles along the east coast of the city state, is one of the Singaporeans' most popular excursion locations. That is why you should avoid visiting it at the weekend! A stop in one of the many seafood restaurants is especially recommendable, as this is actually the only place you can eat *Pepper Crab* in casual surroundings. *www.nparks.gov.sg | bus 16 to Marine Terrace, then further through an underpass under the ECP Highway; bus 36 from Orchard Road or MRT CC 9/EW 8 Paya Lebar, then bus 76*

INSIDER TIP MEMORIES AT OLD FORD FACTORY (0) (*b4*)
Dreams become nightmares: in 1941, the Ford factory in Singapore became the first plant in South-East Asia to produce automobiles. The city has converted the historical buildings into a fascinating memorial site to Singapore's experiences during the Japanese occupation (1942–45). The Japanese renamed the city Syonan-To, 'Light of the South'. But they ruled with such brutality that the Singaporeans have not been able to forget their atrocities to this day. *Mon–Sat 9am–5.30pm, Sun noon–5.30 pm | admission 3 S$ | 351 Upper Bukit Timah Road | www.nas.gov.sg/formerfordfactory | MRT NS 2 Bukit Batok, then bus 173; MRT CC 14 Botanic Gardens, then bus 170/171*

JURONG BIRD PARK
(0) (*b4*)
South-East Asian hornbills or South-American toucans – you'll find almost everything that has feathers in the largest bird park in South-East Asia. It is home to more than 600 species from all over the world including the second-largest penguin show on earth. The largest aviary covers an area of five acres with a tropical forest, waterfall, artificial rain showers and rumbles of thunder that make the colourful tropical birds seek cover. In the *Pools Amphitheater* there's a *Highflyers Show* several times a day in which trained birds perform amazing artistic feats. *Daily 8.30am–6pm | admission adults 28, children 18 S$ | lunch with the parrots noon–2pm, adults 25, children 20 S$ | reservation tel. 63 60 85 60 | combined ticket available, for Zoo, Night Safari and River Safari | 2 Jurong Hill | www.birdpark.com.sg | MRT EW 27 Boon Lay, continue with bus 194 or Singapore Attractions Express (www.saex.com.sg) from many hotels and Orchard Road from 6 S$*

SIGHTSEEING

SINGAPORE ZOO, NIGHT SAFARI & RIVER SAFARI ⭐ (0) (*c3*)

Go on safari day and night: the beautiful Singapore Zoo was conceived as an 'open zoo' – which means that most of the animals are kept in large open enclosures. Often only deep trenches filled with water separate the visitors from those being visited. The *Night Safari* is a world-famous attraction that no visitor to Singapore should miss. You can see the 3600 animals being fed at various times between 9am and 5pm. If you wish you can register for the *Jungle Breakfast (daily 9am–10.30am | admission adults 33, children 23 S$ | book via tel. 63 60 85 60 or saleshotline.wrs@wrs.com.sg)* with the orang-utans. The *Conservation Centre* provides full information on the animals' breeding.

The *River Safari* is a further highlight – a 100-million-S$ tropical jungle you can explore by boat. The journey takes you through 10 global ecosystems such as the Nile Delta, along the Mississippi or up the Amazon. Children love to see the pandas Kai Kai and Jia Jia in their Panda Forest enclosure on the river. There are also the smaller red pandas.

The zoo closes at 6 pm, 75 minutes later the gates to *Night Safari (daily 7.15pm–midnight, tickets on sale until 11pm | admission adults 45, children 30 S$)* open. Torches blaze at the entrance, and the site is bathed in a dim glow; special lamps illuminate the 1000 animals (110 different species) until midnight. Apply insect repellent generously! At the entrance there is a small map suggesting various signposted routes. When you get tired, let the railway carry you around. Be sure to leave enough time to get here; the journey from the city takes a good 1¼ hours.

Daily 8.30am–6pm | admission adults 35, children 25 S$; people celebrating their birthday get in free (bring your passport!); Park Hopper combined tickets for Zoo, Night Safari, River Safari and Jurong Bird Park are better value | 80 Mandai Lake Road | tel. 62 69 34 11 | www.wrs.com.sg | www.zoo.com.sg | bus 171 Mandai Lake Road, then cross the road and continue with bus 138 to the terminus; MRT NS 16 Ang Mo Kio, continue with bus 138; MRT NS 4 Choa Chu Kang, then continue with bus 927 | The Singapore Attractions Express collects you from some hotels and underground stations (www.saex.com.sg)

SPOTLIGHT ON SPORTS

The annual night-time Formula 1 race sends scenes of the city into the living rooms of billions of people around the world. If you are interested in sport in Singapore, you will find all you need to know on the *Singapore Sports Council (www.ssc.gov.sg)* website. Singapore's pride and joy is the *Singapore Sports Hub* (0) (*N2*)*(www.sportshub.com.sg)*, the national stadium which hosts major sporting events. The roof can be opened, the seats are cooled and there's room for 55,000 spectators. The Padang is the main sports arena in the city centre. *Singapore Cricket Club (www.scc.org.sg)* still plays on its old ground and this is also where rugby teams fight it out *(www.scrugbyseens.com)*. Water-sports fans can watch sailing regattas in the windy winter months and dragon-boat races *(www.sdba.org.sg)* and surfing *(www.wakeboard.com)* all year round.

61

FOOD & DRINK

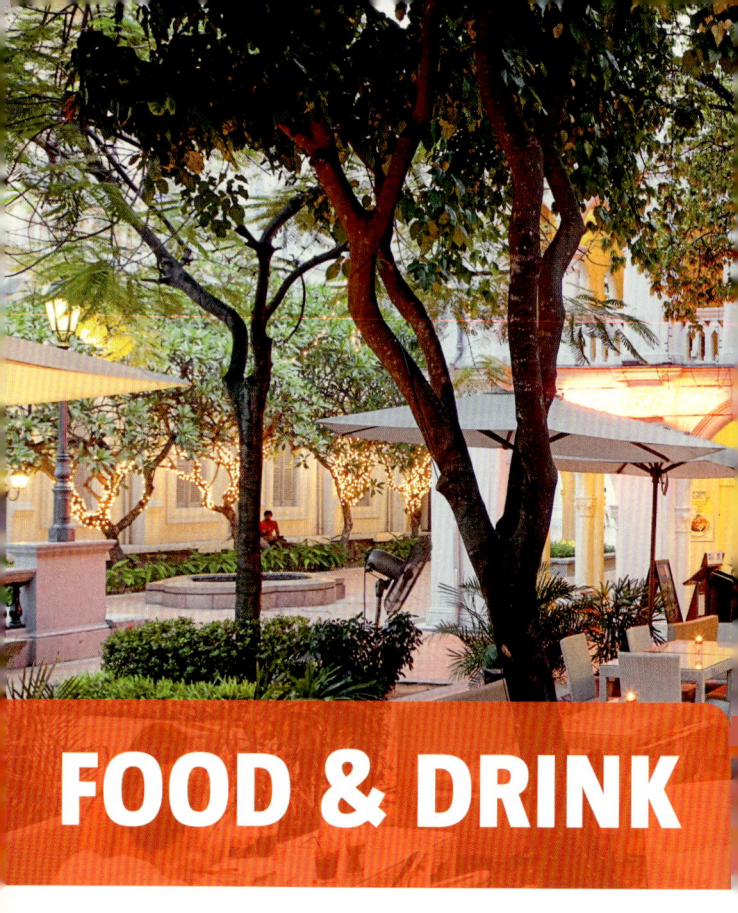

Darn tasty – that's what most people say after a stroll through Singapore's street kitchens and restaurants. Food is the nation's passion. Good cooks are highly respected. You can taste all the cuisines Asia has to offer, but also the best of Australian and European cooking.

The rule is: INSIDER TIP it is better to eat less but do it more often. The servings are often smaller than at home – this applies especially to street booths. That will also make it easier for you to try out all the different national styles of cooking.

The best way to do that is in one of the so-called hawker centres, a collection of small cookshops, usually in the basement or upper floors of large shopping centres and at regular food markets. You sit down on plastic chairs to eat after you have chosen a dish directly from one of the pans; drinks are sold at an extra booth.

In addition to Chinese, Indian and Malay cooking, Singapore has its own unique style: *Peranakan* cuisine, which developed along the Straits of Malacca. The Peranakan culture was established by the early immigrants and combines Chinese with Malay and European influences. In Singapore, you can dine for 4 S$ or 400 S$. Seven percent value-added tax (GST) and a service charge of 10 percent are added to the prices on the menu. Nobody ex-

The magic word is: variety. Singapore is a melting pot for all the cuisines of our world – from China to Italy and Malaysia to France

pects to be tipped. If you order alcohol, it will be very expensive because of the high taxes. A beer can easily cost 7.50 S$.

CAFÉS & TEA HOUSES

INSIDER TIP 40 HANDS (134 C4) (*F5*)
This retro café in a shophouse from the 1930s, in the heart of the fashionable Tiong Bahr district, serves one of the best coffees in town. There are also sandwiches and hotdogs at lunchtime. *Daily 7.30am–7pm, open longer Thu–Sat | 78 Yong Siak Street | www.40handscoffee.com | MRT EW 17 Tiong Bahru*

CAT CAFÉ NEKO NO NIWA
(136 B3) (*J4*)
Cuddling and coffee for anyone who is missing their beloved pet. 13 well-

63

CAFÉS & TEA HOUSES

TWG, the oasis in the middle of the hustle and bustle of shopping in the mall

groomed, headstrong cats allow you to share the café, including coffee and cake, with them. *Mon, Wed–Fri 11am–10pm, Sat/Sun 10am–10pm | admission from 12 S$ | 54a Boat Quay | #2 | www.catcafe.com.sg | MRT EW 14, NS 26 Raffles Place*

CEDELE (129 D4) (*F2*)
Chain of cafés in many shopping districts; the most popular place for Western women in Singapore. Cedele serves organic cakes and fair-trade coffee. For example: *daily 10am–10pm | Wheelock Place | 501 Orchard Road | #03–14 | www.cedeledepot.com | MRT NS 22 Orchard*

PS. CAFE AT HARDING
(128 A4) (*C2*)
Artists and writers congregate here under the tropical trees to enjoy brunch or afternoon tea, the Australian-style food and the gigantic chocolate cakes. *Thu 8am–11pm, Fri/Sat 8am–1am | 28b Harding Road, Tanglin Village | tel. 6479 33 43 | MRT NS 22 Orchard, then bus 7, 77, 106, 123, 174 from Orchard Boulevard*

TEA CHAPTER
(135 F4) (*H6*)
Probably the most famous tea house in Chinatown. You can experience a **INSIDER TIP** tea ceremony too and buy the choice leaves. *Daily 11am–11pm | 9/11 Neil Road | www.tea-chapter.com.sg | tel. 6226 1175 | MRT NE 4 Chinatown*

TOAST BOX
(129 F4–5) (*G2*)
Here you'll get only classic Singaporean food – but that's a bit of an understatement: the classic breakfast of kopi (coffee) or teh (tea) and kaya toast (with coconut and egg jam). Great to watch: the typical pouring of coffee in high arcs. *In many large shopping centres, e.g. daily 7.30am–9.30pm | The Paragon | #02–08a | www.toastbox.com.sg | MRT NS 22 Orchard*

FOOD & DRINK

TWG ★ *(129 E4) (⌘ F2)*
The charm of good old Europe in the heart of Singapore's most modern shopping centres: the TWG tea house has developed into a popular meeting place in the ION and Marina Bay Sands complex. Not without reason: the start-up created by young entrepreneurs has become an (expensive) institution that sells many of its own unique blends. *Daily 10am–10pm | ION | 2 Orchard Turn | #02-21 | www.twgtea.com | MRT NS 22 Orchard*

HAWKER CENTRES & FOOD COURTS

Most of the snack centres with their many small booths open early in the morning for breakfast and work until late at night. The most stylish hawker centre is the ★ *Lau Pa Sat Festival Market (136 B4) (⌘ J5–6) (MRT DT 17 Downtown)* on Robinson Road. There was already a market here in 1822. As part of the redevelopment of Chinatown, the Singapore Tourism Board revamped *Smith Street (135 F4) (⌘ H5) (MRT NE 4 Chinatown)* and turned it into a strip of restaurants *(MRT NE 4 Chinatown)*.

A fine *food court* is on the roof of the *Vivo City (138 C2) (⌘ D8)* shopping centre, directly by the sea: the *Food Republic @ Vivo City (# 3 | 1 Harbour Front Walk | MRT NE 1 Harbourfront)* is laid out like an old Chinese village. The very good *Maxwell Road Food Centre (135 F4) (⌘ H6) (MRT DT 19, NE 4 Chinatown)* in Chinatown resembles an open market. You'll also find some very good *hawker centres* alongside the Esplanade Culture Centre in ● *Makansutra Gluttons Bay*. In the basement (B4) of the *ION Orchard* centre, every day at 11am, you can follow the **INSIDER TIP** *Local Food Trail (tel. 62 38 82 28)* to get to know the local specialities.

RESTAURANTS: EXPENSIVE

THE BLACK SWAN
(136 B4) (⌘ J5)
Western luxury behind a Singaporean art-deco façade. Bankers meet here for

---

MARCO POLO HIGHLIGHTS

★ **TWG**
Favourite meeting place for tea in the best shopping centre in town → p. 65

★ **Lau Pa Sat Festival Market**
Hawker food in a fairy-tale hall → p. 65

★ **The Clifford Pier**
An air of the glorious days of ocean liners with fine Asian specialities thrown in → p. 66

★ **The Knolls**
Enjoy the sunset on a terrace designed by Norman Foster → p. 67

★ **Supertree by Indochine**
The food is mediocre, the view is world-class → p. 68

★ **Din Tai Fung**
Watch as they make the dim sums, which then taste delicious too → p. 69

★ **The Intan**
Delve into Singapore's Peranakan eating culture → p. 69

★ **The Song of India**
Excellent Indian cooking – served with charm in a historical colonial house → p. 69

65

RESTAURANTS: EXPENSIVE

lunch, chic couples for dinner over champagne. *Mon–Fri 11.30am–2.30pm, tea 2pm–5pm, Mon–Sat 5pm–10.30pm | 19 Cecil Street | tel. 81813305 | www.theblackswan.com.sg | MRT EW 14, NS 26 Raffles Place*

COLONY (137 D2) (*K4*)
Ring in Sunday with a *Vintage Champagne Brunch*! Feast your way for hours through delicacies from seven different kitchens – oysters, eggs Benedict with lobster, Wagyu beef. Let time drift by bet-

FAVOURITE EATERIES

Resting and roasting
Australia in Little India: you no longer need to jump into an(other) airplane to experience the coffee culture of Melbourne. Designers, filmmakers and authors like meeting up here – the beans in the former hardware store INSIDERTIP *Chye Seng Huat Hardware* **(131 E3)** (*L1*) *(Tue–Fri 9am–7pm, Sat/Sun 9am–10pm | 150 Tyrwhitt Road | www.cshhcoffee.com | MRT EW 11 Lavender | Moderate)* are roasted in ancient machines. And you can certainly taste the difference.

Captain's table
Wanderlust in the flesh. In the past this was the pier for ocean liners to dock and set sail. Today the atmosphere in the tall hall is still a little reminiscent of the 1920s, only the travel trunks are missing. ★ *The Clifford Pier* **(136 C3)** (*J–K5*) *(daily noon–2.30pm, tea 3.30pm–5.30pm, dinner 6.30pm–10pm, late supper Sun–Thu 10pm–midnight, Fri/Sat 10pm–1am | 80 Collyer Quay | Clifford Pier | tel. 65 97 52 66 | www.fullertonbayhotel.com | MRT EW 14, NS 26 Raffles Place | Expensive)* feels like an invitation to the captain's table on a cruise ship, including the hushed music of the house band. The kitchen caters to both Asian and European tastes, the food is usually light and delicious.

Duck in a spin
Back to the future: this place looks like it's stuck in the 1960s. And everything is spinning – including the Peking duck. Sitting on top of the flour mill silos, INSIDERTIP *Prima Tower Revolving Restaurant* **(139 D2)** (*Q5*) *(Mon–Sat 11am–2.30pm, Sun 10.30am–2.30pm, daily 6.30pm–10.30pm | 201 Keppel Road | tel. 62 72 88 22 | www.pfs.com.sg | MRT NE 1 Harbourfront | then bus 10, 100 towards city centre | Expensive)* serves fine Chinese cuisine. And then there's the panoramic view over the city. It's best at lunchtime: the view stretches into the distance, the prices are rock bottom.

Mr Chan reaches for the stars
Queuing, eating off paper plates, sitting on hard benches? Is this what a Michelin star means in Singapore? Yep. Those who maintain arrogance will miss the chance of super tasty chicken. Since Chan Hon Meng cooked his way to a Michelin star at his hawker stand *Hong Kong Soya Sauce Chicken Rice* **(135 E–F4)** (*H5*) *(Thu–Tue 10am–7pm | Blk 335 Smith Street | #02–127 | Chinatown Complex | Budget)*, he has sold even more chicken and the queue in front of his street kitchen is longer than ever. So come early, or he might be sold out.

FOOD & DRINK

The classy surroundings at The Knolls make it hard to focus on the fabulous food

ween courses. Enjoy the music. And keep reaching for that Champagne glass – as much bubbly as you can drink is included in the price. *Sun noon–3.30pm | 188 S$ | 7 Raffles Av. | #3 | The Ritz-Carlton, Millenia Singapore | tel. 6434 5288 | www.ritzcarlton.com/en/hotels/singapore/dining/colony | MRT CC 4, DT 15 Promenade*

IGGY'S (129 D4) (*E–F2*)

The tiny restaurant with the strong Japanese influence in the kitchen is one of the city's best. The open kitchen is larger than the dining room, which seats only 40 guests. Reservation essential! *Mon, Thu–Sat noon–1.30pm and Mon–Sat 7pm–9.30pm | The Hilton Hotel | 581 Orchard Road | #3 | tel. 6732 2234 | www.iggys.com.sg | MRT NS 22 Orchard*

JAAN (136 B1) (*J3*)

One of the 50 best restaurants in Asia, with a spectacular view from the 70th floor. Head chef Julien Royer offers sublime fusion cuisine. *Mon–Sat noon–2.30pm and 7pm–10pm | Equinox Complex Swissôtel The Stamford | #70 | 2 Stamford Road | tel. 6837 3322 | www.jaan.com.sg | MRT NS 25, EW 13 Cityhall*

THE KNOLLS ★

(138–139 C–D5) (*Q7*)

It is difficult to imagine a more beautiful view – and it would be equally difficult to beat the food. You can have your meal sitting on the sea-view terrace of this colonial house on Sentosa, which was restored by leading architect Norman Foster. After dinner, the ● **INSIDER TIP** **lounge on the first floor** is the ideal place to relax with a drink by candlelight. The cuisine is modern Asian. *Daily 7am–11pm | in the Capella Hotel on Sentosa | tel. 6513 4275 | www.capellasingapore.com | from Vivo City (MRT CC 29, NE 1 Harbourfront) with the Sentosa Express (S2 Imbiah) or by bus; also pick-up service*

PUNJAB GRILL

(137 D–E 3–4) (*K–L5*)

Although the name might not lead you to expect very much, master chef Jiggs Kalra's cooking will carry you back to the India of old. He has modernised the cuisine of North India with great finesse. *Daily 11.30am–3.30pm and 6.30–11pm | Marina Bay Sands | #B1–01a, Galeria Level | tel. 6688 7395 | www.punjabgrill.com.sg | MRT CE 1, DT 16 Bay Front*

67

RESTAURANTS: MODERATE

SKY ON 57 ☼ (137 D3–4) (🗺 K–L5)
Chef Justin Quek offers French/Asian cuisine for gourmets. The breathtaking view from the *Skypark* of the *Marina Bay*

Fusion specialist above the rooftops of Singapore: Justin Quek from Sky on 57

Sands down onto the city and the sea is thrown in for free. The *bar (daily 11am–11.45pm)* is a gem in its own right. *Mon–Fri 7am–10.30am, Sat/Sun 7am–11am, daily noon–5pm and 6pm–10.30pm | Sands Sky Park Tower 1 | #57 | in the Marina Bay Sands complex | tel. 66 88 88 57 | www.marinabaysands.com/restaurants/sky-on-57.html | MRT CE 1, DT 16 Bay Front*

SUPERTREE BY INDOCHINE ★ ☼
(137 E4) (🗺 L5)
A one-of-a-kind location: the Supertree is only at the *Gardens by the Bay*. The restaurant and rooftop bar are situated on two levels in the metal tropical trees, high above the gardens. It is actually too loud here and the food is so-so. But it's true: you have to visit at least once. *Sun–Thu noon–1pm, Fri/Sat noon–2am | 18 Marina Gardens Drive | #03–01 | Gardens by the Bay | tel. 66 94 84 89 | indochine-group.com/home/locsingapore-supertree.php | MRT CE 1, DT 16 Bayfront*

THE TIPPLING CLUB (136 A5) (🗺 H6)
Do you want to have your steak melted and your fish as a drink? If you do, the Tippling Club is the place for you – this is where Ryan Clift prepares molecular food. Some people come just to enjoy the INSIDER TIP ▸ cocktails. *Mon–Fri noon–3pm, Mon–Sat 6pm–open end | 38 Tanjong Pagar Road | tel. 64 75 22 17 | www.tipplingclub.com | MRT EW 15 Tanjong Pagar*

TÓNG LÈ PRIVATE DINING ☼
(136 C3–4) (🗺 J5)
Many consider this to be the best Chinese gourmet restaurant in Singapore at the moment. Alongside exquisite food served in an intimate atmosphere, there's also a fantastic view of the sea. Reservations only. *Mon–Sat 11.30am–3pm, 6pm–11pm | OUE Tower 08 and 10 | 60 Collyer Quay | tel. 66 34 32 33 | www.tong-le.com.sg | MRT EW 14, NS 26 Raffles Place*

RESTAURANTS: MODERATE

BROTZEIT ☼
(138 C2) (🗺 D8)
If you have had enough of chicken and rice, you might like to try the dripping and liver sausage sandwiches at Brotzeit in the Vivo City. They are reasonably priced and there is a free view of the water. *Mon–Thu noon–midnight, Fri/*

FOOD & DRINK

Sat noon–1.30am, Sun 11am–midnight | 1 Harbourfront Walk | #01–149–151 | Vivo City | tel. 62 72 88 15 | www.brotzeit.co | MRT NE 1, CC 29 Harbourfront | branches: 313@Somerset (Orchard Road) and in the Raffles City shopping centre

DIN TAI FUNG ★
(137 D3–4) (*K–L5*)

Dim Sum live: here you can watch the chefs at work while you're queuing for a table. It's worth the wait: the mini dumplings are a dream, and the service is hard to beat, too. *In many shopping centres, e. g. Marina Bay Sands | 2 Bayfront Av. | #B2–63 | Sun–Thu 10.30am–10.30pm, Fri/Sat 10am–11.30pm | tel. 66 34 99 69 | www.dintaifung.com.sg | MRT CE 1, DT 16 Bayfront*

INSIDER TIP EAST COAST SEAFOOD CENTRE (0) (*d4*)

This is the perfect place to try Singapore's national dish ● *Black Pepper Crab*. But it's an acquired taste. The entire row of restaurants along the coast specialises in seafood. The view of the ocean is romantic but the restaurants themselves provide a rather sober Chinese atmosphere with plastic stools and neon lighting. 1206 *Upper East Coast Road | preferably by taxi*

THE INTAN ★ (0) (*d4*)

Here you will be able to delve deep into Peranakan culture: first of all you are shown the authentic house and then served a home-made Peranakan dish for lunch, at tea-time or for dinner. Only by appointment. *69 Joo Chiat | tel. 64 40 11 48 | MRT EW 7 Eunos, then bus 7, 24, 67*

NANBANTEI (129 E4) (*F1*)

Hard to find, but it's worth the search: a tiny restaurant in a shopping centre, but the Japanese restaurant has its regular clients. The fresh salmon rolled in bacon and the raw mackerel are absolutely delicious. The seat at the counter directly in front of the charcoal grill is great. *Daily noon–2.30pm, 6–10.30pm | 14 Scotts Road | Far East Plaza | #05–132 | tel. 67 33 56 66 | www.nanbantei.com.sg | MRT NS 22 Orchard*

THE SONG OF INDIA ★
(129 E3) (*F1*)

One of the most exquisite Indian restaurants in the city. You will be delighted by the charm of the old colonial house although you might find the interior decoration a bit kitschy. But you will not be able to fault chef Millind Sovani's excellent cooking. *Daily noon–3pm, 6–11pm | 33 Scotts Road | tel. 68 36 00 55 | www.thesongofindia.com | MRT NS 22 Orchard*

INSIDER TIP SPRING COURT
(135 F3) (*H5*)

Singapore's oldest family-run restaurant serves traditional Chinese cooking at reasonable prices. The locals love to eat the fish dishes. *Daily 11am–2.30pm, 6pm–10.30pm | 52–56 Upper Cross Street | tel. 64 49 50 30 | www.springcourt.com.sg | MRT NE 4, DT 19 Chinatown*

TRUE BLUE (136 B1) (*J3*)

Chef Baba Ben, as the Singaporeans call Benjamin Seck, cooks in the traditional Peranakan style – a mixture of Chinese, Malay and European cuisines. The recipes still come from his mother Nyonya Daisy Seah. The restaurant is located next to the Peranakan Museum. *Daily 11am–2.30pm, 6–9.30pm | 47/49 Armenian Street | tel. 64 40 04 49 | www.truebluecuisine.com | MRT CC 2 Bras Basah | MRT EW 13, NS 25 Cityhall, then bus 197*

THE WHITE RABBIT (128 A4) (*C2*)

Chef Daniel Sia serves modern European food with a strong touch of Britain in the

69

RESTAURANTS: MODERATE

LOCAL SPECIALITIES

Bah Kut Teh – spicy herb soup with pork and offal

Bak Kwa – shredded pork, brushed with honey, then grilled: doesn't look very appetising, but tastes delicious

Chai Tow Kway/Carrot Cake – a kind of pancake with spring onions and sweet black sauce; not at all like the usual carrot cake

Char Kway Teow – fried flat noodles with sweet black sauce from the wok, with small Chinese sausages, soy sprouts, eggs and garlic

Chicken Rice – gently cooked chicken with various sauces: pure poetry! Originally from the Chinese province of Hainan, it is now Singapore's national dish

Dim Sum – dumplings with meat, shrimp or vegetable filling, steamed in typical small baskets

Hokkien Mee – yellow noodles fried in a wok: with pork or squid and vegetables

Kaya Toast – sweet breakfast pudding made with milk, eggs and lots of sugar

Laksa – the noodles in the famous spicy soup are thick and yellow; served with pieces of chicken or fish, tofu cubes and coconut milk or tamarind juice (photo left)

Nasi Lemak – classic Malay breakfast of sticky rice cooked in coconut milk and wrapped in a banana leaf; served with small sardines and plenty of chili

Rojak – tropical salad of cucumber, pineapple, mango, grilled tofu, tamarind juice, pieces of fried noodles with shrimp paste and chopped peanuts

Roti Prata – Indian pancake made with thin batter and served with a variety of fillings – most of them vegetarian. Stuffed with lamb or chicken, the pancakes are known as Murtabak; usually comes with curry sauce

Satay – chunks of chicken, lamb, beef or squid marinated in hot spices and then grilled over charcoal, traditionally served with peanut sauce, cucumber and raw red onion (photo right)

former garrison chapel. If the food's too expensive for you, you can't go wrong with the cocktails. Tue–Fri noon–2.30pm, 6.30–10.30pm, Sat/Sun 10.30am–2.30pm, 6.30–10.30pm | 39c Harding Road | tel. 64 73 99 65 | www.thewhiterabbit.com.sg | MRT NS 22 Orchard, then bus 7, 77, 106, 123 from Orchard Boulevard

FOOD & DRINK

RESTAURANTS: BUDGET

INSIDER TIP 328 KATONG LAKSA
(138 A6) (*M S2*)

You will not come across any tourists in this eatery. The street restaurant is in the heart of Katong, the old Peranakan district. 328 Katong Laksa won the 'Laksa War' against the neighbouring restaurants and Singaporeans come from the other side of town to enjoy the tasty soup that only costs 4 S$ here. *Daily 8am–10pm | 51–53 East Coast Road/Ceylon Road | bus 14 from Orchard Road*

NEW EVEREST KITCHEN (130 C3) (*M J1*)

No-frills ambience but tasty Nepalese-Tibetan food: if you eat here, you feel like you are at the base of an 8000-m (26,000-ft)-high mountain. The *Momos* (dumplings stuffed with meat) are just as tasty as the *Ladyfingers* (fried okra). In the heart of Little India. *Wed–Mon 11am–3pm, 5pm–11pm | 518 Macpherson | tel. 68 44 41 70 | www.neweverestkitchen.com*

KOMALA VILAS RESTAURANT
(130 C4) (*M J1*)

The most popular – and probably best – Indian vegetarian restaurant in the city. Here, you will be served all kinds of bread, a great variety of rice dishes and lentils and spinach in many variations. *Daily 11am–3.30pm, 6pm–10.30pm | tel. 62 93 69 80 | www.komalavilas.com.sg | 76–78 Serangoon Road | MRT NE 7 Little India*

INSIDER TIP OUR VILLAGE
(136 B3) (*M J5*)

This restaurant on the rooftop terrace of a shophouse on Boat Quay scores with an unbeatable combination of good food and a fantastic panorama. You leave the hustle and bustle behind you as soon as you enter the welcoming terrace where you will be served dishes from North India and Sri Lanka. *Daily 6pm–11.30pm | minimum charge 35 S$ per person | 46 Boat Quay | tel. 65 38 30 58 | MRT EW 14, NS 26 Raffles Place*

SINGAPORE ZAM ZAM (131 E5) (*M K2*)

A well-established Arab restaurant opposite the Sultan Mosque: the world of the *Murtabak*, freshly baked, salty pancakes filled with minced lamb, onions or egg. *Daily 8am–11pm | 697 Northbridge Road | tel. 62 98 62 30 | MRT DT 14, EW 12 Bugis*

TRAPIZZA (138 B4) (*M P6*)

Trapeze and pizza: Singapore's first trapeze school belongs to the restaurant. The unassuming pizzeria's tables and chairs are placed on the sandy beach of Sentosa island, the food is delicious, and your gaze will sweep over the sea. *Daily 11.30am–9.30pm | 101 Siloso Road | Sentosa | tel. 63 76 26 62 | MRT NE1 Harbourfront, then the bus (blue/red/green line) to the terminus at Siloso Beach*

LOW BUDGET

Visit one of the countless *hawker centres* at intersections and in the basement of almost all shopping centres. You will be able to savour all of the delicacies Asia has to offer at prices starting at 4 S$. You needn't worry about the quality. The *hawkers* are closely inspected.

If you are thirsty, you can always ask for ● *ice water*. The refreshing drink is usually served free of charge to accompany your meal in the restaurants in the city – but many tourists forget to ask for it. In any case, it is perfectly safe to drink.

SHOPPING

WHERE TO START?
Orchard Road (129 D–F 4–5, 130 A–B 5–6) *(ɰ E–H 1–3)*: Start your spree on one of the most beautiful shopping avenues in the world. The heat and heavy downpours, however, mean a lot of Singapore's shopping takes place in air-conditioned precincts. Start in the luxury shops in **ION Orchard**, move on, under or above ground, past hundreds of shops to the **Takashimaya** department store. Cross the street, ending up at **The Paragon** or **Tangs**.

Many people think that the ringing of the cash registers is actually the secret national anthem of the city state.

If you don't end up schlepping bags back to your hotel room, you must be a real shopping pooper. The most famous shopping boulevard in Singapore is ● *Orchard Road (129 D–F 4–5, 130 A–B 5–6) (ɰ E–H 1–3)*. There are several department stores with thousands of retail shops in this district alone; and the number is rising all the time. Things are sold wherever possible in Singapore. Even the *Esplanade* cultural centre has a whole row of small boutiques. *Marina Bay Sands* is the top address for lovers of luxury art-

Spending money as the elixir of life: 'I spend, therefore I am' is the motto of the Singaporean's favourite leisure-time activity

icles; the architectural highlight *Vivo City* has shops with a sea view. You will discover international chains such as Body Shop, Uniqlo and Zara in most of the malls. The shops are open seven days a week, usually from 10am to 10pm. At times, such as during the Christmas and Chinese New Year's festivities, the shopping centres stay open until 11pm. It is still possible to find bargains: ladies' shoes and clothing are often cheaper in Singapore than in Europe; the same applies for electronic articles. Be careful about prices that appear to be below the dealer's cost price; there is usually a catch. The accessories for the supposedly super-cheap video camera are often missing or there is no international guarantee. But things are generally very civilised in Singapore. Nevertheless, you should not pay for

BOOKS

anything until you receive the goods! You can bargain in small shops but, as a rule, the large department stores in the inner city have fixed prices. These are often 10–20 percent above those you could get elsewhere after long-drawn-out haggling. In order to avoid irritation later, look for the 'case trust' and 'QJS' signs on the shops where you make your purchases; these are awarded by the consumer protection organisation and the Union of Jewellers as an assurance of quality. If you still have complaints, call the toll-free *Tourist Hotline (Mon–Fri 9am–6pm | tel. 1800 7 36 20 00)*. A seven-percent Goods and Service Tax (GST) is added to most articles and services. Visitors can have the tax refunded if their purchases exceed 100 S$. For electronic processing of *tax refunds* you do not only get a receipt when you buy something, but also an 'e-TRSTicket' when you present your passport. Take this to the self-help kiosk at the border and have the amount of tax refunded to your credit card. You'll find details at *www.iras.gov.sg*.

BOOKS

BOOKS ACTUALLY (134 C4) (*F5*)
This literary bookshop is also a favourite meeting place. Situated in one of Singapore's most attractive streets, you can lose track of time here or at the café next door. *Sun/Mon 10am–6pm, Tue–Sat 10am–8pm | 9 Yong Siak Street | www.booksactually.com | MRT EW 17 Tiong Bahru*

Where shopping is raised to an art form: colourful sculptures at the entrance to the ION centre

KINOKUNIYA ★
(129 E5) (*F–G2*)
This is considered the largest bookshop in South-East Asia and also has a stock of books and magazines from many foreign countries. *391 Orchard Road | #04–20/20A/20B/20C/21 | Ngee Ann City | kinokuniya.com.sg | MRT NS 22 Orchard*

TIMES (129 F5) (*G2*)
Local bookstore chain with English-language literature, loads of magazines and stationery. Many outlets, e. g. Times Bookstores at Centrepoint. *176 Orchard Road | Centrepoint | #04–08/09/10/11 |*

SHOPPING

www.timesbookstores.com.sg | MRT NS 23 Somerset

LADIES' SHOES

The latest models are frequently half the price they cost in Europe. However, they are usually only available in sizes up to 6½ (US. 9). The widest selection is offered at the following stores: *Metro* (129 F4–5) (*ω G2*) (*290 Orchard Road | in Paragon*), *Tangs Orchard* (129 E4) (*ω F2*) (*310 Orchard Road*) and *Takashimaya* (129 E5) (*ω F2*) (*391 Orchard Road | Ngee Ann City*). All: MRT NS 22 Orchard

SHOPPING CENTRES

313@SOMERSET ★
(129 F5) (*ω G2*)
This department store has become the Singaporeans' favourite: it has four floors with the best shops in the city. And the *Food Republic food court* on the fifth floor is like a trip to all the countries in Asia, while the *Brotzeit* and *Marché* restaurants also cater to European tastes. *313 Orchard Road | www.313somerset.com.sg | MRT NS 23 Somerset*

THE CATHAY (130 B5–6) (*ω H–J3*)
Singapore's young crowd flock to The Cathay. The new mall behind the art-deco façade of a 1935 cinema has amusement arcades and cinemas under the roof and boutiques on the lower floors. *2 Handy Road | MRT CC 1 NS 24 NE 6 Dhoby Ghaut*

ION ORCHARD ★ ● ⚜
(129 E4) (*ω F2*)
Luxurious with lots of space to relax. You will be able to spend days in the main attraction on Orchard Road. There are restaurants, a *food court* in the basement and a post office. The design is ultra-modern. You are sure to lose your way – and that is just what the shop owners want. *2 Orchard Turn | www.ionorchard.com | MRT NS 22 Orchard*

MARINA BAY SANDS ★
(137 D3–4) (*ω K–L5*)
Be astonished and shop: the world's top luxury brands under a single (large) roof. There is even a copy of a section of Venice: almost authentic gondolieri will punt you along a canal running through the middle of the building. The store's own skating rink only appears to cool you down: its surface is made of plastic instead of ice. There is no lack of top-class restaurants and there are less expensive chain stores and restaurants in the rear section of the

---

MARCO POLO HIGHLIGHTS

★ **Kinokuniya**
For bookworms – not only when it's wet outside → p. 74

★ **313@Somerset**
The Singaporeans' favourite address → p. 75

★ **ION Orchard**
Singapore's exclusive mall with more than 300 shops → p. 75

★ **Marina Bay Sands**
The newest and most luxurious shopping centre: you can easily spend a full day here → p. 75

★ **Tanglin Village (Dempsey Hill)**
Today the in-crowd meets where soldiers used to drill → p. 79

★ **Mustafa**
Everything you ever wanted to buy – around the clock → p. 80

SHOPPING CENTRES

Singapore's shopping centres tend towards forming clusters, especially on Orchard Road

mall. *www.marinabaysands.com | MRT CE 1, DT 16 Bayfront*

NGEE ANN CITY
(129 E5) (*F–G2*)

The Japanese department store chain *Takashimaya* has taken over one wing of this temple to consumerism. The top floors are reserved for the exclusive boutiques of Armani and Co.; in the cellar, there is a good kitchenware department with woks and Asian tableware. Other attractions here include: good restaurants, hairdressers, the gigantic Kinokuniya bookshop and galleries. On Chinese holidays, you can taste 🟢 local delicacies on stands set up in the cellar. *391 Orchard Road | MRT NS 22 Orchard or bus 7, 77 from Orchard Boulevard*

ROBINSONS THE HEEREN
(129 F5) (*G2*)

The upmarket department store in the Robinsons chain offers fine wares from all over the globe and brands you'll find nowhere else in Singapore. Super-stylish displays. *260 Orchard Road | www.robinsons.com.sg | MRT NS 23 Somerset*

TANGLIN MALL
(128 C4) (*E2*)

Meeting place for many foreign managers' wives for coffee and shopping. They know why: *Shopping at Tiffany's* and *N's Boutique* sell INSIDER TIP designer clothing at outlet prices. *Daily 10am–9pm | 163 Tanglin Road | MRT NS 22 Orchard, then bus 7, 77, 123 from Orchard Boulevard*

INSIDER TIP YUE HWA
(136 A3) (*H5*)

You can still feel the special charm of the 1980s in this Chinese department store behind the original façade – and it is only here, in the heart of Chinatown, that you will be able to find a fine selection of genuine silk underwear, *cheongsams* (Chinese dresses) and traditional Chinese medicine. *70 Eu Tong Sen Street | MRT NE 4, DT 19 Chinatown*

SHOPPING

ELECTRONIC GOODS

If you prefer fixed prices, you should try the *Best Denki*, *Challenger* and *Harvey Norman* chains with many branches in the major shopping centres. Photo shops provide professional advice. Be careful about shopping in the *Orchard Towers* (129 D4) (*F1*) and *Lucky Plaza* (129 E4) (*F2*); you might get ripped off.

LORDS CAMERAS AND WATCHES
(129 E4) (*F2*)

An exception in the Lucky Plaza: cameras at reasonable prices, with reliable service – but do not forget to bargain. *304 Orchard Road | #01-79 Lucky Plaza | MRT NS 22 Orchard*

SIM LIM SQUARE
(130–131 C–D5) (*J2*)

This is a place where Singapore's computer experts like to shop. Sim Lim Square is a huge department store full of electronic shops from deep in the basement all the way up to the roof. As a rule, the prices here are fixed – but you can almost always manage to get a small discount. In 2015 a number of dealers were prosecuted and the police had to step in. *1 Rochor Canal Road | MRT EW 12 Bugis*

CLOTHING

You can buy international brand articles in all of the shopping centres and on *Orchard* and *Scotts Roads*. The best places to buy cheap t-shirts are in the shops in Little India and in *Bugis Village (4 New Bugis Street | MRT EW 12, DT 14 Bugis)*. Singapore promotes young design in a big way. The *National Design Centre* (p. 78) INSIDER TIP *Workshop Element* at *313@Somerset* (p. 75) or *Mu* at *260 Orchard Road* offer clothes by local fashion designers.

BRITISH INDIA (137 D3–4) (*K–L5*)

Here, you can still feel all of the charm of colonial days. The brand with the elephant makes exquisite fashion with a touch of tropical apparel; it is very expensive but some of the pieces are really original – and there's usually a sale on. *Sun–Thu 10am–11pm, Fri/Sat 10am–midnight | 2 Bayfront Av. | #B1–81 | The Shoppes at Marina Bay Sands | MRT CE 1, DT 16 Bayfront*

HAJI LANE (131 E5) (*K2*)

Shop here, in the middle of the trendy quarter Kampong Glam. A small lane full

LOW BUDGET

Sports shoes, but also eyewear, are to be had at INSIDER TIP *Queensway Shopping Centre* (1 Queensway/Alexandra Road) (132 B2–3) (*A4*) at considerably lower prices than in the sports outlets in the city. Unique atmosphere: haggling is a must. Get there by taxi

Song & Song shops don't look good, but it's the price that counts. Where else can you find Adidas shirts for 15 S$ or Nike tennis skirts for 20 S$? Range on offer changes daily. E. g. *304 Orchard Road* (129 E4) (*F2*) (Lucky Plaza | MRT NS 22 Orchard), *245a Holland Av.* (0) (*c4*) (MRT CC 21 Holland Village)

Used gold instead of new: it's worth rummaging for cheap jewellery in the city's many pawnshops. They charge by weight and have mostly 24-carat gold on offer. The design is usually Asian, but you'll find classics too.

77

ART & ANTIQUES

of small, hip labels but also vintage fashion and an over-20s clientele – always on the lookout for the latest trend. *MRT EW 12, DT 14 Bugis*

INSIDER TIP NATIONAL DESIGN CENTRE
(131 D6) (*K3*)

New design from Singapore and the rest of the world: In the shops *Keepers* (daily noon–7pm | #02–03) and *Kapok* (daily 11am–9pm | #01–05) you'll find lots of fancy things, from jewellery to soaps, clothes and accessories. *Daily 9am–9pm | 111 Middle Road | MRT CC 2 Bras Basah*

LOUIS VUITTON (137 D3) (*K5*)

It is impossible to count all of the luxury shops in Singapore, but there is only one floating on the water. The French brand's flagship store can be reached through an underwater tunnel or over a bridge. You'll find a couple of precious books and old Vuitton designs in the tunnel. *Sun–Thu 10am–11pm, Fri–Sat 10am–midnight | 2 Bayfront Av. | #B1–38/39, #B2–36/37/37 A | Crystal Pavilion North | MRT CE 1, DT 16 Bayfront*

INSIDER TIP ONG SHUNMUGAM
(0) (*0*)

Not cheap, but worth every penny: the award-winning Cheongsam designs (high-necked Chinese dresses) by the Singaporean designer of the same name. *Sat noon–7pm, Mon–Fri noon–2pm, later and Sundays by appointment per email | 43 Jalan Merah Saga | info@ongshunmugam.com | ongshunmugam.com | MRT CC 21 Holland Village*

SHANGHAI TANG (129 E5) (*F–G2*)

The Singapore branch of the fashion chain from Shanghai has everything you can find in the main shops in China: expensive fashion with an exotic touch and the colours of Asia. Shanghai Tang was founded in 1994 by the Hong Kong businessman and playboy David Tang Wing-Cheung and regards itself as the first global lifestyle brand from the Middle Kingdom. *391 Orchard Road | #03–06/07 | Ngee Ann City | MRT NS 22 Orchard*

TONG TONG FRIENDSHIP STORE
(131 D6) (*K3*)

You'll find reasonably priced Chinese Cheongsams with a modern feel here, often with large, graphic patterns. The designer moves successfully between western and eastern styles. *100 Beach Road | #01–04 | Shaw Towers | www.tongtong.sg | MRT CC3 Esplanade*

ART & ANTIQUES

Singapore is still a good place to find the almost obligatory Buddha for your modern minimalist apartment. There are many shops where you can look and rummage around for something special on *South Bridge Road* (136 A3–4) (*H5*) and *Pagoda Street* (136 A3–4) (*H5*) in Chinatown. *Tanglin Shopping Centre* (129 D4) (*E1*) is also a good address for Buddha statues and South-East Asian art. If you're a really big spender, why not take a walk through the new *Gillman Barracks* art centre – once used by the army, now home to over a dozen world-famous galleries.

GILLMAN BARRACKS
(132 B5) (*A6*)

Singapore's art district could not be in a prettier location. A state-aided project sees 17 galleries housed in renovated barracks in the middle of the jungle. The guided tours and 'art after dark' events are real hits. Plus restaurant. *Tue–Sun noon–7pm, special events also till late | 9 Lock Road | www.gillmanbarracks.com |*

SHOPPING

MRT CC 27 Labrador Park | bus 175 opposite Alexandra Point, stop no. 15 059

TANGLIN SHOPPING CENTRE
(129 D4) (*E1*)
Naga Arts and Antiques, Apsara and *Antiques of the Orient* have opened their doors in this shopping centre. *Antiques of the Orient* specialises not only in antiques but also in old maps and photographs. *19 Tanglin Road | MRT NS 22 Orchard, then bus 36 from Orchard Boulevard*

FURNITURE

It is also worth making a trip to Chinatown if you are looking for furniture. There are only a few genuine antiques – but even the reproduced cabinets can also be very attractive.

JUST ANTHONY (O) (*d3*)
An institution in Singapore: a large warehouse with restored Chinese furniture, as well as copies made using old wood; away from the centre. *Daily 9am–6.30pm | 379 Upper Paya Lebar Road | www.justanthony.com | MRT NE 12, CC 13 Serangoon, then bus 22, 43, 58*

TAN BOON LIAT BUILDING
(134–135 C–D 2–3) (*F4*)
Here you'll find old furniture. But so much more too – from candlestick holders to clay pottery. A series of galleries have come together in an old factory building. The *Journey East, Asia Passion, Red House, Eastern Discoveries* and *Fair Price Antiques* shops are worth a visit, but you'll have to bargain over the prices. *Daily from noon | 315 Outram Road | MRT EW 16, NE 3 Outram Park*

TANGLIN VILLAGE (DEMPSEY HILL) ★
(128 A5) (*C2*)
More and more restaurants are moving into the barracks on the former military base, but there are still some antique shops and galleries there. If you need a break during the process, there are plenty of good restaurants, cafés and wine bars in which you can relax. *Diagonally*

Island of bags: Louis Vuitton resides on an island in Marina Bay

TAILORS & FABRICS

opposite the Singapore Botanic Gardens | MRT NS 22 Orchard/Orchard Boulevard | then bus 7, 77, 106, 123, 174

Oceans of silk in People's Park

TAILORS & FABRICS

Forget the 24-hour offers; you will only be annoyed later when you see the crooked seams and realise that what you bought does not really fit. Most of the tailors in the hotel arcades work swiftly and well. Prices for a high-quality suit start at around 500 S$ in Singapore. You will find the best selection of fabrics, including dazzling materials from India, silks and batiks, on *Arab Street* (131 D4–E5) (*K H2*) (MRT EW 12, DT 14 Bugis)

INSIDER TIP CYC (136 C1) (*K3*)

Singapore's oldest shirt maker can satisfy the most demanding customers. You can buy not only the best men's shirts in town, but fashionable ladies' blouses, too. Prices start at 130 S$. The tailor will even be happy to renew collars and cuffs years later. *328 Newbridge Road | #02–12 | Raffles Hotel Arcade | MRT EW13, NS5 City Hall*

MUSTAFA ★ (131 D3) (*K1*)

You shouldn't be averse to crowds if you want to shop at Mustafa. It is full and you'll have to jostle. But there's nothing you can't get in this gigantic, chaotic Indian department store, which is open around the clock. The food and fabric departments are particularly impressive, but you'll also find anything else you can think of at very cheap prices here. *145 Syed Alwi Road | www.mustafa.com.sg | MRT NE 8 Farrer Park*

INSIDER TIP PEOPLE'S PARK (135 F3) (*H5*)

A place for real explorers: you can rummage around and haggle to your heart's content in the cloth market in Chinatown. Silk and batik can be tailored on the spot, and there are also small stands selling the most beautiful buttons. Many shops do not open until the afternoon. *100 Upper Cross Street | MRT NE 4, DT 19 Chinatown*

ROSSI (137 D1) (*K3–4*)

Rossi has been part of Singapore's garment-making world for three generations. However, tailoring the exquisite Italian fabric takes time. *9 Raffles Blvd. | #1–36 | Millenia Walk | tel. 63 34 18 00 | MRT CC 4, DT 15 Promenade*

SOUVENIRS

Colourfully painted wood carvings of fruit and animals, stick puppets from Indonesia, pewter goods from Malaysia and Chinese seal stamps, porcelain figures, place mats and jade in all forms can be found in the many small shophouses in Chinatown.

SHOPPING

Herbal teas also make popular souvenirs. Little India, with Arab Street and Bugis, is a treasure trove for souvenir hunters.

EU YANG SAN
(136 A4) (*H5*)
This shop for traditional Chinese herbal medicine was already founded in 1879. *269 South Bridge Road | MRT NE 4, DT 19 Chinatown*

LITTLE INDIA ARCADE
(130 C4) (*J2*)
This market is brimming with fabrics, pashminas, fashion jewellery as well as Indian needlework. There's sure to be something unusual here to take home with you. The INSIDER TIP henna tattoos, which the artists paint freehand on the skin, are cheap and particularly beautiful. *48 Serangoon Road | MRT NE 7 Little India*

INSIDER TIP NAIISE (129 F5) (*G2*)
Singaporeans say 'Can Lah' if something is going well. Now they print phrases like this on T-shirts – and they look good. Naiise sells design articles as souvenirs – many local designers are represented in the huge retail space, including cushions and T-shirts printed with local phrases. *Daily 11am–10pm | 277 Orchard Road | #02–02/24 Orchard Gateway | naiise.com | MRT NS 23 Somerset*

PRINTS (129 E4) (*F2*)
You are in Singapore and discover that your diary is almost full. No problem! Go to Prints; they can help you with their incredible selection. The small shop has the most beautiful diaries and notebooks, photo albums and pocket calendars – but they are not exactly cheap. E. g. *ION Orchard (2 Orchard Turn | #04–26 | www.prints-international.com | MRT NS 22 Orchard)*

RAFFLES HOTEL SHOP
(136 C1) (*K3*)
Stealing from the room isn't on. The shop in the exclusive Raffles Hotel sells tasteful but rather pricey souvenirs that often belong to the furnishing of its rooms. *1 Beach Road | MRT EW 13, NS 5 City Hall*

RISIS
Would you like to take some Singapore orchids home with you and have them live forever? *Risis* is the place where you can buy Singapore's national flower plated with gold. Branches: *Singapore Botanic Gardens* (128 A2) (*C1*) (*Cluny Road | MRT NS 22 Orchard | then bus 7, 77, 106 from Orchard Boulevard*), *C. K. Tangs* department store (129 E4) (*F2*) (*310 Orchard Road | #B1–17 | MRT NS 22 Orchard*)

ROYAL SELANGOR
(137 D3–4) (*K–L5*)
The traditional pewter studio was founded in Kuala Lumpur in Malaysia. After years of only selling dusty tankards and kitsch, Australian designers spruced up the programme. E. g. *10 Bayfront Av. | #B2–92 | Marina Bay Sands | www.royalselangor.com | MRT CE 1 Bayfront*

SIFR AROMATICS (131 E5) (*K2*)
The place to buy perfumed oils in a huge range of scents, produced by this Singaporean institution, and above all: completely alcohol-free. They can mix up a copy of any perfume here. *42 Arab Street | MRT EW 12, DT 14 Bugis*

INSIDER TIP SUPERMAMA
(131 E5) (*K2*)
Souvenirs of a different kind: the Singapore Icons series on fine, blue-and-white Japanese porcelain is a completely different kind of gift to take home. *Daily 11am–8pm | 265 Beach Road | www.supermama.sg | MRT EW 12, DT 14 Bugis*

ENTERTAINMENT

WHERE TO START?

The bad news to begin with – you will have to make a choice. The good news: it is impossible to make a wrong decision – you can find everything you are looking for. You should start at the **rooftop terrace of the Fullerton Bay Hotel (136 C3) (*J–K5)** and then head for one of the many nearby nightspots. There is a risk that you will not feel like moving on, however. Many people have spent more than half the evening up here.

Years ago, the name of the city had a certain double meaning attached to it – many people called Singapore 'sin galore'.

That all changed when the city state became independent in 1965. The new government cleaned things up, introduced censorship, made drug dealing a capital offence and broke up criminal rings. This made the city one of the safest in the world. But also a bit boring. It didn't stay that way for long, though. By the first night-time Formula 1 race in 2009, Singapore had begun to show what it is really capable of: a tropical metropolis that rocks, one that turns balmy evenings into

Photo: Party zone: Clarke Quay

Non-stop fun: swinging Singapore has long been one of the most fashionable party capitals of the world

long nights and where everybody finds what they are looking for once the sun goes down! The government continues to clamp down but has managed to cast off its image of being a bit of a wet blanket. The tourists and gamblers in the casino generate income. This led to the birth of the concept of 'Swinging Singapore'. The concept is bearing fruit: new bars, pubs and clubs are shooting up all over town. Today, Singapore also offers a wide range of cultural activities. Information on events is given in the local press such as the 'Straits Times'. 'Timeout' magazine or its website is even better.

There's something for everyone: the city's flashiest – and sometimes overpriced – entertainment area is around *Boat Quay* (136 B–C 2–3) (*ω G4–5*). The in-crowd now tends to meet a few hundred yards

83

BARS & PUBS

Brewed in the house: Brewerkz

further upstream at ⭐ *Clarke Quay* (136 A2) *(⌘ H4)* and *Robertson Quay* (135 D2) *(⌘ G4)*. The more mature prefer the bars, pubs and restaurants in *Tanglin Village (Dempsey Hill)* (128 A4–5) *(⌘ C2)*. The former barracks provide a mix of rustic charm and haute cuisine in the shade of tropical trees. Singapore's youth lets their hair down in the bars along *Mohamed Sultan Road* (135 E1–2) *(⌘ G4)* until well after midnight. The area around *Duxton Road* (135 E–F5) *(⌘ H6)* in Chinatown and nearby *Club Street* (135 F4) *(⌘ H5)* is the preferred stomping ground for the city's nouveau riche crowd and expats. *Kampong Glam*, *Little India* and *Bukit Pasoh* are becoming increasingly attractive with the experimental and alternative scene.

The cafés around *Emerald Hill* (129 F5) *(⌘ G2)* on Orchard Road mainly attract tourists. The former *Chijmes Monastery* (130 C6) *(⌘ J3)*, with its restaurants and bars, on the other hand is popular with locals and tourists alike. The venerable *Raffles Hotel* (136 C1) *(⌘ K3)* with the *Long Bar* is directly opposite. Here the toasts are made with the fitting drink, the *Singapore Sling*. It was poured for the first time in 1915 in the Long Bar.

BARS & PUBS

Happy hour makes the high prices in the centrally located pubs a little more tolerable. Some establishments reduce the prices for individual drinks but the 2-for-1 principle, where you get two glasses of beer or wine for the price of one, is more common (usually 5pm–8pm).

1-ALTITUDE ⭐ ☼ (136 B3) *(⌘ J5)*

Chill at 282 m (925 ft) above the sea: from this vantage point, the whole city lies spread out at your feet. And there's loud music in your ears. No shorts allowed. On the floor below you can dance the night away at *Altimate* (p. 85). *Mon–Thu 6pm–1am, Fri/Sat 6pm–3am | admission fees vary | 1 Raffles Place | # 63 | www.1-altitude.com | MRT NS 26, EW 14 Raffles Place*

28 HONGKONG STREET
(136 A–B 2–3) *(⌘ H4)*

Hip bar behind a nondescript façade. The barkeeper is known far and wide for his brilliant cocktails; style reminiscent of Manhattan. *Mon–Thu 5.30pm–1am, Fri/*

ENTERTAINMENT

Sat 5.30pm–3am | 28 Hong Kong Street | www.28hks.com | MRT NE 5 Clarke Quay

INSIDER TIP BAR STORIES
(131 E5) (*K2*)

Chocolate with cucumber juice and champagne? No problem. The barman here will mix any cocktail you want. *Sun–Tue noon–8pm, Wed–Sat noon–1am | 55/57a Haji Lane | MRT EW 12, DT 14 Bugis*

BREWERKZ (135 F2) (*H4*)

Large pub-restaurant, which also brews its own beer. It tastes great and is less expensive than in many other pubs. *Mon–Thu noon–1am, Fri–Sat noon–3am, Sun 11am–1am | 30 Merchant Road | #01–05 | Riverside Point | MRT NE 5 Clarke Quay*

KINKI ROOF TOP BAR
(136 B–C4) (*J5*)

If the roof terrace at the Fullerton Bay Hotel is too expensive, you'll love it here: the view over Marina Bay is the same, but the guests are younger, and graffiti adorns the walls. *Mon–Thu 5pm–midnight, Fri/Sat 5pm–open end | 70 Collyer Quay | #02–02 | www.kinki.com.sg | MRT NS 26, EW 14 Raffles Place*

LEVEL33 (136 C4) (*K6*)

Enough beer for everyone in the highest city brewery in the world. The view over Marina Bay and the island of Sumatra is stunning. The home-brewed beer is complimented by modern European food. *Sun–Wed 11.30am–midnight, Thu–Sat 11.30am–2am, Sun noon–midnight | 8 Marina Blvd. | #33–01 | Marina Bay Financial Centre Tower 1 | www.level33.com.sg | MRT DT 17 Downtown*

INSIDER TIP POTATO HEAD FOLK
(135 E4) (*H6*)

Chilling on four floors: a burger restaurant, a cocktail bar and a rooftop bar provide the perfect setting for a relaxed evening. *Tue–Sun 11am–12pm | 36 Keong Saik Road | www.ptthead.com | MRT EW 16, NE 3 Outram Park*

CLUBS & DISCOTHEQUES

Dance the night away on Wednesdays: some of the discos in Singapore are empty from Sunday to Thursday. On these days, the prices, which usually include one drink, are not as high. However, most are packed at the weekend, and often members-only late on.

ALTIMATE (136 B3) (*J5*)

Luxurious nightclub under *1-Altitude*. The view over Singapore is fantastic. As

---

MARCO POLO HIGHLIGHTS

★ **Clarke Quay**
The best place to go out and have fun on the Singapore River → p. 84

★ **1-Altitude**
The highest open-air bar → p. 84

★ **Timbre@The Arts House**
Live music and good food, right on Singapore River → p. 87

★ **Cocoon**
Indulge yourself protected by terracotta guards → p. 86

★ **Zouk**
Singapore's most famous discotheque → p. 87

★ **Esplanade**
Culture for all tastes in South-East Asia's largest concert house → p. 88

85

CLUBS & DISCOTHEQUES

is the view of the rich and beautiful. *Fri/Sat 10pm–2am | 1 Raffles Place | # 61 | www.1-altitude.com | MRT NS 26, EW 14 Raffles Place*

ATTICA (135 F2) (*H4*)
Discotheque over two floors with many lounges on the party pier Clarke Quay. *Wed/Thu 10.30pm–3am, Fri/Sat 10.30pm–4am | 3a River Valley Road | #01–03 | Clarke Quay | www.attica.com.sg | MRT NE 5 Clarke Quay*

B28 (135 F4) (*H6*)
Jazz and whiskey bar in Chinatown. Jazz bands play from Wednesdays to Saturdays and there's a choice of 200 single-malt whiskeys. *Mon–Sat 5pm–midnight | 28 Ann Siang Hill | www.btwentyeight.com | MRT NE 4, DT 19 Chinatown*

BLUJAZ CAFE (131 E5) (*K2*)
Jazz bar with live performances by local and international musicians. In the middle of trendy Kampong Glam. *Mon–Thu noon–1am, Fri noon–2am, Sat 4pm–2am | 11 Bali Lane | www.blujazcafe.net | MRT EW 12, DT 14 Bugis*

INSIDER TIP CANVAS
(136 B2) (*J4*)
This club aims to unite art, fashion and music. Performers include local artists such as drag queen Kumar. *Tue 5pm–1am, Wed/Fri 5pm–3am, Sat 6pm–4am | 20 Upper Circular Road | The Riverwalk | #B1–01 | www.canvasvenue.sg | MRT NE 5 Clarke Quay*

COCOON ★ (136 A2) (*H4*)
Enormous terracotta sentinels guard the entrance that leads to the Cocoon Bar on the ground floor and *Madame Butterfly Restaurant* upstairs. Opulence with opium couches, silk cushions and crystal chandeliers. *Sun–Thu 3pm–3am, Fri/Sat 3pm–6am | Merchant's Court | 3a River Valley Road | #01–02 | indochinegroup.com | MRT NE 5 Clarke Quay*

FASHION TV CLUB SINGAPORE
(135 F2) (*H4*)
This club completes the trio on Clarke Quay with *Attica* and *Zouk*, playing mainly house and R&B. *Wed 9pm–4am, Thu–Sat 10pm–4am | 3b River Valley Road | f-club.sg | MRT NE 5 Clarke Quay*

FOR BOOKWORMS & FILM BUFFS

Singapore – A Biography – the book by Mark Ravinder Frost and Yu-Mei Balasingamchow is a wonderful kaleidoscope of the history of the city state

12 Storeys – the Singaporean director Eric Khoo Kim Hai's film provides a fascinating, somewhat satirical, view of life in the government-subsidised housing of the average person in the city (1997). Khoo's film 'Be with Me' was presented at the 2005 Cannes Festival

I not stupid – has become a legendary saying in the city state. The critical filmmaker Jack Neo Chee Keong takes an analytical look at Singapore society in this work (2002)

In the Footsteps of Stamford Raffles – this updated version of the book on the life and times of the founder of Singapore Sir Stamford Raffles (1781–1826) by British ethnologist Nigel Barley was published in 2010

ENTERTAINMENT

Zouk, superlative dance floor: three discos, international DJs, always packed

TANJONG BEACH CLUB
(139 D6) (*R8*)

Chilling in deckchairs on the beach with a view of the sea, wild parties, cocktails and small dishes – the beach club has an Ibiza feeling. *Mon noon–10pm, Tue–Fri 11am–10pm, Sat 10am–10pm, Sun 10am–11pm | 120 Tanjong Beach Walk | 120 Tanjong Beach Walk | MRT NE 1, CC 29 Harbourfront, then further with the Sentosa Express to Beach Station, and from there with the Beach Train*

TIMBRE@SUBSTATION AND TIMBRE@THE ARTS HOUSE

You can also find things like this in the strict city state: the independent culture centre *Timbre@Substation* (136 B1) (*J3*) (*Sun–Thu 6pm–1am, Fri/Sat 6pm–2am | 45 Armenian Street | The Substation Garden | MRT CC 2 Bras Basah*) gets many local groups up on stage. Offshoot ★ *Timbre@The Arts House* (136 B2) (*J4*) (*Mon–Thu 6pm–1am, Fri/Sat 6pm–2am | 1 Old Parliament Lane/High Street | MRT EW 13, NS 25 City Hall*) is located on the Singapore River, next to the Parliament, with an open-air stage and restaurant. *www.timbregroup.asia/timbresg*

ZOUK ★ (135 D2) (*H4*)

Singapore's legendary nightclub, which has just moved to party central Clarke Quay, is always full and attracts the best DJs from all over the world. The largest dance floor in Zouk is big enough for almost 2000 guests and plays trance, techno and house. The smaller, in-house *Phuture* offers hip-hop and R&B. Zouk also puts on *Zouk Out*, the beach party on Sentosa. *Wed 9pm–3am, Thu 9pm–2am, Fri/Sat 9pm–4am | 3c River Valley Road | #01–05/06 The Cannery | zoukclub.com | MRT NE 5 Clarke Quay*

CINEMA

The Singaporeans are great film fans. There are cinemas on the upper floors of many of the shopping centres on *Orchard Road*, in *Vivo City* and in the renovated

87

CONCERTS, THEATRE, BALLET

art-deco theatre *The Cathay*. There is a complicated classification system with the advisory ratings *G* (general) *PG* (parental guidance) and *PG13* (not recommended for children under 13) and age restrictions *NC16* (no children) and *M18* (only for mature audiences). Cinema programme at *movies.insing.com*

CONCERTS, THEATRE, BALLET

There are performances of classical and modern plays, concerts, musicals and ballet every day of the week. Most take place in *Esplanade* (136 C2) (*K4*). Enchanting: the elaborately restored and sustainable *Victoria Theatre and Concert Hall* (136 B2) (*J4*) (11 Empress Place) is an attractive venue. Tickets for most cultural events are sold by the central ticketing service *sistic* (e. g. | Mon–Sat 10am–8pm, Sun noon–8pm | 313 Orchard Road | #B1, Concierge Counter | 313@Somerset | ticket hotline 63 48 55 55 | www.sistic.com.sg | MRT NS 23 Somerset).

CHINESE STREET OPERA
(135 F4) (*H5*)

Stages made of bamboo scaffolding and tarpaulins are put up on the streets on festive occasions (especially during the Festival of the Hungry Spirits). That is when the opera stars in their spectacular costumes and elaborate make-up recount legends from China's history in their shrill falsetto voices for hours on end. If you happen to be in Singapore when there is no Chinese festival, you can still get a taste of China's operatic art: every Friday and Saturday evening, the *Chinese Theatre Circle* (Fri/Sat 7pm–9pm | admission incl. dinner 40 S$ | 5 Smith Street | tel. 63 23 48 62 | www.ctcopera.com.sg | MRT NE 4 Chinatown), a traditional Chinese troupe, performs popular Cantonese operas in its tea house in Chinatown.

CONCERTS

The Singapore Symphony Orchestra was founded in 1979 and has given more or less regular performances on Friday and Saturday nights since then. You can obtain information on concerts from ★ *Esplanade* (136 C2) (*K4*) (www.esplanade.com) or at www.sso.org.sg. The *Esplanade* is also the venue of many guest performances by international soloists and orchestras. Especially delightful: the Sunday concerts at the romantic location of INSIDER TIP *Shaw Foundation Symphony Stage in the old Botanic Gardens* (128 A2) (*O*) (www.sbg.org.sg), a party for the whole family. The programme ranges from jazz via classical to pop music and is often announced on banners in the inner city. The music fes-

LOW BUDGET

Those who are after rock music head for the *Esplanade* (136 C2) (*K4*) (www.esplanade.com | bus 77, 171, 174, 36). No, you will not have to fork out 100 S$ for a ticket. Singapore's rock musicians get together for a free session on the open-air stage behind the building directly on the water (Fri–Sun 7.30pm–10pm).

Wednesdays are more than fair on the 'fairer' sex. It's *Ladies Night* in Singapore. Most bars and discos offer women free drinks and admission, only the men have to pay. The motto is 'bubbles and heels'. Times and locations on event pages such as www.citynomads.com or www.timeout.com/singapore

ENTERTAINMENT

tivals in *Fort Canning Park* (136 A–B 1–2) (*H–J 3–4*) are even more romantic. The *Nanyang Academy of Fine Arts* (tel. 65 12 40 00 | www.nafu.edu.sg) and the **INSIDER TIP** *Singapore Chinese Orchestra* (www.sco.com) organise regular performances of classical Chinese music. If you are interested in Indian music and dance performances, you should consult the *Singapore Indian Fine Arts Society* (tel. 62 99 59 29 | www.sifas.org).

INSIDER TIP LAUGH WITH KUMAR
Singapore's top drag queen makes fun of the government and everything close to Singaporean hearts. Kumar can get away with more than anybody else, he's an institution. Kumar performs in various places across the city, such as *Canvas* and *The Bank*, but puts in regular appearances at the *Hard Rock Café* (129 D4) (*E2*) (shows: Mon 11.30pm–1am | 50 Cuscaden Road | #04–01 | HPL House | book tickets in advance under tel. 62 35 52 32 | MRT NS 22 Orchard).

THEATRE

Theatrical performances in Singapore continue to be subject to government censorship. Fans of experimental theatre should visit the *Action Theatre*

Legends from the Middle Kingdom: Chinese street operas are a unique experience

(130 C6) (*J3*) (42 Waterloo Street | tel. 68 37 08 42 | MRT EW 12 Bugis | www.action.org.sg) in a restored pre-war bungalow, or *The Substation* (136 B1) (*J3*) (45 Armenian Street | tel. 63 37 75 35 | www.substation.org | MRT NS 25, EW 13 City Hall | MRT CC 2 Bras Basah, then bus 197). Currently, the best English-language stage in Singapore is the *Singapore Repertory Theatre* (135 E2) (*H4*) (DBS Arts Centre | 20 Merbau Road | tel. 67 33 81 66 | www.srt.com.sg | MRT NE 5 Clarke Quay)

89

WHERE TO STAY

Anything is possible in Singapore – from top-notch lodgings to boutique hotels in trendy areas. The Marina Bay Sands complex alone offers more than 2500 beds – and of course the famous pool on the roof.

Book a stay in a renovated colonial building like the classy Raffles, make a small designer hotel in a former shophouse like The Scarlett your home from home or spend the night in a luxurious beach hotel like the Capella. The city state also wishes to attract backpacking tourists and now promotes the establishment of cheap hotels. In light of the low cost of bus, MRT or taxi travel, it can be worthwhile staying a little outside the centre. If Singapore is just a break in your journey, look for a stopover hotel. That can score you up to 50 percent discount. The *Singapore Hotel Association* operates a counter at Changi Airport that is open 24 hours a day and organises last-minute rooms at reduced rates in hotels that are not fully booked. You can also contact hotels on the Internet via *www.stayinginsingapore.com.sg*.

HOTELS: EXPENSIVE

CAPELLA SINGAPORE ★
(138–139 C–D5) (*Q7*)

It cannot get more beautiful than this. The colonial building that was extended by Norman Foster has a panoramic view across the open sea. The rooms and restaurant facilities are first-class. *116 rooms, suites, apartments | from 500 S$ |*

Accommodation in a shophouse? Charming, reasonably priced hotels are now vying with the ultramodern luxury establishments

Sentosa island | tel. 63 77 88 88 | www.capellasingapore.com | from Vivo City (MRT CC 29, NE 1 Harbourfront) with the Sentosa Express (S2 Imbiah) or by bus; pick-up service is available

FAIRMONT SINGAPORE/ SWISSÔTEL THE STAMFORD
(136 C1) (*J3*)

The two high-rise hotels *Fairmont* (80 Bras Basah Road | tel. 63 39 77 77 | www.fairmont.com) and *The Stamford* (2 Stamford Road | tel. 63 38 85 85 | www.swissotel.com) built on top of the Raffles City shopping centre together have a total of 2049 rooms. The taller tower houses the Swissôtel The Stamford. The view from the rooms on the upper floors over the city and islands is spectacular. The hotels have a total of 16 restaurants between them; right at the top are the *Jaan* and the *Equinox*. www.rafflescityhotels.com | MRT NS 25, EW 13 City Hall, CC 3 Esplanade

HOTELS: EXPENSIVE

A lobbyist at the 1929 in Chinatown

INSIDER TIP NAUMI (131 D6) (*K3*)
The luxury boutique hotel has only 40 suites. But they've really got what it takes: each is individually decorated, and for your morning workout each room has a yoga mat and a selection of electronic 'toys' such as Xbox or Wii to choose from. A butler is on hand around the clock. Service is writ large at the Naumi. *41 Seah Street | tel. 6 43 60 00 | www.naumihotel.com | MRT NS 25, EW 13 City Hall | MRT CC 3 Esplanade*

PARKROYAL ON PICKERING
(136 A3) (*H5*)
Situated between Chinatown, the financial district and the pubs and clubs on the Singapore River, this new hotel is a green oasis, welcoming guests with hanging gardens outside. Relax after your shopping spree in the spa *St. Gregory*. *367 rooms | 3 Upper Pickering Street | tel. 68 09 88 88 | www.parkroyalhotels.com/en/hotels-resorts/singapore/pickering.html | MRT NE 4, DT 19 Chinatown*

RAFFLES HOTEL ★ (136 C1) (*K3*)
This legendary hotel is even more luxurious since its magnificent refurbishment. *104 suites from 650–6000 S$ | 1 Beach Road | tel. 63 37 18 86 | www.raffles.com | MRT NS 25, EW 13 City Hall*

ROYAL PLAZA ON SCOTTS
(129 E4) (*F1*)
You couldn't stay more centrally in Singapore's shopping district Orchard Road. The hotel is functional and reasonably priced for its location and is, furthermore, non-smoking. With swimming pool. *511 rooms | 25 Scotts Road | tel. 67 37 79 66 | MRT NS 22 Orchard | www.royalplaza.com.sg*

THE WAREHOUSE HOTEL
(135 D2) (*G4*)
Pay attention, this is a real treasure! Bags of rice were once stored here. Today the converted storehouses offer the finest modern industrial design, right on Robertson Quay. *37 rooms | 320 Havelock*

WHERE TO STAY

Road | tel. 68 28 00 00 | www.thewarehousehotel.com | MRT NE5 Clarke Quay

HOTELS: MODERATE

1929 ★
(135 E4) (*ℳ H5*)

Accommodation here is in a restored building in the heart of Chinatown, with chic, designer-furnished rooms. With swimming pool. *32 rooms | 50 Keong Saik Road | tel. 63 47 19 29 | www.hotel1929.com | MRT EW 16, NE 3 Outram Park | MRT NE 4, DT 19 Chinatown*

COPTHORNE KING'S HOTEL, FURAMA RIVERFRONT, HOLIDAY INN ATRIUM, MIRAMAR, RIVER VIEW
(135 D2) (*ℳ G4*)

These five hotels located close to each other in the Clarke Quay pub district, but far away from Singapore's shopping and business streets, have a total of 1965 rooms. That means that the prices for an overnight stay are fairly reasonable considering the comfort they offer. With the exception of the Furama Riverfront, all the hotels have a swimming pool. *Copthorne King's Hotel (403 Havelock Road | tel. 67 33 00 11 | wwwcopthornekings.com.sg), Furama Riverfront (405 Havelock Road | tel. 63 33 88 98), Holiday Inn Atrium (317 Outram Road | tel. 67 33 01 88 | www.holiday-inn.com), Miramar (401 Havelock Road | tel. 67 33 02 22 | www.miramar.com.sg), River View (382 Havelock Road | tel. 67 32 99 22 | www.riverview.com.sg). MRT NE 5 Clarke Quay, then bus 51*

GALLERY HOTEL ★
(135 E2) (*ℳ G4*)

Singapore's first boutique hotel. A colourful spot in the heart of the fashionable Clarke Quay district with a spectacular pool on the roof. *223 rooms | 1 Nanson Road | tel. 68 49 86 86 | www.galleryhotel.com.sg | MRT NE 5 Clarke Quay, then bus 51*

HOLIDAY INN EXPRESS CLARKE QUAY
(135 E2) (*ℳ H4*)

The new hotel from the chain includes breakfast and wi-fi. It may stand at a

---

MARCO POLO HIGHLIGHTS

★ **Oasia Hotel Downtown**
A green tower in the middle of Chinatown invites you to stay the night
→ p. 94

★ **1929**
Youthful chic in an old shophouse in Chinatown → p. 93

★ **Gallery Hotel**
In the fashionable Clarke Quay area and stylish all the way up to the swimming pool on the roof → p. 93

★ **The Scarlet**
Small but very elegant – and in the middle of Chinatown → p. 95

★ **Capella Singapore**
Reside in elegance on the beach on Sentosa → p. 90

★ **Raffles Hotel**
A magnificent resurrection: the institution among Singapore's hotels
→ p. 92

★ **Adler Hostel**
Princely accommodation for the tight budget. Singapore's first luxury hostel → p. 96

★ **YMCA International House**
Not really a youth hostel but a good hotel at a giveaway price → p. 97

HOTELS: MODERATE

junction, but it is right in Singapore's entertainment district on the Singapore River. *442 rooms | 2 Magazine Road | tel. 65 89 80 00 | www.ihg.com | MRT NE 5 Clarke Quay*

IBIS SINGAPORE ON BENCOOLEN (131 C5) (*J2*)
Very good location between the Colonial Quarter and Little India. The hotel lobby is almost ostentatious, the rooms are of good Ibis standard. *538 rooms | 170 Bencoolen Street | tel. 65 93 28 88 | www.accorhotels.com | MRT CC 2 Bras Basah*

ORCHARD HOTEL (129 D4) (*E1*)
This hotel is in just the right place for visiting Orchard Road and the Botanic Garden. Many restaurants and shopping malls are within walking distance. *656 rooms | 442 Orchard Road | tel. 67 34 77 66 | www.millenniumhotels.com | MRT NS 22 Orchard Road*

PERAK HOTEL (131 D4) (*J2*)
This small, traditionally furnished hotel and guesthouse in a renovated Peranakan house in Little India is tastefully decorated. It is privately run and the friendly staff are happy to give tips about all of the

MORE THAN A GOOD NIGHT'S SLEEP

Red-green future
Tarzan would have no problem visiting Jane in her room here. The red skyscraper of ⭐ 🌀 *Oasia Hotel Downtown* **(135 F5)** (*H6*) *(314 rooms | 100 Peck Seah Street | tel. 68 81 88 88 | www.stayfareast.com/en/hotels/oasia-hotel-downtown-singapore | MRT EW 15 Tanjong Pagar | Expensive)* in Chinatown is covered in vegetation from top to bottom. It looks cool, and it is. The tower is considered an example of green construction. Inside you'll enjoy a series of pools and a sky garden. You'll hardly notice that the rooms are rather small.

Up on the roof with Lady Luck
Why not play the tables of the casino in the cellar until you can afford one of the rooms in the three towers above? The whole world knows the rooftop pool at 🌀 *Marina Bay Sands* **(137 D3–4)** (*K–L5*) *(2560 rooms | from 350 S$ | 10 Bayfront Av. | tel. 66 88 88 97 | www.marinabaysands.com | MRT CE 1, DT 16 Bayfront | Expensive)* from Instagram and Facebook. As the Botanic Garden is only a stone's throw away, and a whole world of shopping opens up in the basement, you could make yourself comfortable here for a week without stepping outside – but that would be a shame.

Sleepwalking
Never mind the wandering, you're here to party. **INSIDER TIP** *Wanderlust* **(130 C4)** (*G1*) *(29 rooms | 2 Dickson Road | tel. 63 96 33 22 | www.wanderlusthotel.com | MRT NE 7 DT 12 Little India | MRT DT 22 Jln Besar | Moderate)* was created from a former school by four of Singapore's most famous designers and architects. Choose well before booking: every room here looks different. The result is a highly modern boutique hotel in the heart of Little India. Where, come to think of it, you don't actually need a hotel, because you're not here to sleep – but to wander, from club to club.

WHERE TO STAY

It can't be topped – in any sense of the word: Marina Bay Sands hotel

things to be discovered in the neighbourhood. *34 rooms | 12 Perak Road | tel. 62 99 77 33 | www.peraklodge.net | MRT NE 7, DT 12 Little India*

THE SCARLET ★ (135 F4) (*H6*)

The location in the heart of Chinatown is great; the decoration breathtaking: the red brocade and opulent gold and black create a Baroque atmosphere, the porters wear livery. The shophouses along an entire street were connected and renovated to create this hotel. *5 suites, 79 rooms | 33 Erskine Road | tel. 65 11 33 33 | www.thescarlethotel.com | MRT NE 4, DT 19 Chinatown*

SILOSO BEACH RESORT (138 B4) (*P6*)

Fancy staying a little outside the city? Why not try the seaside promenade on the leisure island of Sentosa? The resort is the only one in Singapore with a spring-fed landscape pool and does all it can to protect natural resources. *182 rooms | 51 Imbiah Walk | tel. 67 22 33 33 | www.silosobeachresort.com | MRT S3 Beach (Sentosa)*

THE SULTAN (131 E4–5) (*J2*)

Stepping out at The Sultan: ten old colonial houses were combined to make this hotel, which boasts the *Singjazz Club* and *Wonderbar* in the new trendy district Kampong Glam. *64 rooms | 101 Jalan Sultan | tel. 67 23 71 01 | www.thesultan.com.sg | MRT EW 12, DT 14 Bugis*

VILLAGE HOTEL ALBERT COURT (130 C4) (*J2*)

Small, cosy hotel near Little India, known for its friendly atmosphere. *136 rooms | 180 Albert Street | tel. 63 39 39 39 | www.stayfareast.com | MRT NE 7 Little India*

VILLAGE HOTEL BUGIS (131 E5) (*K2*)

Most of the 393 rooms have a fine view of the old Malay district. The hotel is in the programmes of numerous touroperators. It has a swimming pool and also extremely competitive prices, as it is located quite a way from the major shopping streets. *390 Victoria Street | tel. 62 97 28 28 | www.stayfareast.com | MRT EW 12 Bugis*

HOTELS: BUDGET

HOTELS: BUDGET

ADLER HOSTEL ★ (135 F3) (*H5*)

A hostel, but a prize-winning, luxurious one. It is located in a renovated shophouse in the centre of Chinatown and is furnished with antqiue furniture and local arts and crafts. *2 dormitories with 16 beds each | 259 South Bridge Road | tel. 62 26 01 73 | www.adlerhostel.com | MRT NE 4, DT 19 Chinatown*

INSIDER TIP HANGOUT@MT.EMILY
(130 B4) (*H2*)

The modern but inexpensive lodge received an award from Singapore's tourism authority. The rooms are air-conditioned and have private bathrooms; the dormitories have beds for five to seven guests. One special point is that the operators donate one dollar of the room price to charity organisations. The *Wild Rocket Restaurant* (www.wildrocket.com.sg) in the same building serves modern, light Singaporean cuisine. *54 rooms | 10 A Upper Wilkie Road | tel. 64 38 55 88 | www.hangout-hotels.com | MRT CC 1, NE 6, NS 24 Dhoby Ghaut, then bus 64, 65, 139*

ROBERTSON QUAY HOTEL
(135 E2) (*H4*)

The building is not especially attractive from the outside, but it is in a fine location directly in Singapore's amusement area and even has a rooftop pool. Orchard Road and the commercial districts are also just a short distance away. *150 rooms | 15 Merbau Road | tel. 67 35 33 33 | www.robertsonquayhotel.com.sg | MRT NE 5 Clarke Quay*

INSIDER TIP THE ROYAL PEACOCK
(135 E4) (*G–H6*)

The 73 rooms and six suites are hidden in a renovated row of houses in the heart of Chinatown. Located in what was once the city's red-light district, the Peacock is now surrounded by bars and restaurants. *55 Keong Saik Road | tel. 62 23 35 22 | www.royalpeacockhotel.com | MRT EW 16, NE 3 Outram Park*

SANTA GRAND HOTEL EAST COAST
(138 B6) (*S1*)

This modest hotel in the heart of Katong, the colourful, traditional quarter outside the city centre of Singapore, offers you good value for money. The hotel's own Peranakan restaurant rates as one of the best in town. *73 rooms | 171 East Coast Road | tel. 63 44 68 66 | www.santagrandhotels.com | MRT EW 8, CC 9 Paya Lebar, then bus 40*

LOW BUDGET

It is not absolutely essential to stay in a hotel in Singapore. You can even pitch a tent in this tropical metropolis – and it is completely free of charge in the *East Coast Park* **(0)** (*O–S3*) *(tel. 1800 04 71 73 00 | www.nparks.gov.sg | bus 16 to Marine Terrace, then through the underpass to the East Coast Park | www.nparks.gov.sg)*. There, you just have to set up the tent you brought with you and a park attendant will come along and take down your particulars.

Nice-sounding name and cheap beds in the dormitory: the *Betel Box* **(138 A5)** (*R1*) *(200 Joo Chiat Road | tel. 62 47 73 40 | www.betelbox.com | CC 9, EW 8 Paya Lebar)*. The hostel in the Peranakan district Katong offers simple beds from 20 S$. Family rooms cost 80 S$.

WHERE TO STAY

STRAND (130 C6) (*J3*)
The 130 functionally equipped rooms have televisions with a video programme; there is also a lounge with live music and a coffee shop. Excellent location in the centre of town. *25 Bencoolen Street | tel. 63 38 18 66 | www.strandhotel.com.sg | MRT CC 1, NS 24, NE 6 Dhoby Ghaut, then bus 64, 65*

YMCA INTERNATIONAL HOUSE ★
(130 B6) (*H3*)
You do not have to be a Christian, or young, or even male to be able to stay in one of these two guesthouses, but you do have to be quick. The very attractive price of the rooms means that they are in great demand – especially those in the centrally located *International House*. The surprisingly lavish – in this price category – amenities with swimming pool, squash courts, fitness centre, coffee shop and international direct-dial telephones in the simply furnished rooms can also be found in the more distant *YMCA Metropolitan (128–129 C–D1) (*O*) (92 rooms | 60 Stevens Road | tel. 68 39 83 33 | www.mymca.org.sg | MRT NS 22 Orchard, then bus 190)*. *106 rooms | 1 Orchard Road | tel. 63 36 60 00 | www.ymcaih.com.sg | MRT CC 1, NS 24, NE 6 Dhoby Ghaut*

Inexpensive but comfortable: YMCA International House

APARTMENTS, PRIVATE ROOMS & HOSTELS

Renting rooms in private homes is still not as widespread in Singapore as it is in many other of the world's metropolises. Here, this new branch is only developing slowly. This is because the rents paid for the old Chinese shophouses are so high – often more than 15,000 dollars a month – that it simply does not add up to offer only a few rooms to guests. However, you can try your luck on several Internet sites including *www.airbnb.com, www.easyroommate.com.sg | www.ibilik.sg | www.wimdu.com/singapore*.

Hostels are an economical alternative in the city state. Among those providing beds and simple rooms are the *Chic Capsules (13 Mosque Street | tel. 83 80 05 00 | chiccapsules.singaporee.space | MRT NE 4, DT 19 Chinatown)* in the heart of Chinatown. One alternative is Singapore's 'first indie boutique hostel': *Shophouse – The Social Hostel (48 Arab Street | tel. 62 98 87 21 | www.shophousehostel.com | MRT EW 12, DT 14 Bugis)* by the large mosque in the new in quarter Kampong Glam.

97

DISCOVERY TOURS

1 SINGAPORE AT A GLANCE

START: ① Botanic Gardens
END: ⑭ 1-Altitude

Distance:
➡ 21 km/13 mi (8.5 km/5.3 mi on foot)

1 day
Actual walking time
2 hours

COSTS: approx. 40 S$ without food and drink
WHAT TO PACK: Sunscreen and water, if you don't want to stop off specially too often; in the rainy season, an umbrella

IMPORTANT TIPS: For individual stages of the tour, take a taxi, rickshaw or the underground.

From tai chi under tropical trees to a nightcap in one of the most beautiful rooftop bars in South-East Asia – in the coming hours you'll get to know Singapore in all its variety. Naturally, this also includes the districts of Chinatown and Little India. But it's also worth exploring its colonial heritage and the famous Raffles Hotel.

You can find these tours as an app at: go.marco-polo.com/sin

Would you like to explore the places that are unique to this city? Then the Discovery Tours are just the thing for you – they include terrific tips for stops worth making, breathtaking places to visit, selected restaurants and fun activities. It's even easier with the Touring App: download the tour with map and route to your smartphone using the QR Code on pages 2/3 or from the website address in the footer below – and you'll never get lost again even when you're offline.

TOURING APP

→ p. 2/3

07:30am The best way to work off the effects of your long flight is with some **INSIDER TIP** early-morning Chinese sport in the fresh air: in Singapore's old ❶ **Botanic Gardens → p. 58** there are a number of groups which offer free tai chi, gymnastics or fan dance. You can join in wearing your normal clothes. **The simplest way is to head for the large open space at the Visitor Centre (Cluny Park Gate),** where dozens of early-morning exercisers get together when it's not raining. After that you will have earned your breakfast against this green backdrop. The **Casa Verde**

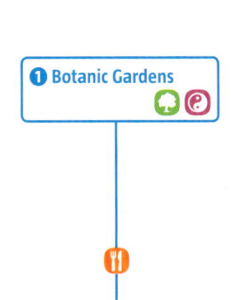

❶ Botanic Gardens

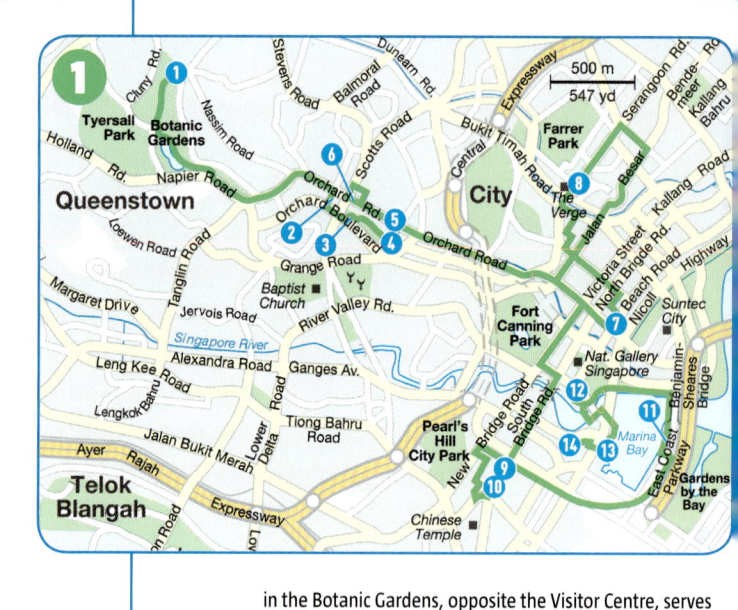

in the Botanic Gardens, opposite the Visitor Centre, serves baguettes as well as Asian rice dishes. Afterwards, take a walk through the garden underneath the magnificient tropical trees. The dazzling display of blossoms and their early-morning scent will get your day off to a good start. **Follow the signs to the Tanglin Gate. Cross the road and take the bus (7, 77, 106, 123, 174) in front of the Gleneagles Hospital as far as the Thai Embassy in the city centre. Cross Singapore's main thoroughfare, Orchard Road → p. 35, at the pedestrian crossing and keep to the left.** At the junction, enter the glass pyramid on ❷ **Wheelock Place**. The escalator takes you down to the second basement level – now you are standing in the heart of Singapore's shopping district, in the exclusive ❸ **ION Orchard → p. 75** centre which has over a hundred shops. Still underground, protected against the rain and the sun, stroll over to the traditional ❹ **Takashimaya → p. 76** department store, which is the place to go for Asian brands. **After that, cross over the street from Takashimaya** and visit the attractive shopping centre ❺ **The Paragon → p. 36** as well as the traditional Singaporean department store ❻ **Tangs**.

12:00pm **In front of the Marriott Hotel next door to Tangs take a taxi and drive up Orchard Road into the old Colonial Quarter** and on to your next destination, the

DISCOVERY TOURS

7 Raffles Hotel → p. 36, a gem from the colonial era. Brunch is served in the Billiard Room. The quality of the food is outstanding; some people come here especially for the INSIDER TIP desserts. The **souvenir shop → p. 81** behind the restaurant is delightful but expensive. **Outside Raffles, hire a rickshaw (they usually stand at the corner of Beach Road/Bras Basah Road) and have yourself chauffeured along 8 Serangoon Road → p. 28**, the main street through Little India. From here, drift off into the side streets following the scent of jasmine and curry. **A taxi will bring you quickly back to Chinatown → p. 44**, where the city has its origins. Wander through the narrow streets, don't trust the tailors who make tantalising offers of suits, but do peep into the cooking pots of the many street food vendors. Chinatown is where the various cultures come together: at its heart is the Hindu **9 Sri Mariamman Temple → p. 48** where priests, worshippers and tourists celebrate a noisy get-together. If your legs are starting to ache, stop for a coffee break in one of Singapore's oldest bakeries: diagonally opposite the Sri Mariamman Temple is the traditional baker's **10 Tong Heng** *(285 South Bridge Road)*, famous for its warm egg tarts. If you are on a diet, plump for the Tea Chapter → p. 64 to witness a traditional Chinese tea ceremony. Then travel by underground railway from Chinatown station to Bayfront as far as **11 Marina Bay Sands → p. 43**. Singapore's new landmark development includes the largest casino in the city and countless luxury boutiques. It is most famous, however, for its rooftop terrace high above the hotel. Some have dubbed it the 'ironing board', others say it resembles a boat. Nowhere, though, will you get a more beautiful view of the sunset.

07:00pm Now stroll past the stages of the Esplanade → p. 40 along the romantic path beside the bay as far as The Arts House → p. 31. Here, choose a table on the terrace of the **12 Timbre@The Arts House → p. 87** for a fabulous view across the brightly lit banking district. If you're not particularly hungry, go for the tapas; if you could do with something more substantial, there are noodles or fish. **After dinner, cross over Cavenagh Bridge with its splendid cast-iron framework and go through the underpass at the Fullerton Hotel to return to the bay.** To your right is the Fullerton Bay Hotel. The pretty rooftop terrace at ★ **13 The Lantern** is the perfect place to chill out – and mark the start of the evening with a sensational view over Marina Bay. To round things off, head up high onto

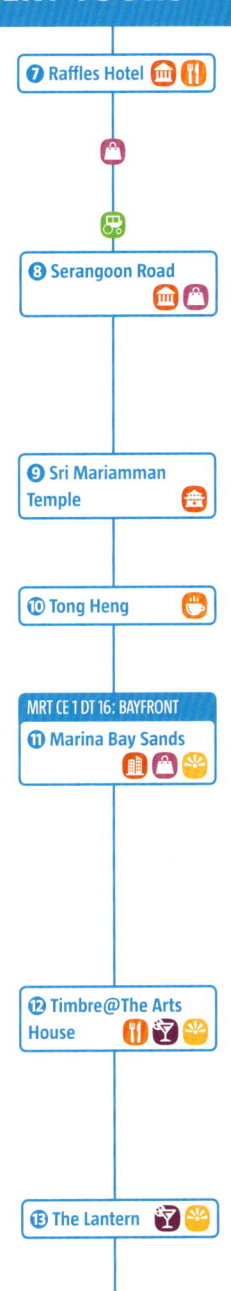

7 Raffles Hotel

8 Serangoon Road

9 Sri Mariamman Temple

10 Tong Heng

MRT CE 1 DT 16: BAYFRONT
11 Marina Bay Sands

12 Timbre@The Arts House

13 The Lantern

101

14 1-Altitude

the rooftop bar of the **14 1-Altitude → p. 84**. Hot rhythms at the open-air disco and cool drinks in the night-time breeze – experience the tropics at their most beautiful.

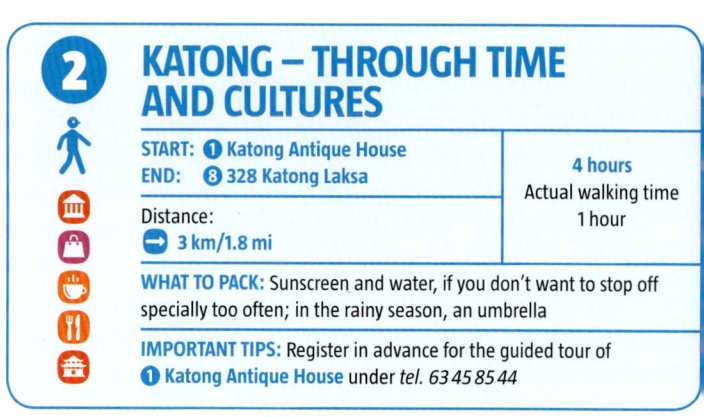

2 KATONG – THROUGH TIME AND CULTURES

START: 1 Katong Antique House
END: 8 328 Katong Laksa

Distance:
➡ 3 km/1.8 mi

4 hours
Actual walking time
1 hour

WHAT TO PACK: Sunscreen and water, if you don't want to stop off specially too often; in the rainy season, an umbrella

IMPORTANT TIPS: Register in advance for the guided tour of **1 Katong Antique House** under *tel. 63 45 85 44*

Walk for an afternoon in the footsteps of the early Singaporeans – Katong is the district of the Peranakan. This is the name of the ethnic group which developed out of the early Chinese, European and Malay settlers. They have left their mark on 'Little Singapore', as Katong is known – with their food, their architecture as well as their clothing.

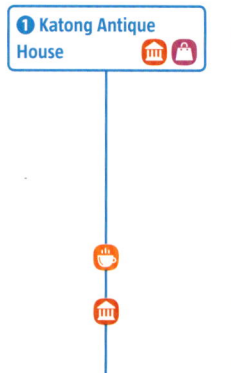

1 Katong Antique House

Stroll along both sides of East Coast Road – the main axis in Katong – for a close look at Singapore and its unique architecture. Do not expect to see anything spectacular, but you will gain an insight into everyday life. The walk begins at around 2pm at **1 INSIDER TIP Katong Antique House** *(208 East Coast Road | MRT NS 22 Orchard, then bus 14)*. You will discover a world all of its own behind the modest wooden door of this pale yellow house: Peter Wee, whose father once owned a whole street of houses here, will lead you through the Museum of Peranakan Culture *(approx. 45 mins.)*. There is a small shop selling genuine, but expensive Peranakan antiques on the ground floor. **Turn left when you leave the small museum.** You will immediately come across the **Chin Mee Chin Confectionery** *(closed Mon)*, one of Singapore's traditional bakeries. **Continue walking until you come to a narrow street which is worth taking a closer look at:** old, single-storey former officers' quarters still stand here. Now painted in bright colours, the small villas were built on pillars to protect them from flood waters. At the next set of traffic lights you come

DISCOVERY TOURS

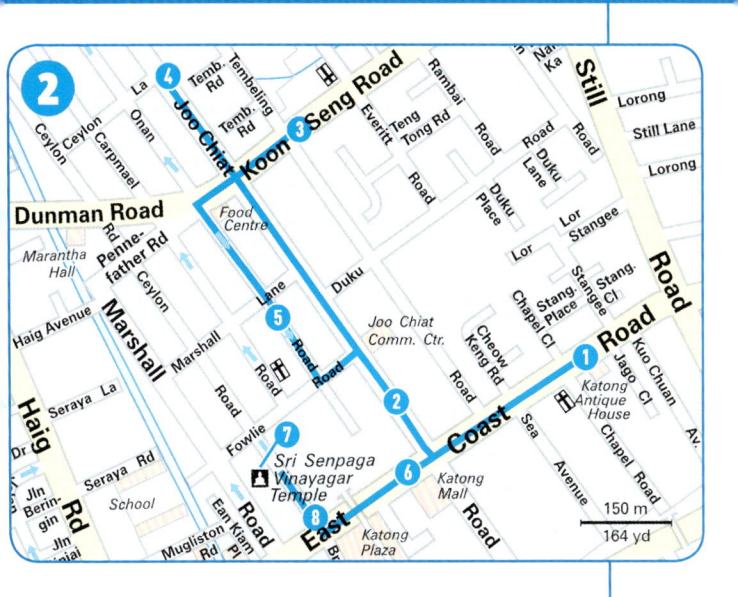

to Brotzeit, a pleasant restaurant catering mainly to European tastes. **Cross the road here and turn into ❷ Joo Chiat Road**. The sweetest temptation awaits you on the right-hand side on the corner: **Awfully Chocolate**. The shop is decorated completely in white and sells little else but all manner of dark chocolate – expensive, but good quality. And things stay sweet: further along, on the left-hand side, the warm, filled dim sum dumplings on sale at **D'bun Freshly Handmade Bun Specialist** *(no. 356)* are also delicious. **A good way further up the road on the left is the Ann Tin Tong Medical Hall** *(no. 320)*, a 70-year-old chemist's which employs a doctor and still mixes its teas and tinctures on the premises. **Just a few steps away on the right, you come to ❸ Koon Seng Road**. Its ensemble of houses is unique in Singapore. Their façades, decorated with stucco, combine Victorian and Chinese elements. The house fronts bear symbols of happiness and long life, such as bats, dragons, deer and dogs. They are made even more attractive by the application of old tiles which were imported at great cost from Europe. **Walk back a little way up Joo Chiat Road. A few hundred yards further on, you will discover one of the last paper-figure makers in Singapore,** ❹ **Chiang Pow Joss** *(no. 252)*, on the left-hand side, at the corner with Ceylon Road. Using small bamboo canes, glue and coloured paper, he and his employees build en-

❷ Joo Chiat Road

❸ Koon Seng Road

❹ Chiang Pow Joss

103

tire dioramas and make copies of cars, mobile phones and other articles to accompany the dead in their graves. He has no objection to you looking over his shoulder while he is at work. Grave goods may not be everyone's thing, but the figurines are perfectly respectable gifts that can be bought for a few cents. **Continue your stroll a little further up the road.** Its many small cafés, shops and restaurants ensure it stays interesting. An old Chinese temple stands diagonally opposite the paper-figure maker's shop. It is worth a look for the way it was constructed – these elongated bungalows on pillars used to line the entire street. The row of houses on the left-hand side *(from no. 174)* are fine examples of art-deco architecture in modern Singapore. **Once you've seen enough, simply turn round and head back to the Dunman Food Court** and then turn left into ❺ **Onan Road**. You now walk through a typical Singaporean residential district with mango trees in the front gardens until you reach the main road again.

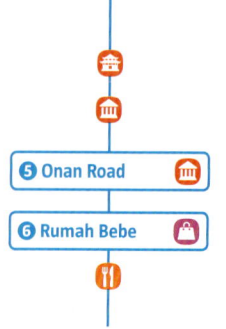

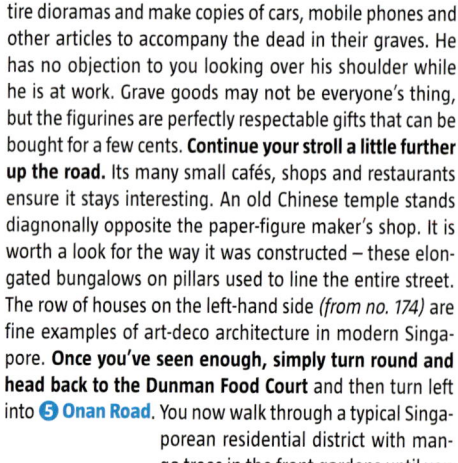

Victorian meets Chinese: architecture on Koon Seng Road

Turn left into Fowlie Road and then right onto Joo Chiat Road. From here you can get back onto East Coast Road again. Stay on the right until you reach ❻ **Rumah Bebe** *(www.rumahbebe.com)*, the 'House of Bebe'. This is an excellent place to buy some beautiful souvenirs. The owner, Bebe Seet, is a real expert in the traditional art of embroidering shoes and clothes with pearls. She even gives 'beading' lessons in her house *(around 250 S$ including materials)*. **Rumah Kim Choo** and **Kim Choo's Kitchen** are right next door. Here, the glutamate which is otherwise used extensively as a flavour enhancer in Singapore is replaced with a home-made broth made with chicken bones, ginger and garlic – and the food tastes really good. Restaurateur Desmond Wong will be happy to answer any questions you still have on the fascinating Peranakan culture after your walk. **Turn right onto Ceylon Road and wind up your walk through the**

104 You can find these tours as an app at: go.marco-polo.com/sin

DISCOVERY TOURS

cultures with a dash of Hinduism. This is the location of the ❼ **Sri Senpaga Vinayagar Temple**, built by Indian Tamils in 1875 underneath a senpaga tree in honour of the elephant god. **Head back onto East Coast Road** and bring the evening to a traditional close: the hot noodle soup at the famous snack-bar ❽ **328 Katong Laksa → p. 71** right on the corner is the best you'll find anywhere in the city.

- ❼ Sri Senpaga Vinayagar Temple
- ❽ 328 Katong Laksa

3 ROMANTIC SINGAPORE

START: ❶ Elgin Bridge
END: ❼ Makansutra Gluttons Bay

Distance: ➡ 2 km/1.2 mi

3.5 hours
Actual walking time 30 minutes

WHAT TO PACK: Water, if you don't want to stop off specially too often; in the rainy season, an umbrella

IMPORTANT TIPS: The ❹ pleasure cruisers leave every 15 minutes, daily between 9am and 10.30pm.

An Asian metropolis is seldom romantic, but usually colourful and full of hustle and bustle. Singapore's Colonial Quarter develops a very special charm after nightfall (daily at around 7.30pm). Of course, you can also do the three-hour-and-a-half walk during the day, but it is especially captivating in the evening, when the old lanterns twinkle under the tropical trees.

The starting point of this walk is at ❶ **Elgin Bridge** *(MRT NE 5 Clarke Quay)*, close to Singapore's Parliament House, which connects South and North Bridge Roads. It was the first bridge in Singapore (1823) and is an important artery in the city since it acts as a link between Tua Po and Sio Po – the large and the small city, in the dialect of the Fujian Chinese. These indicate Singapore's administrative district and Chinatown, the commercial district on the other side of the river. **The Parliament is on your left-hand side as you stand on the left bank of the river looking towards the brightly illuminated skyscrapers of the financial institutions. To the side of the Parliament, go down the few steps to the river** and take a break on one of the many benches to admire the magnificent panorama. **Stroll a little further along the river bank as far as the floodlit ❷ statue of Singapore's founding father, Sir Thomas Stamford Raffles**, who came ashore here in 1819.

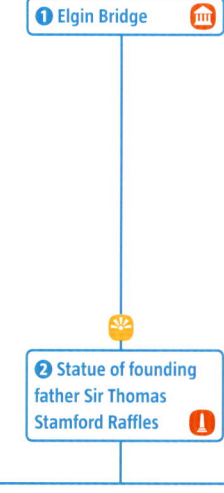

- ❶ Elgin Bridge
- ❷ Statue of founding father Sir Thomas Stamford Raffles

105

③ Asian Civilisations Museum

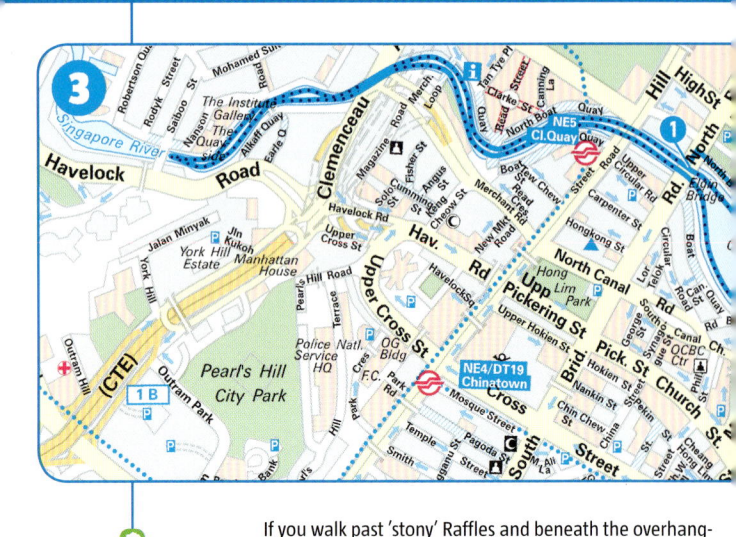

④ Pleasure cruisers

⑤ Cavenagh Bridge

⑥ Esplanade

If you walk past 'stony' Raffles and beneath the overhanging branches and aerial roots of the tropical trees, you will soon reach the painstakingly renovated ③ **Asian Civilisations Museum → p. 32**. On the steps you are greeted by silent witnesses to the past: sculptors Chern Lian Shan and Malcolm Kok have positioned life-size statues of the coolies and merchants who laid the foundations for Singapore's prosperity along the river many years ago. The Indian Chettiar, the money-lenders, negotiate with a female stockbroker who appears to have just come out of one of the bank towers on the opposite side of the river. The museum is well worth a visit and is open until 9pm on Fridays. **Afterwards, turn left and cross the bridge to the opposite bank of the river.** A number of ④ **pleasure cruisers** *(24 S$)* are moored at the Fullerton Hotel. The 40-minute trip could hardly be more romantic. At the same time, you can find out a lot about the history of the old commercial docks. **Back on land, cross the historical, beautifully floodlit** ⑤ **Cavenagh Bridge** (1868) and return to the other side of the river. Singaporean couples like to be photographed under the trees to the left and right when they get married; the bank towers in the background are thought to auger prosperity. **Continue along the riverside path that now makes two slight curves before leading into a tunnel. The Queen Elizabeth Walk along Esplanade Park starts on the other side. If you walk further along the bay and then under the highway bridge, you finally arrive at the brightly lit** ⑥ **Esplanade → p. 40**. INSIDER TIP Singaporean bands

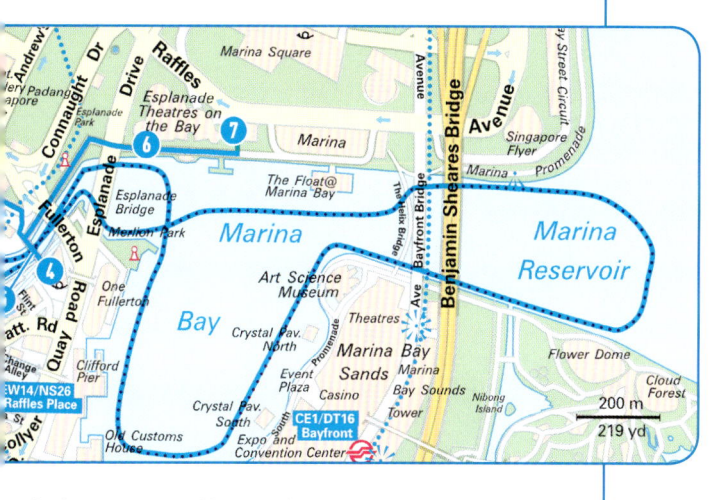

DISCOVERY TOURS

give free concerts on Friday, Saturday and Sunday evenings on the open-air stage by the water. On the right, behind the building, there is also an open-air *hawker centre*. In ❼ **Makansutra Gluttons Bay → p. 65** the government has brought together the best hawker restaurants in Singapore. For just a few dollars, you can enjoy a delicous evening meal under the starry tropical skies.

❼ Makansutra Gluttons Bay

④ THE SOUTHERN RIDGES – CITY IN A GARDEN

START: ❶ Hort Park
END: ❽ Vivo City

3 hours
Actual walking time
1.5 hours

Distance:
➡ 4.5 km/2.8 mi

Difficulty:
📶 easy

WHAT TO PACK: Be sure to take water and sunscreen with you; in the rainy season, an umbrella.

IMPORTANT TIPS: It's a good idea to begin the walk early, before the sun gets too hot. Drink plenty of water and take lots of breaks on your way.

Singapore considered itself a garden city for many years. It now officially calls itself a 'City in a Garden'. In the course of this development, the individual hiking paths were linked to form a circular route around the inner city – the ⭐ Southern Ridges. The path is extremely well thought-out and does not require any special preparations.

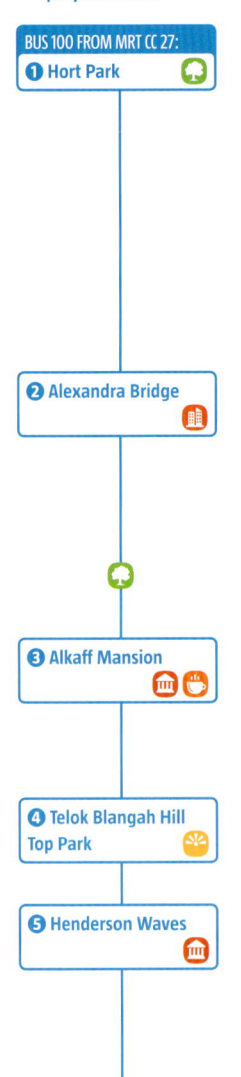

BUS 100 FROM MRT CC 27:

① Hort Park

② Alexandra Bridge

③ Alkaff Mansion

④ Telok Blangah Hill Top Park

⑤ Henderson Waves

Take a taxi or bus to the car park of the ① Hort Park *(Alexandra Road)* **at around 9am.** The park itself is a large exhibition area where Singapore's garden specialists show what they are capable of. You will be enchanted by the artistically-designed gardens, fountains and examples of façade greening systems on display. It was here that experiments were carried out to ensure that the glass roof constructon of the enormous greenhouses in the Gardens by the Bay would let sufficient light but not too much direct sun into the cool glass houses. Singapore's new gallery district is developing in the former Gillman Barracks → p. 78 a little further along Alexandra Road towards the harbour. **However, you stay in the park and cross** the metal **② Alexandra Bridge** which curves elegantly in the form of a leaf above Alexandra Road. LED lights immerse the bridge in a sea of colours after night falls. **When you reach the end of the bridge, follow the steel construction, at the same height as the treetops. Continue up the secure metal steps for about 20 minutes and keep your eye on your surroundings.** You will discover birds and lizards and, if you look closely through the trees, whole herds of monkeys. But please don't feed them; they can become aggressive. **On your way up the mountain, you pass the ③ Alkaff Mansion** *(10 Telok Blangah Green | alkaff.com.sg)*. The old colonial house from 1918, once owned by an Arab merchant, now houses an Italian restaurant *(Mon–Fri 11.30am–3pm, Mon–Sun 6pm–11pm | Expensive)*. Have a coffee to get your strength back. **If you continue along the path you will soon reach the highest point in the ④ Telok Blangah Hill Top Park**. This is the perfect place to catch your breath and admire the panoramic view over Singapore through the dazzling bougainvillea bushes. **This is also where you set out for the ⑤ Henderson Waves** – an amazing wooden bridge that arches 36 m/118 ft above Henderson Road and links the Telok Blangah Hill Park with Mount Faber. The American architect Daniel Libeskind designed the towers shining in the sun on the right, which appear to rise out of the jungle in front of the harbour. Children love the alcoves formed by the curves of the wooden bridge which was built using yellow South-East Asian bakau wood.

DISCOVERY TOURS

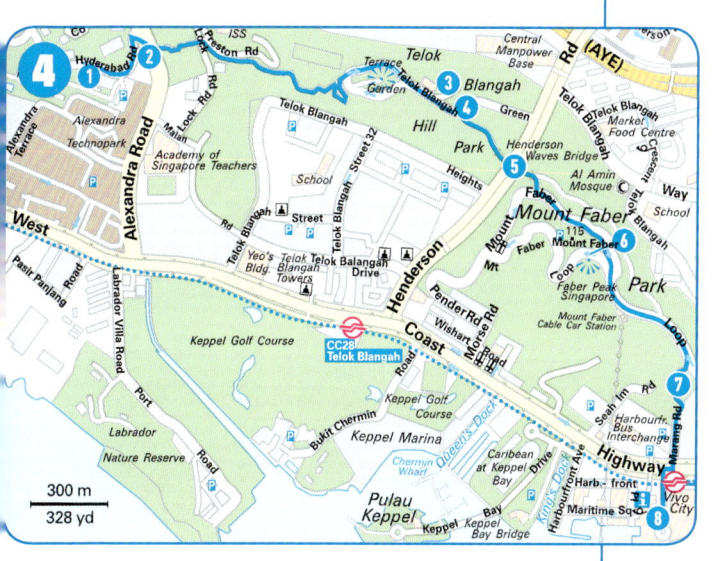

You have now reached ❻ **Mount Faber → p. 54**. If the weather is fine, you'll be able to see as far as Sumatra. The jungle here covers an area of more than 56 hectares/ 138 acres. The **Faber Peak Singapore → p. 54** with its restaurants and bars is located at the very top of Singapore's 'own' mountain. From here, there is a stunning view of Sentosa, the important harbour and the busy Straits of Malacca, the main shipping route to China and Japan. The harbour is responsible for seven percent of Singapore's economic output. You can also take the cable car over to Sentosa from here, but save this for another day, as you still have the interesting descent ahead of you: the ❼ **Marang Trail** is the least developed section of the path for tourists. Sometimes, after a tropical storm, the odd tree can lie across the steps. **Follow the signposts along the road, over the crest of the mountain to Car Park B and then to the right, behind the building and down into the valley.** If you are lucky, you might be here when the saga trees are wearing their dazzling red pearls – they are often used to make jewellery. **Now the path goes steeply down towards the harbour.** The jungle only opens up to give a view of it at the very last moment: you realise you are back in civilization when you turn the last bend and suddenly catch sight of the glaringly white Vivo City shopping centre, plus the underground station and six-lane harbour road.

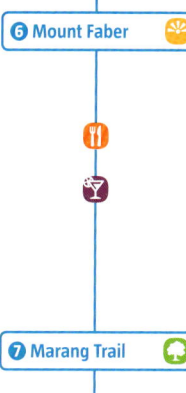

❻ Mount Faber

❼ Marang Trail

109

Back in the cool of civilization: a refreshing end to your walk at Vivo City

8 Vivo City

The path downhill takes around a quarter of an hour. Cross the road and walk through the attractive shopping centre 8 Vivo City → p. 57 – take care not to catch cold, though, if you're still sweating from your walk; the air-conditioning is pretty powerful. There are dozens of cafés along the waterside of Vivo City in which you can relax and round off your ramble through the 'city garden' with a good cup of coffee or an ice cream.

5 TIONG BAHRU – DIP INTO THE MELTING POT

START: **1** Tiong Bahru underground station END: **9** Tiong Bahru Market	**4 hours** Actual walking time 30 minutes
Distance: ➡ 2 km/1.2 mi	

WHAT TO PACK: Water and sunscreen; in the rainy season, an umbrella.

IMPORTANT TIPS: Most cafés and shops are closed on Mondays.

Tiong Bahru is Singapore at its most attractive – as a melting pot. In no other quarter is the mixture of young and old, Singaporean and foreigner, in-crowd and social-housing resident as noticeable as here. The magnificent architecture is

DISCOVERY TOURS

unique, some is reminiscent of the Paris or Berlin of the early 1920s, but with an Asian touch. We recommend you visit Tiong Bahru on a Saturday morning and mingle with the crowds.

Take the underground railway to ❶ Tiong Bahru station. When you leave the station by the Tiong Bahru Plaza exit, keep to the left. Cross Tiong Bahru Road at the pedestrian crossing and go on down to the left. Then turn right into Kim Pong Road. All of a sudden, the view around you changes completely: gone are the high-rise complexes; before you lies an ensemble of delightful white art-deco buildings. They were built between the late 1930s and the 1950s, originally as social housing. Because they appeared so modern in the eyes of the Singaporeans and due to their wing-like form, they were nicknamed the 'Aero-Flats'. **At the end of the road you come to two fine restaurants on Moh Guan Terrace;** or are there actually three? The rear section of the eatery on the left-hand side, the traditional Chinese noodle restaurant **Hua Bee** *(daily 7am–2.30am)*, becomes a modern, Japanese restaurant *(daily noon–3pm and 6pm–midnight)* – in this way the leaseholders reduce the high rents. The noodles are just as good as the Japanese dishes. On the right-hand side is the Australian-style Flock Café *(daily 8am–6pm)*. Walk past the café and take a stroll down ❷ **Yong Siak Street**. This is where young entrepreneurs have opened shops and restaurants in old houses. To the left is the PoTeaTo Bistro Café, a few yards further along, the **40 Hands → p. 63**. Long-standing residents love it here in particular because of the good coffee. Cross over to the other side of the street and browse the shelves at **Books Actually → p. 74**. It's a combination of literature bookshop, local meeting place and antique dealer's. Take a look at the choice of scene and city magazines. A little further on, **Woods in the Books** *(Tue–Sat 11am–8pm, Sun 11am–6pm)* has a large selection of English-language books for children. It's now time, though, for a coffee: wander on down to the INSIDER TIP **Plain Vanilla Bakery** *(Tue–Fri 11am–8pm, Sat 9am–8pm, Sun 9am–6pm)*. The wonderful smell is enough to enchant anyone; but you can also take a peek over the bakers' shoulders as they work. If you wish, you can hire one of the turquoise-coloured bicycles (10 S$/hr) for the rest of the tour.

Keep to the left on ❸ Chay Yan Street. The overhanging roofs of the traditional houses provide welcome shade and

MRT EW 17: TIONG BAHRU
❶ Tiong Bahru

❷ Yong Siak Street

❸ Chay Yan Street

④ Guan Chuan Street

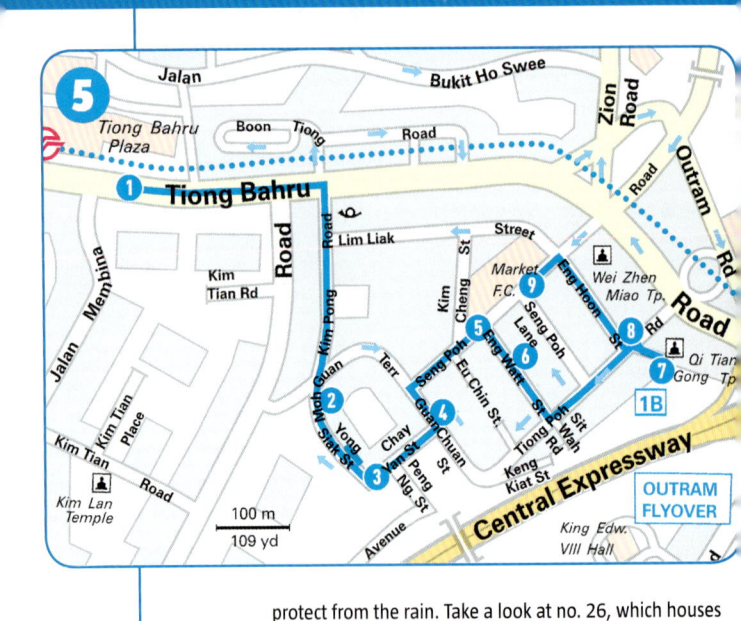

⑤ Seng Poh Road

⑥ Nimble & Knead

⑦ Qi Tian Gong Temple

protect from the rain. Take a look at no. 26, which houses the **White Space Art Asia** *(Tue–Sun 11am–8pm)* gallery. Everywhere in this quarter you will find informative, large signs in English depicting its history; it's worth taking the time to read them. **Now turn left into ④ Guan Chuan Street**, where there's a branch of the well-known **PS. Café** *(daily 11am–11pm)*. If you like Australian cakes and burgers, this is the place to indulge. **A detour to the right takes you onto the district's main thoroughfare, ⑤ Seng Poh Road.** Although Tiong Bahru is now very popular with foreigners, its Chinese roots cannot be overlooked: the houses are decorated with lanterns at Chinese New Year. Again and again you will discover tiny altars set into the walls of the houses. And look out for the staircases, balconies and the shapes of the doors and windows – you won't find anything comparable in the rest of today's Singapore. **Turn right into Eng Watt Street.** If you fancy a massage, look no further. **⑥ Nimble & Knead** promises to give your muscles the once-over until they are as 'soft as dough'. The price for a one-hour foot massage starts at 42 S$. Often half an hour is enough.

Suitably invigorated, continue left onto Tiong Poh Road, which you follow downhill. Diagonally opposite at the road junction stands the ⑦ Qi Tian Gong Temple, the first

112 You can find these tours as an app at: go.marco-polo.com/sin

DISCOVERY TOURS

in Singapore to be dedicated to the monkey god. He is said to bring happiness, prosperity and also ingenuity. Here, at the latest, you will notice that this is no Western metropolis, but a thoroughly Asian city. **Now turn into ❽ Eng Hoon Street** behind you. On the right-hand side you will soon come across the well-known **Tiong Bahru Bakery** – founded by a Frenchman, it is expensive but fantastic. It's worth popping into **Nana & Bird** *(Tue–Fri noon–7pm, Sat/Sun 11am–7pm)* opposite. The boutique, which has two branches in the district, sells clothes and accessories by a number of Singaporean designers. **You reach the heart of the district at the far end of the street:** the **❾ Tiong Bahru Market**. The two-storey building has hardly changed in the last 50 years, despite the recently completed renovation. Here, you will still see older generations, the 'uncles' and 'aunties', doing their shopping. Downstairs, vegetables and meat, household goods and plastic flowers are on sale; upstairs is one of the best *hawker centres* in the city. More than 20 of the local snack bars are so popular that they have been successfully doing business for over 30 years. Stand no. 82, for example, offers traditional boneless chicken and rice. Two stands further along, at no. 30, there are Wanton noodles. The best idea is just to wander along from one stand to the next and take a peek into the cooking pots. As a rule of thumb: the longer the queue at the stand, the better the food.

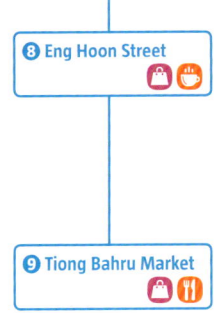

❽ Eng Hoon Street

❾ Tiong Bahru Market

Culmination of the tour: lunch at one of the best *hawkers* in town, Tiong Bahru Market

TRAVEL WITH KIDS

Have you got young ones in tow? Good. Singapore is fond of children. People in the street will smile at your offspring. The two biggest attractions are still the *Zoo* (p. 61) and the *Resort World Sentosa* (p. 55). There are plenty of tips for your trip with children in *www.singaporeforkids.com*; adventures in the city are listed under *www.nparks.gov.sg/activities*.

AND IF IT RAINS

'Trampoline till you drop': *Amped* has large halls full of them, surrounded by thick cushions. Fun for young and old all over the city, e. g. *Mon 10am–7pm, Tue 3pm–10pm, Wed–Fri 10am–10pm, Sat 9am–10pm, Sun 9am–9pm | 12–18 S$, depending on the day | 46 Kim Yam Road | MRT NE 5 Clarke Quay*. Or does your child want to be a banker, pilot or doctor? Then take them to ●★ *Kidzania* (138 C4) (*P6*) (*daily 10am–6pm | admission adults 35, children 2–3 years 25, 4–17 years 58 S$ | 31 Beach View | #01–01/02 | www.kidzania.com.sg | MRT NE 1, CC 29 Harbourfront, then Sentosa Express to Beach Station*) in Sentosa. Here children can play out various careers. The ★ *Singapore Science Centre* (0) (*b4*) (*daily 10am–6pm | admission adults 12, children 8 S$ | 15 Science Centre Road | www.science.edu.sg | bus 335 or 66 from MRT EW 24, NS 1 Jurong East*) is geared to the scientists of the future. If you need to cool down afterwards, head for the artificial ski slope at *Snow City* (skis for hire). The Imax cinema next door shows good films with an educational element – even during the holidays! The *Civil Defence Heritage Centre* (136 B1) (*J4*) (*Tue–Sun 10am–5pm | free admission | Central Fire Station | 62 Hill Street | www.scdf.gov.sg | MRT EW 13, NS 25 City Hall, NE 5 Clarke Quay, then bus 190*) sounds a bit war-like but it's here that the kids can become firefighters (*Sat 9am–11am*).

PLAYGROUNDS

Children can have fun and learn a lot about nature in the ★●◯ *Jacob Ballas Children's Garden* (128 A–B1) (*0*) (*daily 8am–7pm | Botanic Gardens | Cluny Road entrance | www.sbg.org.sg | MRT CC 19, DT 9 Botanic Gardens*) in the old Botanic Gardens. The youngsters can romp around in the fountains in the *outdoor water playground* (138 C2) (*D8*) (*daily 10am–10pm | Telok Blangah Road/Sentosa Gate-*

114

That Jungle feeling! Anybody who thinks that Singapore is not a good place for children is keeping them from some fantastic experiences

way | www.vivocity.com.sg | MRT NE 1, CC 29 S Habourfront) in the courtyard on the second floor of *Vivo City*. There are other INSIDER TIP large pools of water one floor higher up on the roof. There is even a covered playground for small children in the centre of the shopping centre *The Paragon* (129 F4–5) (*G2*) (daily 10am–10pm | 290 Orchard Road | www.paragon.com.sg | MRT NS 22 Orchard Road) on Level 5. The *Hip Kids Club* (daily 10am–10pm | 583 Orchard Road www.forumtheshoppingmall.com.sg | MRT NS 22 Orchard) at the *Forum The Shopping Mall* (129 D4) (*E1*) offers a large, supervised play area for an annual fee of 15 S$.

PURE NATURE

The INSIDER TIP *Tree Top Walk* in the *MacRitchie Reserve* (0) (*c4*) (Tue–Fri 9am–5pm, Sat/Sun 8.30am–5pm | free admission | Upper Thomson Road | at the level of Venus Drive | www.nparks.gov.sg | bus 132 from Orchard Road) runs over a 250-m (273-yd)-long suspension bridge in the treetops. You will probably see lots of monkeys – but remember that it is strictly forbidden to feed them.

At the southern entrance you can hire a kayak at the *Paddle Lodge* (daily 9am–noon, 2pm–6pm | kayak 15 S$/hr | Lornie Road | tel. 62 62 58 00 57 | www.scf.org.sg | MRT NS 22 Orchard, then bus 167 from Orchard Boulevard) for a paddle across the lake under jungle vegetation.

TOURS ● (137 D1) (*K3*)

Super – today you travel by *Duck*! The brightly painted US-Army amphibious vehicles rumble through the Colonial Quarter and then straight into the water; depart on the hour 10am–6pm | adults 37, children from 3–12 27 S$ | 3 Temasek Blvd. | #01–330 | Suntec City | tel. 63 38 68 77 | www.ducktours.com.sg | MRT CC 3 Esplanade

FESTIVALS & EVENTS

Buddhists, Christians, Hindus and Muslims – each religious group is granted two public holidays in Singapore. The major holidays of the religious and ethnic groups are also days off for everyone else, although the shops open their doors (except on Chinese New Year).

EVENTS

JANUARY/FEBRUARY

★ *Chinese New Year:* The excitement can be felt throughout the city days before: houses and streets are decorated in red and gold. Groups of drummers appear, and lion and dragon dancers make their way through the streets. A highlight is the *fireworks display* at the harbour.

FEBRUARY

INSIDER TIP *Thaipusam* the celebrations honouring the Hindu god Muruga are really dramatic: the faithful bore the ends of the wires of the 'Kavadi', cages decorated with peacock feathers, into their skin: the metal constructions are then carried in processions through the streets. Some men walk the two miles from the Sri Srinivasa Perumal to the Sri Thendayuthapani temple wearing shoes of nails.
Chingay Parade: Carnival in Singapore! Dozens of groups and acrobats make their way across the arena at the Formula 1 track and guarantee that the spectators have a good time. Noisy, colourful and with many circus-like interludes.

MARCH/APRIL

INSIDER TIP *Ching Ming Festival*: A Chinese mixture of All Saints' Day and Easter. Mercedes Benz cars, Rolex watches and computers are set ablaze at the cemeteries – but these treasures are only made of paper. The smoke transports them to the other world where they make the life of the departed more luxurious.

MAY/JUNE

INSIDER TIP *Great Singapore Sale*: Of course, you can shop twelve months a year, but it is even more fun during the Great Sale – and you can save money.

JUNE

Dragon Boat Festival: This festival was initiated in memory of the Chinese schol-

Singapore's colourful calendar of festivities is characterised by tolerance: there are two public holidays for each religion

ar Qu Yuan, who drowned himself 2400 years ago because he was so distressed about the corruption in the country – today it is a spectacle on Marina Bay.

AUGUST
Hungry Spirits Festival: Small altars are set up all over town where offerings of fruit are made to the dead. The main centre is Chinatown.

SEPTEMBER/OCTOBER
Thimithi: Believers walk over glowing coals in honour of the goddess Draupathi in the Sri Mariamman Temple.
Formula 1 night-time race

OCTOBER/NOVEMBER
Deepavali: Little India is even more dazzling during the Hindu Festival of Lights. Visitors delight in the food, aromas, dances and colourful clothing of the Indians.

NATIONAL HOLIDAYS

1 Jan	New Year's Day
late Jan/early Feb	
	Chinese New Year
March/April	Good Friday
1 May	Labour Day
late May/early June	
	Vesak Day
late May 2020, mid-May 2021	
	Hari Raya Puasa
9 Aug	National Holiday
mid-Aug 2020, mid-July 2021	
	Hari Raya Haji
mid-Oct/early Nov	
	Deepavali
25 Dec	Christmas

LINKS, BLOGS, APPS & MORE

LINKS & BLOGS

www.timeoutsingapore.com The best website to find out about what is happening in Singapore; put together by the journalists of the city magazine of the same name

www.mrbrown.com A dash of satire about the 'fine city' for those in the know, written in a way that you can still laugh about it in Singapore

www.hungrygowhere.com/singapore For the hungry – the site Singaporeans consult for restaurant tips

www.airconditionednation.com The excellent collection of essays *Singapore: Air-Conditioned Nation* by the journalist Cherian George explains how politics and society function in Singapore

short.travel/sin1 The best blogs about the region arranged by categories including fashion, lifestyle, influence, originality – and food, of course

www.ladyironchef.com The witty restaurant reviews make this one of the top ten food blogs

ieatishootipost.sg This site provides a good overview of Singapore's food scene

sethlui.com Seth Lui does the leg work for you, testing out Singapore's restaurant scene. Practical: you can order results according to price, location and cuisine

singart.com Singapore has developed into an art and culture hotspot – this website helps you to discover it

singaporerebel.blogspot.com Political and socio-critical blogs like this one are usually produced abroad, many of them by disgruntled Singaporeans

Regardless of whether you are still researching your trip or already in Singapore: these addresses will provide you with more information, videos and networks to make your holiday even more enjoyable

www.visitsingapore.com This website (also available as an app) provides information on everything travellers are interested in: sightseeing tours, festivals, theatre shows, concerts, special events, museums, food and drink, shopping, accommodation, public transport, wi-fi and so on. It also has downloadable maps

www.couchsurfing.com/places/asia/singapore/singapore The 'couch-surfing' network links travellers with people in other countries and cities; in this case, with Singapore

www.sgtravelcafe.com Network where Singaporeans exchange views – if you enter the word 'Singapore', you will get the best tips for their hometown

www.lonelyplanet.com/thorntree/forums/asia-south-east-asia-islands-peninsula/singapore The Thorntree Community exchanges experiences and useful tips about Singapore: where you can find really inexpensive accommodation and which Chinese restaurant you should avoid at all cost

VIDEOS & MUSIC

www.youtube.com/watch?v=oYoAC3cLOgI&feature=related This deals exclusively – and humorously – with Singapore's favourite food: Pepper Crab

www.youtube.com/watch?v=OJ1Ya5AwzGc&feature=related Background information and pictures of the construction of the Marina Bay Sands complex

www.youtube.com/watch?v=PVP1GdvD2L4 Although not bang up to date, this introduction to the city from Discovery Channel, including historical pictures, is extremely informative

APPS

iChangi The app for flights to and from Singapore's Changi Airport

gothere.sg Lost your bearings? This app helps you find your way round the city

grabtaxi and easytaxi Use these two apps to call a taxi (almost) anytime, anywhere in Singapore

The Publisher shall not be held responsible for the contents of the links, blogs, apps, etc. listed here

TRAVEL TIPS

ADDRESSES IN SINGAPORE

It takes some getting used to the way addresses are given in Singapore: in large buildings, the floor and room number are given. For example, British Airways' address is shown as 15 Cairnhill Road, #06–05 Cairnhill Place. This means that you will find the office at 15 Cairnhill Road on the sixth floor. The shops and offices on the individual floors also have house numbers – British Airways has got the number 5.

ARRIVAL

Most visitors land at Changi Airport (0) (*e3–4*). There are MRT stations under the terminals. The trains leave for the inner city every twelve minutes between 5.31am and 11.18pm (Orchard by MRT NS 22); the trip costs 1.75 S$. The last MRT from the inner city leaves the Orchard Road Station at 11.25pm.

The air-conditioned buses of line 36 also leave from the basement every ten minutes for the Orchard Road terminus. The fare is 2.50 S$. You must have the exact amount. There are also taxis (transfer time around 20 min, approx. 40 S$), maxi-cabs (for 7 persons from 40 S$), Mercedes limousines (from 45 S$) and hotel buses.

Cruise ships and the ferries to Batam dock at the Cruise Centre *(www.singaporecruise.com.sg)* near Harbourfront Centre (128 C2) (*B8*). The MRT NE departs from there for Orchard Road (CC 1, NS 24, NE 6 Dhoby Ghaut). The ferries to the Southern Islands steam out of Marina South Pier *(MRT NS 28 Marina Pier | www.islandcruise.com.sg)*. Ferries to Bintan depart from the Tanah Merah Ferry Terminal (0) (*e4*) (ideally by taxi). Information on the islands and other excursions under: *www.wildsingapore.com* and *www.nparks.gov.sg*.

Express buses from Kuala Lumpur (min. 5 hours) arrive at Lavender Street Bus Station (131 E–F 2–3) (*L1*) *(MRT EW11 Lavender)* or at the Golden Mile Komplex (131 F5) (*L2*) *(MRT C5 Nicoll Highway)*.

BANKS & CURRENCY EXCHANGE

Avoid changing money in hotels – it can be very expensive. The best exchange rates are offered by the 'Authorized Money Changer' in many shopping centres. Some banks charge high fees for

RESPONSIBLE TRAVEL

It doesn't take a lot to be environmentally friendly whilst travelling. Don't just think about your carbon footprint whilst flying to and from your holiday destination but also about how you can protect nature and culture abroad. As a tourist it is especially important to respect nature, look out for local products, cycle instead of driving, save water and much more. If you would like to find out more about eco-tourism please visit: *www.ecotourism.org*

From addresses to weather

Your holiday from start to finish: the most important addresses and information for your Singapore trip

cashing traveller's cheques. However, the branches of the OCBC Bank exchange free of charge.

The rates for exchanging money in Europe before you leave are unfavourable. Banks in Singapore are usually open Mon–Fri 9.30am–3pm or 4pm, Sat 9.30am–11am. Several branches of the DBS Bank are open until 3pm on Saturdays. As anywhere in the world, the simplest way to get money are cash dispensers. Many of them accept Visa, American Express and MasterCard credit cards, as do most of the larger shops.

CLIMATE, WHEN TO GO

There are two seasons in Singapore but it is always very humid: the dry period (March–Oct) with high temperatures of around 33°C (92°F) and the rainy season (Nov–Feb) when the temperature can fall to 23°C (73°F).

CLOTHING

You should wear loose cotton clothes or other apparel suitable for hot weather. Do not forget an umbrella if you go for a long walk (tropical downpours!). You have to remove your shoes before entering Hindu temples and Muslim mosques.

CONSULATES & EMBASSIES

BRITISH HIGH COMMISSION
(128 B4) (*D2*) 100 Tanglin Road | Singapore 247919 | tel. +65 64 24 42 00 | ukinsingapore.fco.gov.uk

CANADIAN HIGH COMMISSION
(130 B3) (*J5*) One George Street, #11-01 | Singapore 049145 | tel. +65 68 54 59 00 | www.singapore.gc.ca

U.S. EMBASSY
(128 B4) (*D2*) 27 Napier Road | Singapore 258508 | tel. +65 64 76 91 00 | sg.usembassy.gov

BUDGETING

Coffee	£0.50–£2.80/ $0.80–$4.40	for a cup of coffee
Snack	£2–£3/ $3.30–$4.80	for a serving of chicken rice in a food court
Beer	£5–£10/ $7.80–$15.50	for a glass of beer
Boat trip	£7.30–£15/ $12–$24	for a trip to the Southern Islands
Souvenirs	£5–£6/$7–$8	for three table mats made of Chinese fabric
Clothes	£2.50–£11/ $4–$17.50	for a simple t-shirt

CUSTOMS

You can import 1L of alcohol and a small amount of perfume for your personal use tax-free – but no cigarettes! It is forbidden to bring pornographic material and any kind of drugs into the country. *Customs information: (tel. 65 42 70 58 | tel. 63 55 20 00 | www.customs.gov.sg)*. The following goods can be exported duty-free when you leave Singapore: 200 cigarettes or 50 cigars or 250 g tobacco, 1 L of spirits or 4 L wine, 250 g coffee and other good up to a value of £390/450 euros. Travellers to the US who are residents of the country do not have to pay duty on articles purchased overseas up to the value of $800, but there are limits on the amount of alcoholic beverages and tobacco products. For the regulations for international travel for US residents please see *www.cbp.gov*.

The import of crocodile skins into other countries requires a complicated permit in line with the Convention on International Trade in Endangered Species of Wild Fauna and Flora.

ELECTRICITY

Mains voltage 220–240 volt, 50 hertz. Two-pin plugs can be used in most hotel rooms but in general three-pin Commonwealth plugs are common in Singapore (an adapter can be obtained at the front desk and in many shops).

EMERGENCY SERVICES

Police *(tel. 999)*, Ambulance & Fire Brigade *(tel. 995)*.
24-hour emergency service in hospitals: *Gleneagles Hospital (tel. 64 73 72 22); Mount Elizabeth Hospital (tel. 67 37 26 66)* both are centrally located and recommendable.

HEALTH

Vaccinations are not prescribed and are also not necessary unless you arrive from a yellow fever or cholera region. There is no danger of malaria in Singapore but dengue fever does exist. It is completely safe to drink tap water. If you should need a doctor, ask your hotel.

IMMIGRATION

A visa is not required but a passport valid for more than six months is necessary. Your passport will be stamped permitting you to stay for up to 30 days *(extensions from the Immigration Department | tel. 63 91 61 00)*. A two-page *Landing Card* has to be completed before passport control; keep the copy until your departure.

INFORMATION BEFORE THE TRIP

SINGAPORE TOURISM BOARD
– *c/o Singapore Centre, First Floor, Southwest House, 11A Regent Street, London, SW1Y 4LR | tel. +44 (0)20 74 84 27 10 | stb_london@stb.gov.sg*
– *589 Fifth Avenue, Suite 1702, New York, NY 10017 | tel. +1 212 30 2 48 61 | new york@stb.gov.sg*

INFORMATION IN SINGAPORE

SINGAPORE TOURISM BOARD (STB) VISITOR INFORMATION CENTRES
The centres are excellently equipped and it is especially worth visiting the one on Orchard Road.
– Orchard Gateway (130 A5) (*ω G2*) (216 Orchard Road)
– Chinatown Visitor Centre (135 F4) (*ω H5*) (2 Banda Street)
Hotline: *tel. (free) 1800736 20 00*
Get basic information from the website of the Singapore Tourism Board *www.stb.com.sg* and at *www.yoursingapore.com*.

TRAVEL TIPS

INTERNET & WI-FI

The three telephone companies Singapore Telecom (Singtel), Starhub and M1 offer a variety of prepaid cards. They have their own counters at the airport; in town, most money changers and 7 Eleven shops sell cards. All you need is your passport. A local telephone number will allow you to log into the *wireless@SG* hotspots around the city.

PHONES & MOBILE PHONES

International phone calls can be made wherever you see the 'IDD' symbol. You can buy phonecards in telecom shops, post offices, 7-eleven shops and exchange offices (3–50 S$). There are credit-card phones at the airport, in post offices and telecom shops. You can make local calls free of charge from the airport. Dialling code for Singapore: *+65*; dialling code to the UK *+44*, US/Canada *+1*.

POST

The main post offices are *Tanglin Post Office* (128 C4) (*D2*) (*Mon–Fri 8.30am–5pm, Sat to 1pm | 56 Tanglin Road | opposite Tanglin Mall*) and *Orchard Post* (129 E4) (*F2*) (*Mon–Sun 11am–7pm | 2 Orchard Turn | #B2–62 | Ion Orchard*). Your hotel reception will help you send letters abroad. *Singapore Post (www.singpost.com)* makes it possible for you to really surprise your friends and family at home: you can have INSIDER TIP your own photograph printed on a stamp in Singapore and then use it for your holiday post. The 'MyStamp' service is only available at *Singapore Philatelic Museum* (136 B1) (*J4*) (*daily 10am–5pm | 23b Coleman Street | MRT EW 13, NS 25 City Hall*). Bring your chosen motif with you on a USB stick.

CURRENCY CONVERTER

£	SGD	SGD	£
1	1.73	1	0.58
3	5.21	3	1.73
5	8.68	5	2.89
13	22.50	13	7.50
40	69.50	40	23.09
75	130.20	75	43.30
120	208	120	69
250	434	250	144
500	866	500	289

$	SGD	SGD	$
1	1.36	1	0.73
3	4.08	3	2.20
5	6.80	5	3.67
13	17.70	13	9.55
40	54.43	40	29.37
75	102	75	55.07
120	164	120	88
250	341	250	184
500	682	500	367

For current exchange rates see www.xe.com

PUBLIC TRANSPORT

Singapore's underground is air-conditioned and excellently organised. Mobile telephones even work in the tunnels. There are currently five lines: the North East Line (NE), the East West Line (EW), the North South Line (NS), the Circle Line (CC) as well as the Downtown Line (DT). Construction of the sixth line, the Thomson East Coast Line (TEL), is going on and the line will open in five stages from 2019 onwards. MRT fares range from 1S$ to 3 S$, and the trains run in the municipal area from 5.30am to 0.30am.

Buses depart every six to thirty minutes from 5.15am to midnight. The fares range from 1S$ to 3 S$ depending on the distance travelled. You can pay the driver in the bus – but be sure to have the exact amount.

The *EZ-link Card*, or *Easy Card (www.ezlink.com.sg)* for short, is a rechargable ticket for buses and MRT and costs 12 S$. This includes a non-refundable, one-off purchase fee of 5 S$. This card considerably reduces fares.

The *Singapore Tourist Pass* is a special EZ-link Card which is valid for one, two or three days for 10, 16 and 20 S$ and entitles the holder to unlimited travel in the corresponding period. The 10-S$ deposit is refunded when you return the card. Visitors can buy the cards and the useful *Transit Link Guide* (5.90 S$) at the main MRT stations such as NS 22 Orchard Road. Additional information under *www.smsrt.com.sg* and *www.sbstransit.com.sg*.

There are also many different passes with various combinations of public transport and admission to major attractions. One example is the *Tourist Pass Plus (home.ezlink.com.sg/singapore-tourist-pass)*, a combination of the EZ-link Card and admission ticket – this makes admission, for example to the *Zoo* or *Universal Studios*, cheaper. Depending on the combination and period of validity, the pass costs 28 S$ for one day, 38 for three days. It can be bought at the MRT ticket counters at the Dhoby Ghaut (130 B6) (*M H3*) and Orchard (129 E4) (*M F2*) stations.

The *Singapore City Pass (www.singaporecitypass.com)* is valid for one to three days. It provides reduced admission fees to most attractions and cheaper tickets for tours. The price: 69.90 S$ (one

WEATHER IN SINGAPORE

	Jan	Feb	March	April	May	June	July	Aug	Sept	Oct	Nov	Dec
Daytime temperatures in °C/°F	30/86	30/86	31/88	31/88	31/88	31/88	31/88	31/88	30/86	31/88	30/87	29/84
Nighttime temperatures in °C/°F	23/73	23/73	24/75	24/75	24/75	25/77	25/77	24/75	24/75	24/75	24/75	23/73
Sunshine hours/day	5	6	6	6	6	6	6	6	6	5	5	4
Precipitation days/month	13	10	11	11	11	10	10	11	9	13	16	18
Water temperature in °C/°F	27/81	27/81	28/82	28/82	28/82	29/84	28/82	28/82	28/82	28/82	28/82	27/81

TRAVEL TIPS

day), 89.90 S$ (two days) and 158.90 S$ (three days). You can buy the pass at the Singapore Flyer observation wheel *(Tourist Hub #01–05)*.

used like a bus with the *EZ-link Card.* It costs 3 or 4 S$ depending on the route. It starts at Marina Barrage and sails up the Singapore River.

SIGHTSEEING TOURS

Duck & Hippo Tours (adults 43, children 33 S$ | www.ducktours.com.sg) are trips in decommissioned US Army amphibious vehicles through the old part of town and then into Marina Bay – great fun, and not just for younger visitors.

The *SIA Hop-On-Bus (daily 9am–9pm | adults 25, children 15 S$ | www.siahopon.com)* operated by Singapore Airlines offers day tickets for a set route through the city in its programme. All Singapore Airlines' passengers ride for free with the *Singapore Stopover Holiday (SSH) Pass.*

You can book trips in a ● rickshaw at *www.toursinsingapore.com,* e. g. four hours through Chinatown at night including dinner for 68 S$, or one-and-a-half hours through Little India to Arab Street with *Luxury Tours & Travel (49 S$ | tel. 67 33 28 08 | www.b2bluxurytours.com)*, and also under *www.citytours.sg* for a package including the main city sights, often combined with the ticket for the Singapore Flyer observation wheel.

The *Tour East (www.toureast.net/singapore)* organisation, in cooperation with the *Chinatown Visitor Centre,* offers in-depth tours of Chinatown. The three-hour excursion *(28 S$)* features visits to the clans and homeland associations, traditional workshops where masks and combs are made, as well as to cookshops where you can take a look into the pots, *wet markets* and grocery shops.

● *Singapore River Cruise (23 S$ | tel. 63 36 61 11 | www.rivercruise.com.sg)* shows you Singapore from the water. The *River Explorer (www.riverexplorer.sg)* can be

TAXIS

All of the taxis in Singapore are air-conditioned, have an officially-sealed taximeter and are inexpensive in comparison with Britain. Cars from Grab, which you can book via the app, are often even cheaper. Taxis can be flagged down on the street and you will find taxi ranks in front of all the main shopping centres and hotels. Telephone reservations: *Comfort & City Cab tel. 65 52 11 11; SMRT Taxi tel. 65 55 88 88; Premier tel. 63 63 68 88; Grab (www.grab.com); taxi hotline 63 42 52 22.*

Information on all taxi telephone numbers and prices can be found under *www.taxisingapore.com.* Prices and supplements are also listed on a sticker on the rear side window of the taxi. As a rule, taxi drivers do not cheat customers, but they occasionally give tourists foreign coins as change. Please note that it is compulsory to wear seat belts.

TIME

Singapore Time (SGT, no daylight saving time in summer) is eight hours ahead of GMT, twelve hours behind US Eastern Time (EST) and three hours behind Australian Eastern Time (AEST), one hour less during summer daylight saving time.

TIPS

Tips are generally not expected in Singapore. Taxes and service charge are already included in the price in restaurants or taxis.

STREET ATLAS

The green line indicates the Discovery Tour 'Singapore at a glance'
The blue line indicates the other Discovery Tours
All tours are also marked in the pull-out map

Exploring Singapore

The map on the back cover shows how the area has been subdivided

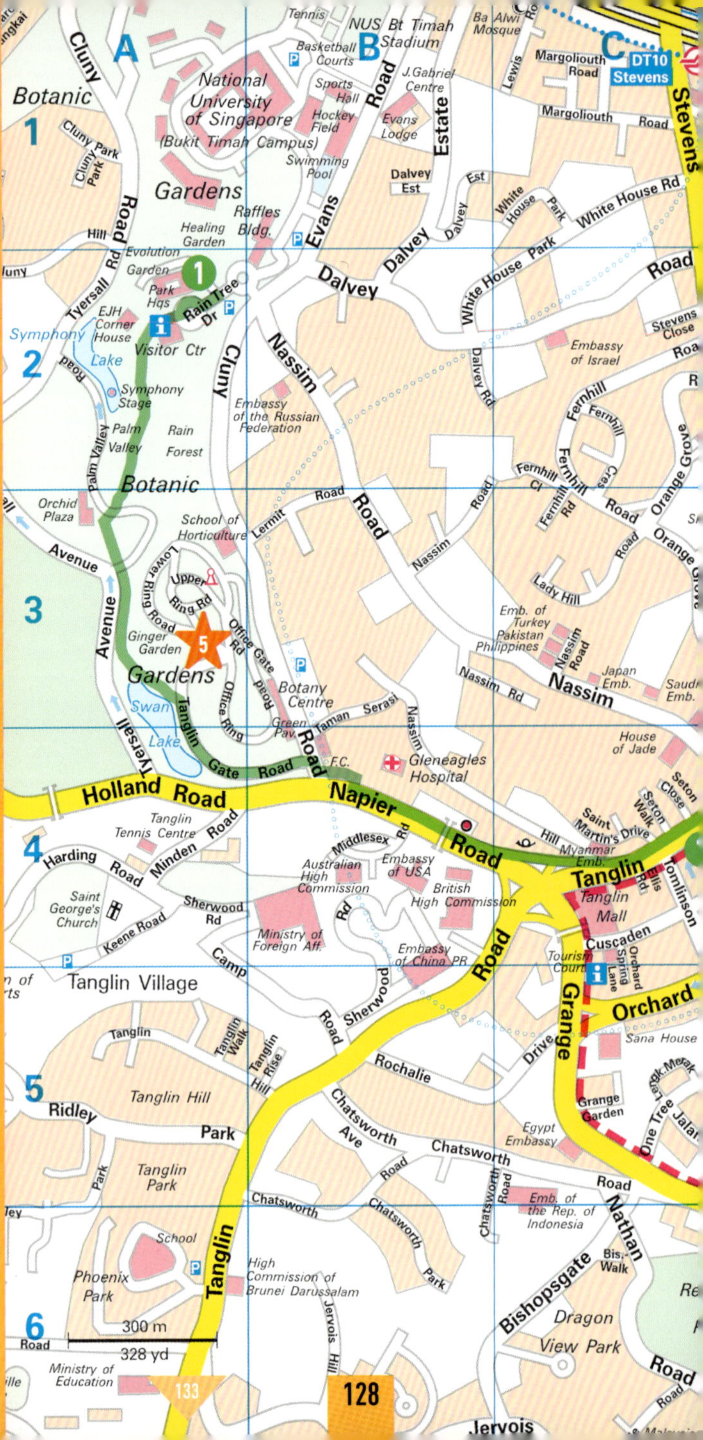

A
B
C
1
2
3
4
5
6
Cluny
Botanic
Gardens
Cluny Park
National University of Singapore (Bukit Timah Campus)
Tennis
NUS Bt Timah Stadium
Basketball Courts
Sports Hall
Hockey Field
Swimming Pool
Ba Alwi Mosque
Lewis
Margoliouth Road
DT10 Stevens
Stevens
J.Gabriel Centre
Evans Lodge
Dalvey Est
Estate
Road
Raffles Bldg.
Healing Garden
Evans
Hill
Evolution Garden
Park Hqs
Rain Tree Dr
Tyersall Rd
EJH Corner House
Visitor Ctr
Symphony Lake
Symphony Stage
Palm Valley
Rain Forest
Botanic
Dalvey
Dalvey Road
White House Park
White House Rd
Stevens Close
Embassy of Israel
Nassim
Cluny
Embassy of the Russian Federation
Dalvey Rd
Fernhill
Fernhill Cres
Fernhill Cl
Fernhill Rd
Orange Grove
Orchid Plaza
Avenue
School of Horticulture
Lermit Road
Nassim Road
Lady Hill
Lower Ring Road
Upper Ring Rd
Office Gate Rd
Ginger Garden
Gardens
Swan Lake
Tanglin Gate Road
Office Ring Road
Tyersall
Emb. of Turkey
Pakistan
Philippines
Nassim Road
Nassim Rd
Japan Emb.
Saudi Emb.
Botany Centre
Green Pav.
Taman Serasi
Nassim
House of Jade
Gleneagles Hospital
F.C.
Seton Close
Seton Walk
Saint Martin's Drive
Holland Road
Napier Road
Tanglin Tennis Centre
Minden Road
Middlesex Rd
Myanmar Emb.
Hill
Tanglin
Tanglin Mall
Ellis Rd
Tomlinson
Harding Road
Australian High Commission
Embassy of USA
British High Commission
Saint George's Church
Sherwood Rd
Keene Road
Ministry of Foreign Aff.
Camp Road
Embassy of China PR
Road
Cuscaden
Tourism Court
Orchard Spring Lane
Orchard
Grange
Tanglin Village
Tanglin
Tanglin Walk
Tanglin Rise
Tanglin Hill
Sherwood Road
Rochalie
Drive
Sana House
Lengkok Merak
Ridley Park
Chatsworth Ave
Chatsworth Road
Chatsworth
Grange Garden
One Tree
Jalan
Egypt Embassy
Tanglin Park
Park
Chatsworth Road
Nathan Road
Emb. of the Rep. of Indonesia
Chatsworth Park
School
Phoenix Park
Tanglin
High Commission of Brunei Darussalam
Jervois Hill
Bishopsgate
Bis. Walk
Dragon View Park
Road
300 m
328 yd
Ministry of Education
Jervois

133

D
E
F
1
2
3
4
5
6
School
Asimont Lane
Methodist Church
Swiss Cottage Est
Goldhill Drive
Goldh. View
Goldhill Rise
Goldhill Ave
Barker Road
Timah
Dunearn Road
Canal
Raffles Counselling Centre
Baptist Church
Robin Drive
Close
Robin Road
Keng Chin Road
Ewe Boon Road
City Towers
Chancery
Jalan Pasiran
Gentle Road
Evelyn Rd
Buckley
Gilstead
Dunearn
Bukit Timah
Balmoral Road
Balmoral Crescent
Balm. Plaza
Jesus Crist of Latter-Day-St.
Sarkies Rd
Balmoral Park
Thai Gallery
Goodwood Hill
Social Devt Unit
Newton Circus
NS21/DT11 Newton
Walshe Road
Raffles Girl School
Draycott
Stevens Road
Goldbell Tower
School
Clemenceau Avenue
Environment Bldg
Cairnhill Garden
Anthony Road
Peck Hay Road
Ardmore Park
Admore Pk
Draycott Park
Draycott Dr
Tanglin Club
Tunisia Consulate
American Club
Goodwood Park
Cairnhill Art Centre
Cairnhill Circle
Cairnhill Rise
Delfi Orchard
Orchard Road
Claymore Dr
Claymore Towers
Royal Thai Emb.
Royal Plaza
Pacific Plaza
Scotts Road
Far East Plaza
Grand Hyatt
Elizabeth
Claymore Hill
Shaw Centre
Forum
Ming Arcade
Hilton
Far East Shopping Centre
HPL House
Four Seasons
Internat. Bldg
Shaw House
Scotts
Marriott Hotel
Tangs Plaza
Nutmeg
Jln Jintan
Jln Lada Puteh
Jln Kayu Manis
Jln Elok
Mount Elizabeth Hospital
Mount Elizabeth Link
Liat Tower
Wheelock Place
ION
NS22 Orchard
Orchard Parksuites
Wisma Atria
Lucky Plaza
Tong Bldg.
The Paragon
Bideford Road
Al-Falah Mosque
Thong Sia Bldg
Hullet Road
Saunders Rd
Emerald Hill
Starhub Centre
Centre Point
Cuscaden Walk
Paterson Rd
Tupai
Angullia
Arnap
Kelawar
Takashimaya Center
Ngee Ann City
Orchard Turn
Orchard Link
The Heeren
Mandarin Sh. Arcade
Wellington Bldg.
School
Faber House
Lengkok Angsa
SIM Paterson Centre
Paterson Hill
Paterson Road
International Schools
Boulevard
Cineleisure
Orchard Bldg
Somerset Rd
Power Bldg
NS23 Somerset
Skate Park
Grange Road
Grange Rd
High Commission of India
Devonshire Road
Exeter Road
Concentre
Tiverton Lane
Dublin Rd
Ministry of Education Teachers Network
Hoot Kiam Road
Irwell Bank Road
Leonie Hill
Muslim Cemetery
Devonshire Bldg
Tong Xian Ting Temple
Tai Wah Bldg
Lloyd Road
Lloyd Gardens
CGH Bldg.
Killiney Road
Baptist Church
Jalan Mutiara
Kaypoh Road
River Valley Road
River Valley Grove
Saint Thomas Walk
134
The Tiara
The Cosmopolitan
St Bernadette

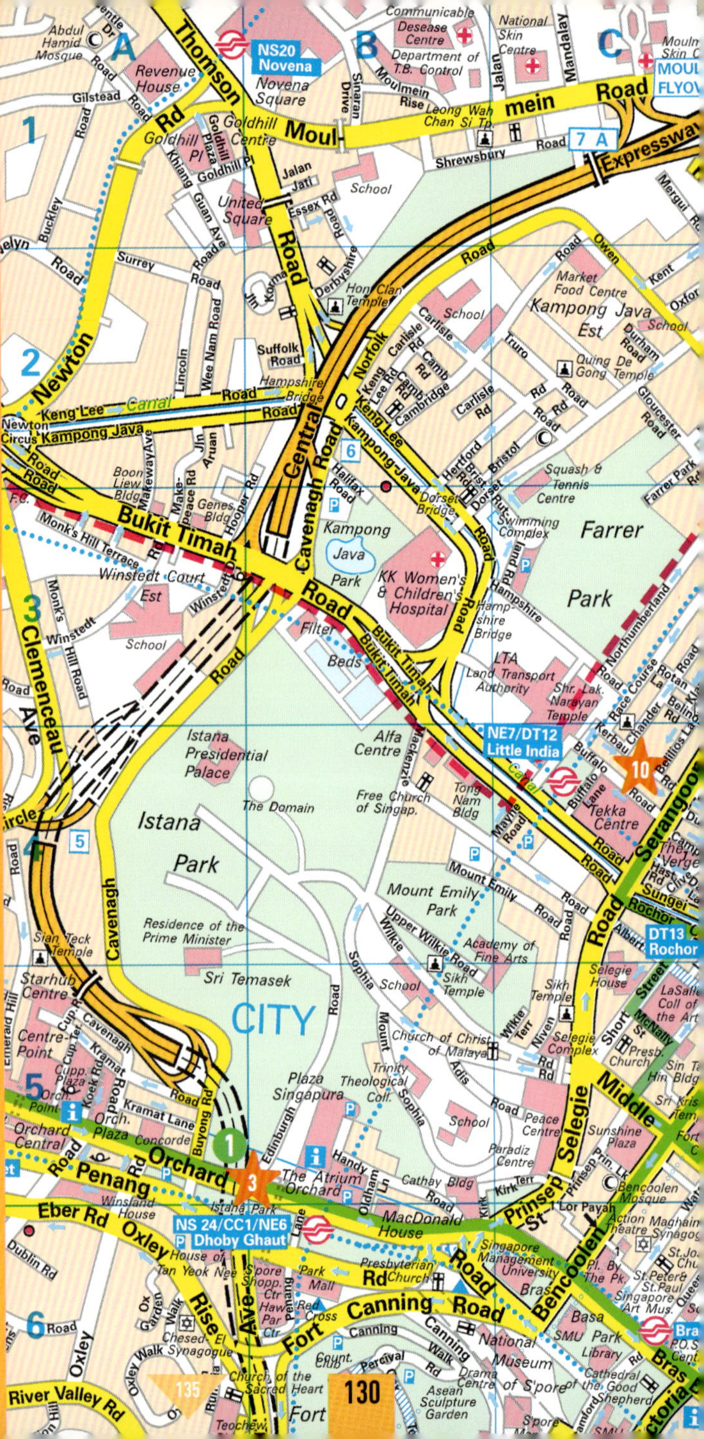

A
B
C
1
2
3
4
5
6
NS20 Novena
Thomson Rd
Revenue House
Novena Square
Abdul Hamid Mosque
Gilstead Road
Communicable Desease Centre
Department of T.B. Control
National Skin Centre
Moulmein Rise
Sinaran Drive
Jalan
Mandalay
Moulmein Road
Leong Wah Chan Si Tp
Shrewsbury Road
7 A
Expressway
Goldhill Centre
Goldhill Plaza
Goldhill Pl
Khiang Guan Ave
Jalan Jati
Essex Rd
School
United Square
Buckley Road
Surrey Road
Thomson Road
Derbyshire Road
Hon Clan Temple
Market Food Centre
Kampong Java Est
Owen
Kent
School
Durham Road
Quing De Gong Temple
Truro
Carlisle
Cambridge
Norfolk
Keng Lee
Gloucester Road
Suffolk Road
Hampshire Bridge
Lincoln
Wee Nam Road
Newton
Keng Lee Canal Road
Kampong Java Road
Newton Circus
Boon Liew Bldg
Makeway Ave
Make-peace Rd
Jln Aruan
Genes Bldg
Hooper Rd
Central
Cavenagh Road
Halifax Road
Kampong Java
Dorset Bridge
Hertford Rd
Bristol
Squash & Tennis Centre
Farrer Park
Farrer Park Rd
Swimming Complex
Bukit Timah Road
Monk's Hill Terrace
Winstedt Court Est
Winstedt Dr
Monk's Hill Road
Winstedt
School
Clemenceau Ave
Kampong Java Park
KK Women's & Children's Hospital
Hampshire Bridge
Filter Beds
LTA Land Transport Authority
Shr. Lak. Narayan Temple
Northumberland
Race Course Road
Chander Rd
Kerbau
Buffalo Road
NE7/DT12 Little India
Tekka Centre
10
Serangoon
Istana Presidential Palace
Alfa Centre
The Domain
Free Church of Singap.
Tong Nam Bldg
Mackenzie
Mayne Road
Istana Park
Mount Emily Road
Mount Emily Park
Upper Wilkie Road
Academy of Fine Arts
Sikh Temple
Residence of the Prime Minister
Sri Temasek
Sian Teck Temple
Starhub Centre
Cavenagh
Sophia Road
School
Church of Christ of Malaya
Wilkie Terr
Niven Rd
Selegie Complex
Selegie House
Sikh Temple
Short St
Presb. Church
Rochor
DT13 Rochor
LaSalle Coll of the Art
CITY
Centre Point
Cuppage Plaza
Koek Rd
Kramat Road
Kramat Lane
Orchard Point
Orchard Central
Orch. Plaza
Concorde
Buyong Rd
Plaza Singapura
Trinity Theological Coll.
Edinburgh
Sophia
Adis Road
School
Peace Centre
Paradiz Centre
Selegie
Middle
Sunshine Plaza
Orchard Road
Penang Rd
Winsland House
The Atrium Orchard
Handy Road
Cathay Bldg
Kirk Terr
Prinsep St
Bencoolen Mosque
Eber Rd
Oxley Rise
Istana Park
NS 24/CC1/NE6 Dhoby Ghaut
MacDonald House
Lor Payah
Action Theatre
Maghain Synagog
Dublin Rd
House of Tan Yeok Nee
Sporee Shopp. Ctr
Park Mall
Presbyterian Church
Singapore Management University
Bras Basah
Pl. By The Pk.
Bencoolen
St.Joseph's Church
St.Peter & St.Paul
Singapore Art Mus.
Road
Oxley
Ox Garden Walk
Chesed-El Synagogue
Oxley Walk
Red Cross
Fort Canning Road
Canning Walk
Canning Rise
Count. Club
Percival Rd
Drama Centre
National Museum of S'pore
SMU Park Library
Cathedral of the Good Shepherd
River Valley Rd
135
Church of the Sacred Heart
Asean Sculpture Garden
Fort
Teochew
S'pore
Victoria

D
E
F
1
2
3
4
5
6
7 C
Singapore Vocational Institute
Eye Hospital
Balestier
Ceylon Sports Club
S'pore Indian Assoc.
S'pore Chinese Sports Club
Khalsa Assoc.
McNair
HS Sanct. Serv.
S'pore
School
Sing Ave
Civil Service Clubhouse
Joo
Sing Joo Walk
Avenue
Tessensohn
Chinese Temple
Race Course
Sri Sivan Temple
Sri Srinivasa Perumal Temple
Sri V. Temple
Tamil Malar
Sakaya Muni Buddha Gaya Temple
Central Sikh Temple
Kwong Wai Siu Free Hospital
Serangoon
Rd
Road
Boon Keng
NE9
Boon Keng
Bendemeer Mall
Mkt. F.C.
Kempas Rd
Peta-ling Rd
Tronoh Rd
Kempas
Idris
Lavender
Bendemeer
Kallang Tengah
Kallang Bahru
Bahru
F.C.
Hiap Huat House
Jalan Lembah Kallang
Cyber Hub
Curch of Victory
Kallang
Beatty
Sch
Wu De Bldg
Thekchen Collin
Sturdee Rd
Jalan Besar
Est
Eminent Plaza
Foch Rd
Casket
Hamilton Rd
Cavan Road
Horne
GEO Technique Bldg
Kallang Junction
Kallang Avenue
Star-light Terr
Perumal Rd
Kitchener Rd
City Square Mall
Marne Rd
Petain
Flanders Sq
Link
Somme Rd
Burmah Rd
Angullia Mosque
Serangoon Plaza
Mustafa Centre
Verdun Rd
Kitchener
Football Assoc of S'pore
Allen. Rd
Jln Besar Stadium
Avenue
Creative Centre
Padang Jeringau
Tai Pei Buddhist Centre
Syed Alwi
Desker
Rowell
Baboo La
Hindoo Rd
Sam Leong Rd
Besar
Plu-mer Rd
Tyrwhitt
Jln Besar Plaza
School
Maude
Road
New World Ctr.
King George's
French Rd
Penhas Rd
Jellicoe
Kallang Rd
Sri Manmathan Temple
Nam Lock
Kampong
EW11
Lavender
Crawford Bridge
ICA Bldg.
Hindoo Rd
Kampong Kapor
Chitty Rd
Weld
India
Jalan
F.C.
Kelan La
Kelantan Road
Townshend
Berseh
Polyclinic
Syed Alwi Bridge
Old Malay Cem
Victoria Bridge
Hong Wen Sch
Eng Cheong Tower
Crawford
Bugis
Street
Crawford Lane
Bus Terminal
Rochor Canal
Muslim Cem
Victoria La
Jalan Kubor
Klapa
Jln
Abdul Gaffoor Mosque
Sim Lim Tower
Sungei
Rochor Centre
Arab
Bus Term.
School
Jln Kledek
Jln Pisang
Plaza Cinema Textile Ctr
Sultan Plaza
Minto Road
Key-point
Hajjah Fatimah Mosque
Golden Mile Complex
Golden Theatre
Golden Mile Tower
Java Rd
Sch.
Istana Kg Glam Malay Her. Ctr.
Kandahar St
Aliwal
Sultan
Muscat St
Sultan Mosque
Wholesale Centre
Ophir
Rochor
Queen
Johore
Victoria
Raffles Hospital
Blanco Court
Bridge
Haji Lane
Bali La
Baghdad St
Bussorah St
Pahang St
Sultan Gate
The Concourse
Highway
CC5
Nicoll Highway
Promenade
EW12/DT14
Bugis
Parkview Square
North
Street
Beach
The Furniture Mall
Parkroyal
The Plaza
The Gateway
Republic Avenue
Marina
PARCO Bugis Junction
Fu Lu Shou
Cheng Yan Pl
Malabar St.
Hylam St.
Tan Quee Lan
Liang Seah St
S'pore Finance House
Nat. Library
Bras Basah Cpl
Mus. of Toys
Purvis St
Seah Street
Beach Road
Kimetal Bldg.
Shaw Towers
Nicoll
Road
Suntec City Mall
Beach Centre
Raffles Hotel
Church La
300 m
328 yd
131
137

132

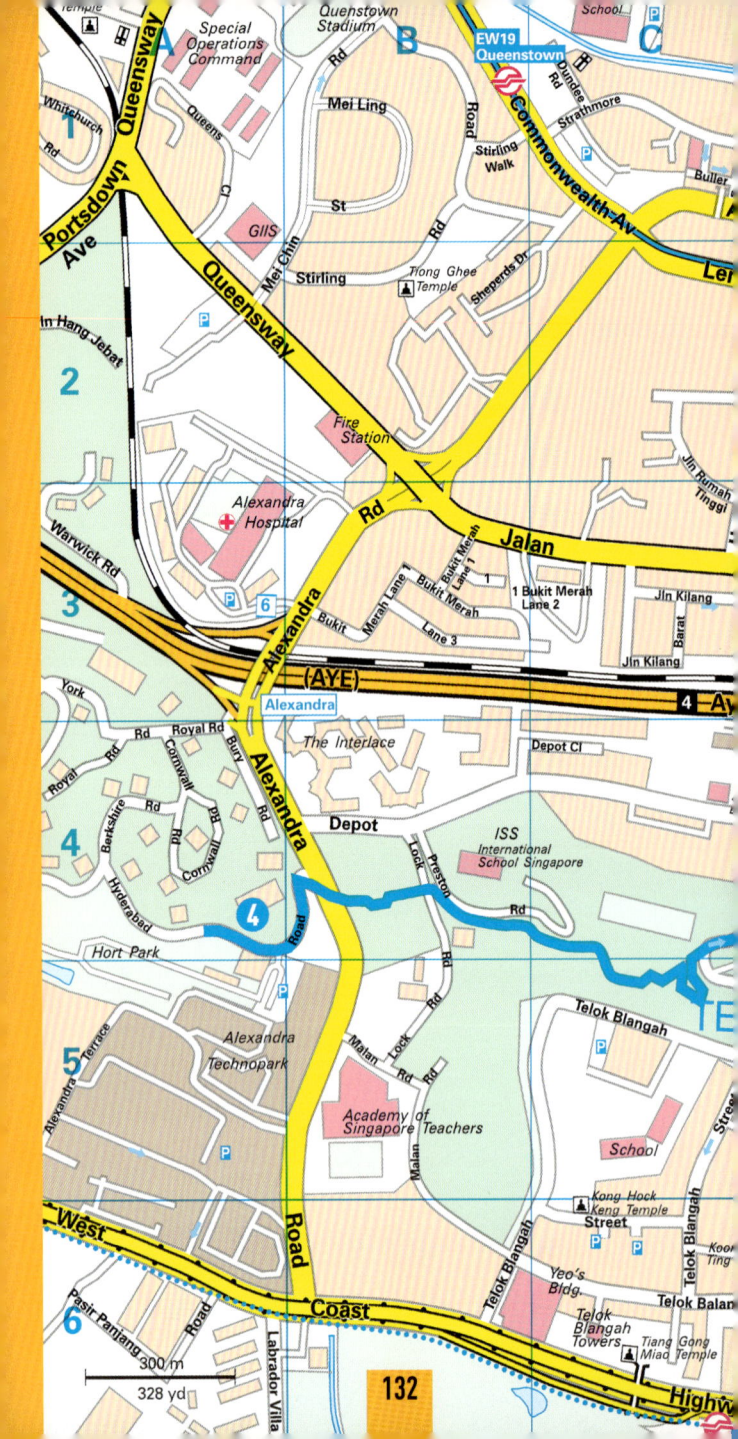

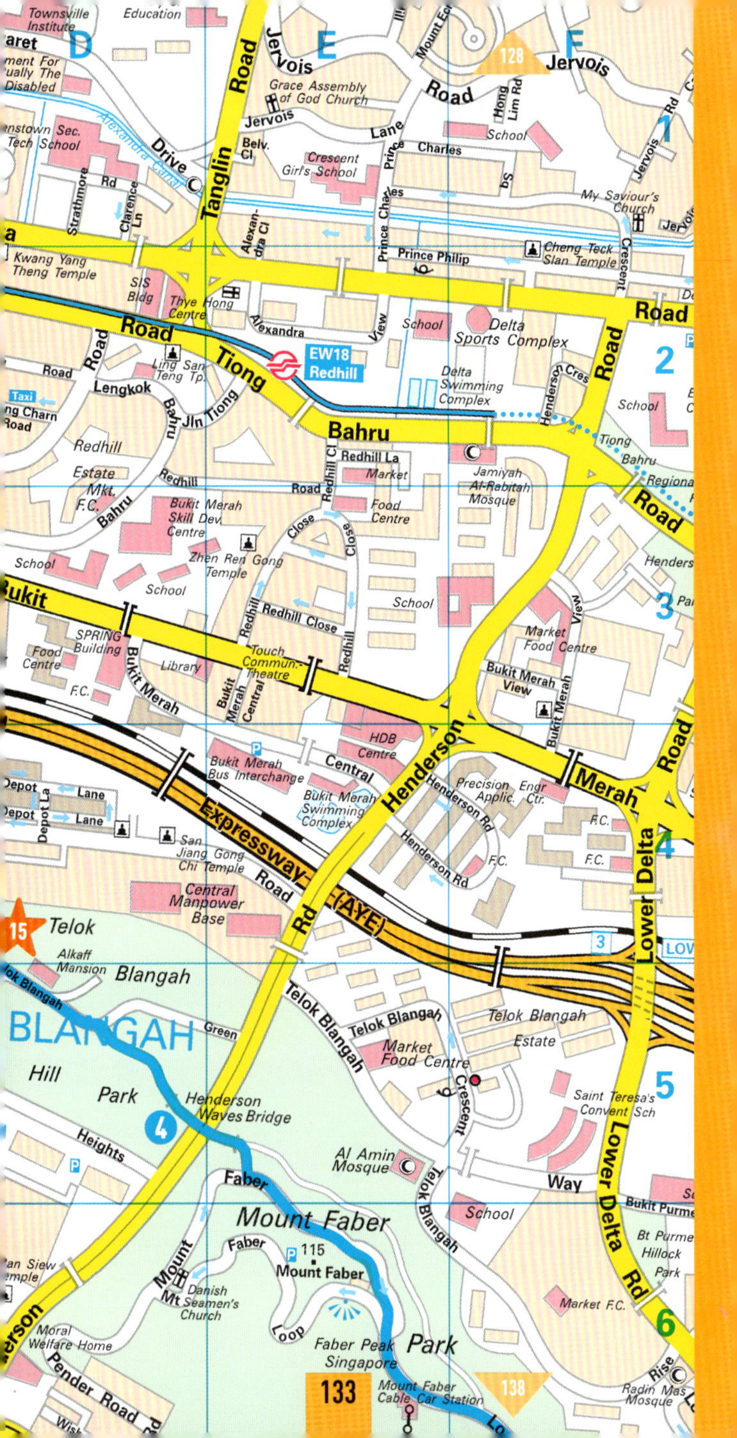

D
E
F
128
1
2
3
4
5
6
Townsville Institute
Education
Jervois Road
Grace Assembly of God Church
Jervois Lane
Tanglin Road
Charles
Hong Lim Rd
School
Crescent Girl's School
Prince Charles Crescent
Prince Philip
My Saviour's Church
Alexandra Canal
Strathmore Rd
Clarence Ln
Belv. Cl
Alexandra Cl
Cheng Teck Slan Temple
Kwang Yang Theng Temple
SIS Bldg
Thye Hong Centre
Alexandra View
School
Delta Sports Complex
Delta Road
Tiong Bahru Road
EW18 Redhill
Ling San Teng Tp.
Lengkok Bahru
Jln Tiong
Delta Swimming Complex
Henderson Cres
Taxi
Redhill Estate
Mkt. F.C.
Redhill Road
Redhill Cl
Redhill La
Market
Food Centre
Jamiyah Al-Rabitah Mosque
Tiong Bahru
Regional
Bukit Merah Skill Dev. Centre
Zhen Ren Gong Temple
School
Redhill Close
School
Henderson
Bukit Merah Road
SPRING Building
Food Centre
F.C.
Library
Touch Commun. Theatre
Bukit Merah Central
Market Food Centre
Bukit Merah View
HDB Centre
Henderson Rd
Bukit Merah Bus Interchange
Bukit Merah Swimming Complex
Precision Engr Applic. Ctr.
Depot Lane
Depot La
San Jiang Gong Chi Temple
Expressway (AYE)
F.C.
Lower Delta Rd
Central Manpower Base
15
Telok Blangah
Alkaff Mansion
Telok Blangah Green
Telok Blangah Estate
Market Food Centre
Telok Blangah Crescent
Saint Teresa's Convent Sch
Telok Blangah Hill Park
Henderson Waves Bridge
4
Telok Blangah Heights
Al Amin Mosque
Telok Blangah Way
Bukit Purmei
Mount Faber Road
Mount Faber
115
Mount Faber
School
Bt Purmei Hillock Park
Danish Seamen's Church
Mt Faber Loop
Market F.C.
Moral Welfare Home
Faber Peak Singapore
Mount Faber Park
Pender Road
Mount Faber Cable Car Station
Radin Mas Mosque
Rise
138

A
B
C
129
300 m
328 yd
1
2
3
4
5
6
Jervois
Hong Lim Rd
School
Jervois Rd
Cable Road
Malaysian High Commission
Holt Road
Shanghai Rd
River Valley Road
Mutiara
St Bernadette Church
The Tiara
Kim Seng
Times
Kellock Road
Zion
Great World City
Valley Park
Fraser Suites
My Saviour's Church
Jervois Close
Metico Centre
Zion Close
Zion Rd
Kim Seng Prom
Cheng Teck Siah Temple
Crescent
Delta Avenue
Delta Road
APSN School
Kg Delta Mosque
Boy's Brig. Headqtr.
F.C.
Delta House
Delta Estate
Delta Sports Complex
Road
Ganges Avenue
Heavy Vehicle Park
Nile Road
Havelock Road
Ganges Centre
Indus Road
Henderson Cres
School
Examin. Centre
F.C.
Beo Cres
Market F.C.
Giok Hong Tian Temple
Tiong Bahru Regional Park
School
Isetan Off. Bldg
Jamiyah Al-Rabitah Mosque
Jalan Bukit Ho Swee Est
F.C.
Taman Ho Swee
Jln Klinik
Bukit Ho Swee
School
Tiong Bahru Plaza
Boon Tiong Road
Henderson
Tiong Bahru
Tiong Bahru EW17
Park
View
Lim Liak Street
Market Food Centre
Kim Tian Rd
Road
Kim Cheng St
Market F.C.
Bukit Merah View
Bukit Merah
Jln Membina
Membina
Mkt. Inst.
Barat
Kim Pong Road
Seng Poh Lane
Kim Tian
Kim Tian Place
Moh Guan Terr
Seng Poh
Eng Watt St
Eu Chin St
Yong Siak St
Chay Yan St
Guan Chuan St
Tiong Bahru Rd
Keng Kiat St
Ng Peng St
Merah
Precision Engr Applic. Ctr.
School
Kim Lan Temple
Road
F.C.
Jalan
Kg Tiong Bahru Est
Tiong Poh Avenue
Mc Alister Flats
MacAlister
F.C.
F.C.
Lower Delta
Kim Tian
1 A
BUKIT MERAH FLYOVER
Market Food Centre
Jalan
Central
3
LOWER DELTA FLYOVER
Kai San Temple
2 C
School
College
Telok Blangah Estate
Wat Ananda Temple
Tai Yeong Kon Temple
Bukit Merah
RADIN MAS FLYOVER
Silat La
Sikh Temple
3
Crescent
Saint Teresa's Convent Sch
Bt Teresa Cl
Carmelite Monastery
Silat Walk
Silat Ave
Bahru
Bukit Teresa
Spooner Road
Way
School
Saint Teresa's High Sch
Road
Lower Delta
School
Bukit Purmei Avenue
Ayer-Rajah
Bt Purmei Hillock Park
Bukit Purmei Rd
2 B
Saint Teresa's Church
Market F.C.
Bukit Purmei
School
KEPPEL VIADUCT
Tanah Kubor Raja
Kampong
Radin Mas Mosque
Rise
Road
Bukit Kasita
139
Keppel Distripark
Keppel

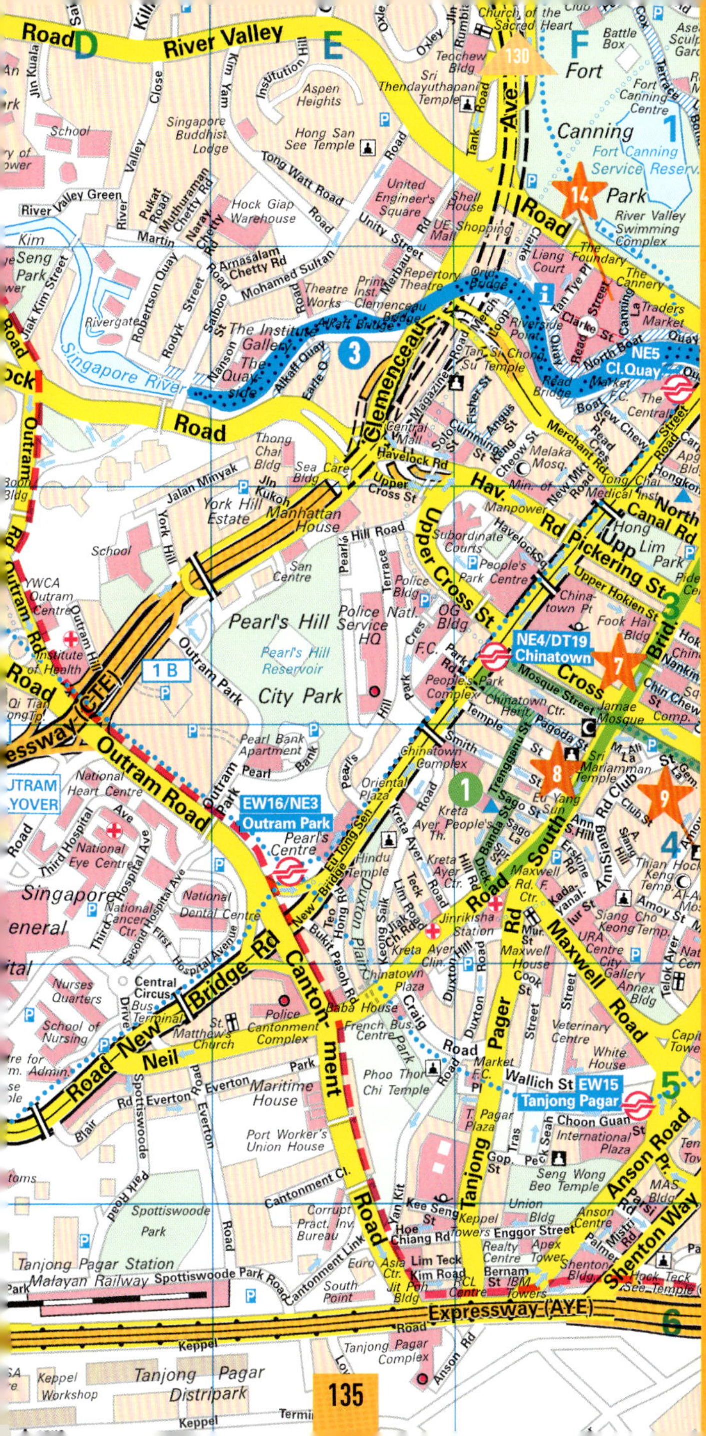

136

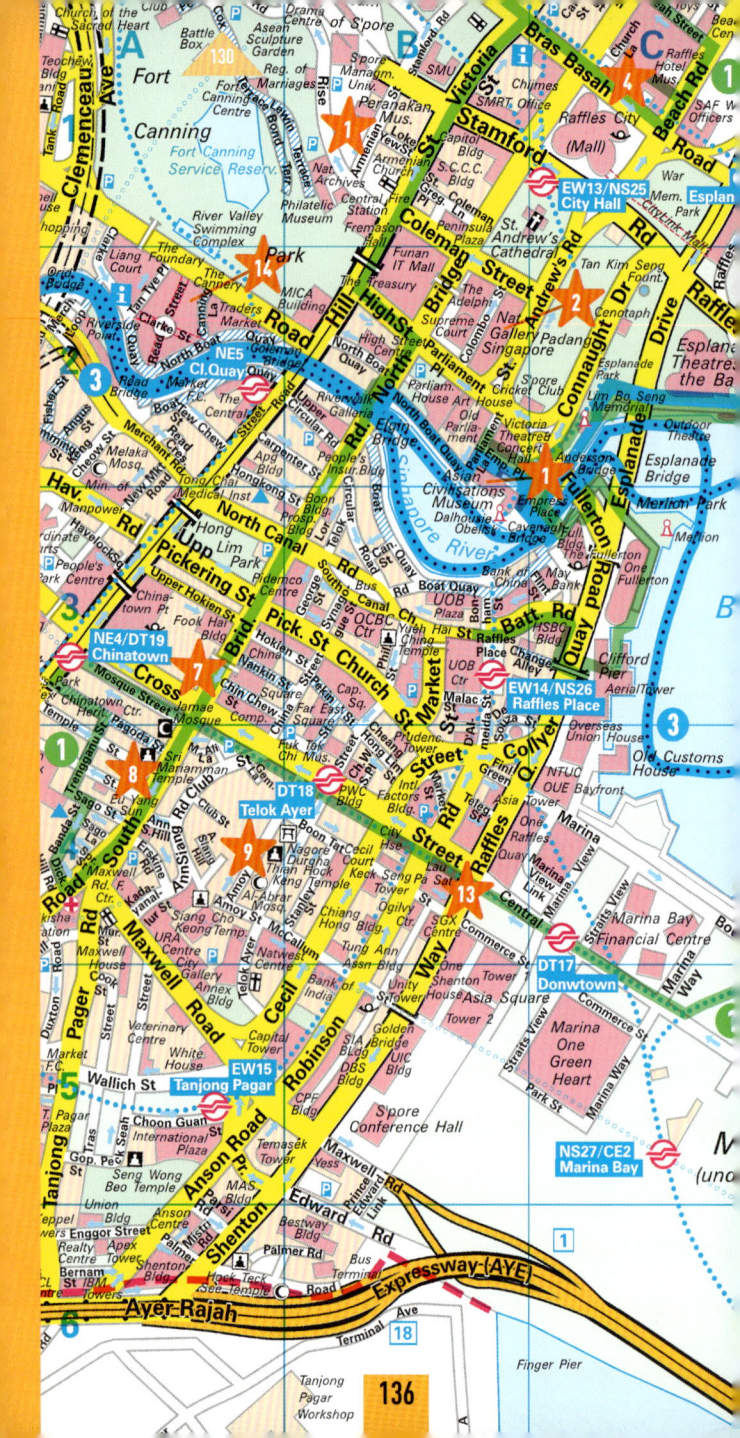

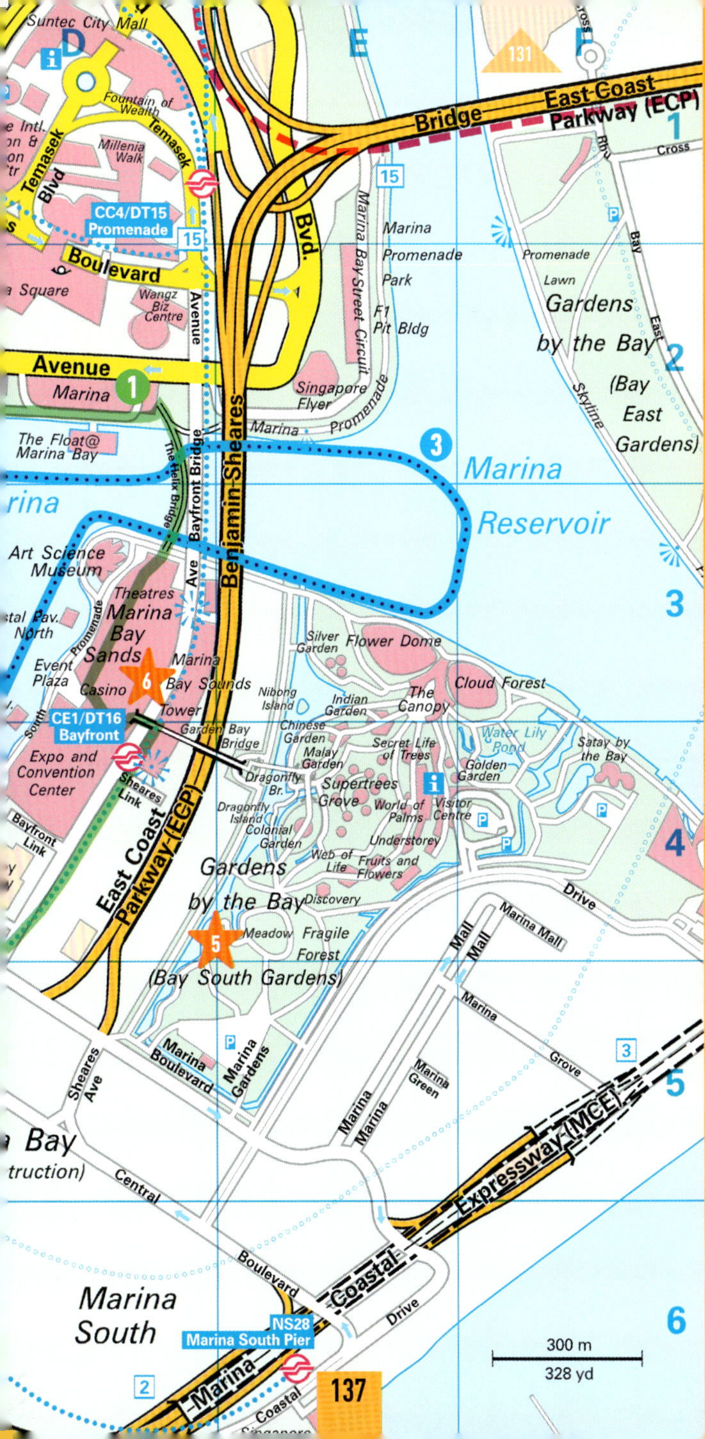

Suntec City Mall
D
E
F
131
East Coast
Bridge
Parkway (ECP)
1
Cross
Fountain of Wealth
Millenia Walk
Temasek
Temasek Blvd
CC4/DT15
Promenade
15
Boulevard
Square
Wangz Biz Centre
Avenue
Bvd.
Marina Bay Street Circuit
Marina Promenade Park
F1 Pit Bldg
Singapore Flyer
Marina Promenade
Promenade Lawn
Gardens by the Bay
(Bay East Gardens)
Bay East
Skyline
2
Marina
1
The Float@ Marina Bay
The Helix Bridge
Bayfront Bridge
Benjamin Sheares
3
Marina Reservoir
rina
Art Science Museum
Theatres
Marina Bay Sands
Ave
Bayfront
3
Promenade
Event Plaza
Casino
6
Marina Bay Sounds
Tower
North
CE1/DT16
Bayfront
South
Expo and Convention Center
Sheares Link
Bayfront Link
Garden Bay Bridge
Silver Garden
Flower Dome
Cloud Forest
Nibong Island
Indian Garden
The Canopy
Water Lily Pond
Satay by the Bay
Chinese Garden
Malay Garden
Secret Life of Trees
Golden Garden
Dragonfly Br.
Supertrees Grove
Dragonfly Island
Colonial Garden
World of Palms
Visitor Centre
Understorey
Web of Life
Fruits and Flowers
4
East Coast Parkway (ECP)
Gardens by the Bay
Discovery
Drive
5
Meadow
Fragile Forest
(Bay South Gardens)
Marina Mall
Mall
Mall
Marina
Grove
3
Marina Boulevard
Marina Gardens
Sheares Ave
Marina Green
5
Marina
Marina
Expressway (MCE)
Bay
truction)
Central
Boulevard
Coastal
Drive
Marina South
NS28
Marina South Pier
Marina
Coastal
2
6
300 m
328 yd

A
B
C
1
2
3
4
133
Telok Blangah Drive
Telok Blangah Towers
Tiang Gong Miao Temple
West Coast Highway
Henderson Road
Moral Welfare Home
Pender Road
Wishart
Morse Rd
Mount Faber
Faber Peak Singapore
The Jewel Box
Mount Faber Cable Car Station
Park
Loop
Silk Village Handicraft Centre
Meth. Church
Hill
Rd
Keppel
CC28 Telok Blangah
Keppel Golf Course
Road
Keppel Golf Course
Keppel Club
Bukit Chermin
Keppel Marina
Chermin Wharf
Queen's Dock
Caribean at Keppel Bay
Drive
Marina
Jetty
Pulau Keppel
Keppel Bay Bridge
Bay
King's Dock
Harbour front Ave
Harb.-front
Harbourfront Towers
Harbourfront Cable Car
Maritime Sq
Harbour Front Centre
Harbour Wk
SPI Bldg
Oil Wharf
Singapore Cruise Centre
Ferry Terminal
Seah Im Rd
Harbourfront Bus Interchange
Telok Blangah
Marang Road
15
Temenggong Rd.
Signal Station
NE1/CC29 Harbour Front
Sentosa Monorail Station
4
VivoCity
Market F.C.
Sekupang, Teluk Senimba, Batu Ampar, Batam Centre, Tanjung Balai
Cruise Bay
Monorail "Sentosa Express"
Fort Siloso (Gun Museum)
Underwater World
Spa Villas
Equarius Water Park
MEMA Maritime Experimential Museum and Aquarium
Hard Rock Hotel
Convent. Ctre
Coliseum
Bull Ring
Sentosa Visitor Centre
Resorts World at Sentosa
11
Ticket Booth
Mega Zip Adventure Park
Mt. Imbiah
62
Imbiah Falls
Imbiah Nature Reserve Walk
Imbiah Hill Road
Butterfly Park
Siloso Road
Shangri - La's Rasa Sentosa Resort
Island Life Centre
Flying Trapeze
Trapizza
Siloso Beach Walk
Sapphire Hall
Cine Blast
4D Magix
Butterfly Park & Insect Kingdom
Cable Car Stn
Tiger Sky Tower
Festive Grand Theatre
Crockfords Tower
Lake of Dreams
Galleria
Madagascar
Hollywood
New York
S1 Waterfront
Universal Studios Singapore
Images of Sporé
Cable Car Road
Skyride
Sentosa Luge
Merlion Tower
S2 Imbiah
Sci Fi City
Road
Beach View
Tresure Res Sentosa
Artillery
Larkhill Rd
Tourism Academy
Mega Zip Adventure Park
Siloso Beach
400 m
437 yd
Beach Arrival Plaza
S3 Beach
Songs of the Sea
Palawan
Palawan Beach
Camping Laguna
Rope Bridge
Palawan Island
Kuan Im Tng Temple
Joo Chiat
Lane
Road
Sim Poh Seng Temple
Pulasan
Lor Nang Ka
Still Road
Lorong
300 m
328 yd
2
Temb. Rd
Joo Chiat Road
Koon Seng Road
Everitt
Teng Tong Rd
Rambai Road
Tembeling
Duku Lane
Duku Place
Lor Stangee
Stangee Place
Stang. Cl
Still Lane
Onan
Carpmael
Ceylon
Penhas
Pennefather Rd
Food Centre
Lane
Duku
Joo Chiat Comm. Ctr.
Chapel Cl
Cheow Keng Rd
Katong Antique House
Kuo Chuan Avenue
Jago Cl
Still Road
Karikal La
Saint Patrick's Rd
Martia Rd
Tan. Rd
Katong Convent School
Marshall Road
Ceylon
Fowlie
Sri Senpaga Vinayagar Temple
East Coast Road
Katong Mall
Sea Ave.
Chapel Rd
Marine Parade Rd
South
Library & Comm. Ctr.
Seraya Rd
School
Mugliston Rd
East Kiam Pl
Katong Shopp. Centre
Katong Plaza
Brooke
Roxy

D
E
F
1
2
3
4
5
6
135
Ayer Rajah Expressway (AYE)
KEPPEL VIADUCT
2 A
MB 2
Purmei
School
Tanah
Bukit
Kasita
Rd
Bahru
Keppel
Distripark
Coast
Highway
Keppel Wharfes Bldg
Suzue-PSA Cold Store
Keppel Workshop
Tanjong Pagar Distripark
Tanjong Pagar Complex
Low Hill Rd
Point
Bldg
Terminal
Avenue
Keppel
Terminal
Ave
Street
Road
Tanjong Pagar Container Terminal
East Wharf
West Wharf
Gate 2 Brani Terminal
Prima Tower
West Wharf
West
Keppel Channel
Brani Terminal Road
Brani
Terminal
Street
Avenue
Pulau Brani
Brani Terminal Building
Brani Terminal Road
Selat Sengkir
Serapong Jetty
Maritime Museum
Ranger Post
Sentosa Golf Club
Serapong Course
Road
Course
Serapong
Historic & Massacre Site of Sentosa
Serapong Lake
Serapong Golf Course
Sentosa
Serapong Hill
85
Mt. Serapong
Lakeshore View
Road
Satellite Tower
Woodwich
Sentosa Earth Satellite Station
Coralarium & Nature Ramble
Recycling Building
SDC Resorts World
SDC Transp.Office
SDC Office
SDC Workshop
Allanbrooke
Allanbrooke Road
Spa Botanica
Bukit
Mansi
The Beaufort Singapore
The Sentosa Resort & Spa
Tanjong
Beach
Walk
Road
Sentosa Golf Club
Tanjong Course
Sentosa Golf Club
Tanjong Beach
Cove Drive
Ocean Drive
Treasure
Ocean Way
Dolphin Fountain
Sentosa Cove Ave
Sentosa Cove Arrival Plaza
Sentosa Cove
Drive
Ocean Way
Cove
Sandy Bridge
Sandy Island
Sandy Island
Way
Pearl Bridge
Pearl Island
Island
Ocean Drive
Cove Grove

This index lists a selection of the streets and squares shown in the street atlas

A
Adis Road **130/B5**
Admore Park **129/D3**
Albert Street **130/C4**
Alexandra Close **133/E2**
Alexandra Road **132/A3-A4-C1**
Alexandra Terrace **132/A5**
Alexandra View **133/E2**
Aliwal Street **131/E4**
Alkaff Quay **135/E2**
Allanbrooke Road (Sentosa) **139/D5**
Allenby Road **131/E3**
Amoy Street **135/F4-136/A4**
Anderson Road **129/D3**
Angullia Park **129/D5**
Angus Street **135/F2-136/A2**
Ann Siang Hill **135/F4-136/A4**
Ann Siang Road **135/F4-136/A4**
Anson Road **135/E6-136/A5**
Anthony Road **129/F3**
Arab Street **131/D4**
Ardmore Park **129/D4**
Armenian Street **136/B1**
Arnap, Jalan **128/C5**
Arnasalam Chetty Road **135/E2**
Artillery Avenue (Sentosa) **138/C4**
Aruan, Jalan **130/A2**
Ayer Rajah Expressway (AYE) **132/C3-134/C6**

B
Baboo Lane **131/D3**
Baghdad Street **131/E5**
Bain Street **131/D6**
Balestier Road **131/D1**
Bali Lane **131/E5**
Balmoral Crescent **129/E1**
Balmoral Park **129/D2**
Balmoral Road **129/D2**
Banda Street **135/F4-136/A4**
Ban San Street **131/D4**
Barker Road **129/E1**
Battery Road **136/B3**
Bay East Drive **137/F1**
Bayfront Avenue **136/C5**
Bayfront Bridge **137/D3**
Bayfront Link **137/D4**
Beach Lane **131/D6**
Beach Road **131/D6-E5-136/C1**
Beach View (Sentosa) **138/C4**
Beatty Road **131/E2**
Belilios Lane **130/C4**
Belinos Road **130/C3**
Belvedere Close **133/E1**
Bencoolen Link **131/D5**
Bencoolen Street **130/C6**
Bendemeer Road **131/E2**
Benjamin Sheares Bridge **137/E3**
Beo Crescent **134/B2**
Berkshire Road **132/A4**
Bernam Street **135/F6-136/A6**
Bernard Street **131/D6**
Berseh, Jalan **131/E4**
Besar, Jalan **131/D4**
Bideford Road **129/F5**
Birch Road **131/D3**

Bishopsgate **128/C6**
Bishopswalk **128/C6**
Blair road **135/D5**
Boat Quay **135/F2-136/A2-B2-B3**
Bond Terrace **135/F1-136/A1**
Bonham Street **136/B3**
Boon Keng Road **131/E1**
Boon Tat Street **136/B4**
Brani Terminal Avenue **138/C3-139/D2**
Bras Basah Road **130/C6-136/B1**
Bristol Road **130/B2-C2**
Buckley Road **129/F1-130/A1**
Buffalo Lane **130/C4**
Buffalo Road **130/C4**
Bugis Street **131/D5**
Bukit Chermin Road **138/A2**
Bukit Ho Swee, Jalan **134/B2**
Bukit Kasita **134/B6-139/D1**
Bukit Mansi Road **139/D5**
Bukit Merah, Jalan **132/B3-134/B3**
Bukit Merah Central **133/D3-E3**
Bukit Merah Lane **132/B3**
Bukit Merah View **133/F3-F4-134/A3-A4**
Bukit Pasoh Road **135/E4**
Bukit Purmei **134/B6**
Bukit Purmei Avenue **133/F6-134/A6**
Bukit Purmei Road **134/B6-139/D1**
Bukit Teresa Close **134/B5**
Bukit Teresa Road **134/B5**
Bukit Timah Road **128/C1-129/E1-130/A3-B3**
Burmah Road **131/D3**
Bussorah Street **131/E5**
Buyong Road **130/A5**

C
Cable Car Road (Sentosa) **138/B4**
Cable Road **133/F1-134/A1**
Cairnhill Circle **129/F4**
Cairnhill Rise **129/F3**
Cairnhill Road **129/E3-F5**
Cambridge Road **130/B2**
Cameron Court **129/D5**
Campbell Lane **130/C4**
Camp Road **128/A4**
Canning Lane **135/F2-136/A2**
Canning Rise **130/B6**
Canning Walk **130/B6**
Cantonment Close **135/E6**
Cantonment Link **135/E6**
Cantonment Road **135/E4**
Canton Street **136/B3**
Carlisle Road **130/B2**
Carpenter Street **135/F2-136/A2**
Carver Street **131/D6**
Cashin Street **131/D6**
Cavan Road **131/E3**
Cavenagh Road **130/A5-A4-B3**
Cecil Street **136/A5**
Central Boulevard **136/B4**
Central Circus **135/D5**
Central Expressway (CTE) **130/B2-134/B5**
Chancery Lane **129/E1**
Chander Road **130/C4**
Chang Charn Road **133/D2**
Change Alley **136/B3**
Chatsworth Avenue **128/B5**
Chatsworth Park **128/B5**
Chatsworth Road **128/B6-B5**
Chay Yan Street **134/C4**
Cheang Hong Lim Street **136/B4**
Cheang Wan Seng Place **136/B4**
Cheng Yan Place **131/D5**
China Street **135/F4-136/A4**
Chin Chew Street **135/F3-136/A3**
Chitty Road **131/D4**
Choon Guan Street **135/F5-136/A5**
Chulia Street **136/B3**
Church Lane **136/C1**
Church Street **136/B3**
Circular Road **136/B3**
Clarence Lane **133/D1**
Clarke Quay **135/F1-136/A1**
Clarke Street **135/F2-136/A2**
Claymore Drive **129/D4**
Claymore Hill **129/E4-D4**
Claymore Road **129/D4**
Clemenceau Avenue **129/F3-130/A3-135/E2-136/A1**
Clive Road **130/C4**
Club Street **135/F4-136/A4**
Cluny Park **128/A1**
Cluny Road **128/A1-A2**
Coleman Lane **136/B1**
Coleman Street **136/B1**
College Road **134/C5**
Collyer Quay **136/B4**
Colombo Street **136/B2**
Commerce Street **136/B4**
Connaught Drive **136/C2**
Cook Street **135/F5-136/A5**
Cornwall Road **132/A4**
Cove Drive (Sentosa) **139/E6**
Cove Grove (Sentosa) **139/E6**
Cove Way (Sentosa) **139/F6**
Cox Terrace **130/B6**
Craig Road **135/E5**
Crawford Lane **131/F4**
Crawford Street **131/F4**
Cross Street **135/F3-136/A3**
Cuff Road **130/C4**
Cumming Street **135/E2**
Cuppage Road **130/A5**
Cuscaden Road **128/C4**
Cuscaden Walk **129/D5**

D
Dalhousie Lane **130/C4**
D'Almeida Street **136/B3**
Dalvey Estate **128/B1-B2**
Dalvey Road **128/B2**
Delta Avenue **134/B1**
Delta Road **134/B2**
Depot Road **132/B4**
Derbyshire Road **130/B2**
Desker Road **131/D3**
De Souza Street **136/B3**
Devonshire Road **129/F5**

STREET INDEX

Dickenson Hill Road **135/F4-136/A4**
Dickson Road **131/D4**
Dorset Road **130/B3**
Draycott Drive **129/D3-E3**
Draycott Park **129/D2**
Dublin Road **129/F6-130/A6**
Dundee Road **132/C1**
Dunearn Road **129/D1-E1**
Dunlop Street **130/C4**
Durham Road **130/C2**
Duxton Hill **135/E5**
Duxton Road **135/F5-136/A5**

E
Earle Quay **135/E2**
East Coast Parkway (ECP) **137/F1-D4**
Eber Road **130/A6**
Edinburgh Road **130/B5**
Elok, Jalan **129/E4**
Emerald Hill Road **129/F5-130/A5**
Enggor Street **135/F6-136/A6**
Eng Hoon Street **134/C3**
Eng Watt Street **134/C3**
Erskine Road **135/F4-136/A4**
Esplanade Drive **134/C3**
Essex Road **130/B1**
Eu Chin Street **134/C3**
Eu Tong Sen Street **135/E4**
Evans Road **128/B2**
Evelyn Road **129/F2**
Everton Park **135/D5**
Everton Road **135/D5**
Ewe Boon Road **129/D1**
Exeter Road **129/F5**

F
Fernhill Close **128/C2**
Fernhill Crescent **128/C2**
Fernhill Road **128/C2-C3**
Finlayson Green **136/B4**
First Hospital Avenue **135/D4**
Fisher Street **135/F2-136/A2**
Flanders Square **131/E3**
Flint Street **136/C3**
Foch Road **131/E2**
Fort Canning Road **130/B6**
French Road **131/E3**
Fullerton Road **136/C2**

G
Ganges Avenue **134/B2**
Gateway Avenue (Sentosa) **138/C4**
Gemmill Lane **135/F4-136/A4**
Gentle Road **129/F1**
George Street **136/B3**
Gilstead Road **129/F2-130/A1**
Gloucester Road **130/C2**
Goldhill Avenue **129/E1**
Goldhill Drive **129/E1**
Goldhill Plaza **130/A1**
Goldhill Rise **129/E1**
Goldhill View **129/E1**
Goodwood Hill **129/E2-E3**
Gopeng Street **135/F5-136/A5**
Grange Garden **128/C5**

Grange Road **128/C5-129/E5**
Guan Chuan Street **134/C4**

H
Haji Lane **131/E5**
Halifax Road **130/B2**
Hamilton Road **131/E3**
Hampshire Road **130/B3**
Handy Road **130/B5**
Harding Road **128/A4**
Hastings Road **130/C4**
Havelock Road **134/B2-C2-135/ E2-F2-136/A2**
Havelock Square **135/F3-136/A3**
Henderson Crescent **133/F2-134/A2**
Henderson Road **133/D6-E4-138/A1**
Hertford Road **130/B2**
High Street **136/B2**
Hill Street **136/B2**
Hindoo Road **131/D4-D3**
Hoe Chiang Road **135/E6**
Hokien Street **135/F3-136/A3**
Holt Road **134/B1**
Hongkong Street **135/F2-136/A2**
Hong Lim Road **133/F1-134/A1**
Hoot Kiam Road **129/D6**
Horne Road **131/E3**
Hospital Drive **134/C5**
Hoy Fatt Road **132/C3**
Hullet Road **129/F5**
Hylam Street **131/D6**

I
Idris Road **131/E2**
Imbiah Hill Road **138/B3**
Imbiah Walk (Sentosa) **138/A3**
Indus Road **134/C2**
Institution Hill **135/E1**
Ironside Link (Sentosa) **139/D4**
Ironside Road (Sentosa) **138/C4**
Irwell Bank Road **129/D6**

J
Jati, Jalan **130/B1**
Jellicoe Road **131/F4**
Jervois Close **133/F1-134/A1**
Jervois Lane **133/E1**
Jervois Road **133/F1-134/A1**
Jiak Chuan Road **135/E4**
Jiak Kim Street **135/D2**
Jintan, Jalan **129/E4**
Johore Road **131/D5**
Joo Avenue **131/D2**

K
Kadayanallur Street **135/F4-136/A4**
Kallang Avenue **131/F2**
Kallang Bahru **131/F1-F2**
Kallang Junction **131/F3**
Kallang Road **131/F3**
Kallang Tengah **131/F1**
Kampong Bahru Road **134/B6-39/D1**
Kampong Bugis **131/F3**
Kampong Java Road **130/A2-B2**
Kampong Kapor Road **131/D4**

Kandahar Street **131/E5**
Kaypoh Road **129/D6**
Kayu Manis, Jalan **129/E4**
Keene Road **128/A4**
Kee Seng Street **135/E6**
Kelantan Lane **131/D4**
Kelantan Road **131/D4**
Kelawar, Jalan **128/C5**
Kellock Road **134/B1**
Kempas Road **131/E1-E2**
Keng Cheow Street **135/F2-136/A2**
Keng Chin Road **129/D1**
Keng Kiat Street **134/C4**
Keng Lee Road **130/B2-A2**
Kent Road **130/C2**
Keong Saik Road **135/E5**
Keppel Bay Drive **138/B2**
Keppel Hill **138/B1**
Keppel Road **135/D6-138/C2-139/E1**
Keppel Terminal Avenue **139/D2-E1-F1**
Kerbau Road **130/C4**
Khiang Guan Avenue **130/A1**
Killiney Road **129/F6-135/D1**
Kim Cheng Street **134/C3**
Kim Pong Road **134/C3**
Kim Seng Promenade **134/C1**
Kim Seng Road **134/C1**
Kim Tian Place **134/B4**
Kim Tian Road **134/B3-B4**
Kim Yam Road **129/F6-135/E1**
King George's Avenue **131/E4**
Kinta Road **131/D3**
Kirk Terrace **130/B6**
Kitchener Road **131/D3**
Klang Lane **130/C3**
Klang Road **130/C3**
Klapa, Jalan **131/E4**
Kledek, Jalan **131/E4**
Klink, Jalan **134/B3**
Koek Road **130/A5**
Korma, Jalan **130/B2**
Kramat Lane **130/A5**
Kramat Road **130/A5**
Kreta Ayer Road **135/E4**
Kubor, Jalan **131/E4**
Kukoh, Jalan **135/E2**

L
Labrador Villa Road **132/A6**
Lada Puteh, Jalan **129/E4**
Lady Hill Road **128/C3**
Lakeshore View (Sentosa) **139/E4**
Larkhill Road (Sentosa) **138/C4**
Larut Road **131/D4**
Lavender Street **131/E2**
Lembah Kallang, Jalan **131/F2**
Lembu Road **131/D3**
Leng Kee Road **132/C2**
Lengkok Angsa **129/D5**
Lengkok Bahru **132/C3-133/D2**
Lengkok Merak **128/C5**
Leonie Hill **129/E6**
Leonie Hill Road **129/E6**
Lermit Road **128/B3**
Lewin Terrace **135/F1-136/A1**

141

Lewis Road **128/C1**
Liang Sean Street **131/D6**
Lim Liak Street **134/C3**
Lim Teck Kim Road **135/E6**
Lincoln Road **130/A2**
Lloyd Gardens **129/F6**
Lloyd Road **129/F6**
Loke Yew Street **136/B1**
Lower Delta Road **133/F5-134/A5**
Lower Ring Road **128/A3**
Low Hill Road **135/E6-139/F1**

M

MacAlister Road **134/C4**
Mackenzie Road **130/B3**
Madras Street **130/C4**
Magazine Road **135/E2**
Makepeace Road **130/A3**
Makeway Avenue **130/A3**
Malabar Street **131/D6**
Malacca Street **136/B3**
Mandalay Road **130/C1**
Manila Street **131/E5**
Marang Road **138/C2**
Margaret Drive **133/F3**
Margoliouth Road **128/C1**
Marian Gardens Drive **137/F4**
Marina Boulevard **136/C4-137/D5**
Marina Coastal Expressway (MCE) **137/F6**
Marina Mall **137/E5-F4**
Marina South Promenade **137/D4**
Marina View **136/C4**
Marina View Link **136/B4**
Marina Way **136/C5**
Maritime Square **138/B2**
Market Street **136/B4**
Marne Road **131/D2**
Martin Road **135/D1**
Maude Road **131/E3**
Maxwell Road **135/F4-136/B5-A4**
Mayne Road **130/C4**
Mayo Street **131/D4**
McCallum Street **135/F4-136/A4**
McNair Road **131/D1**
Mei Chin Road **132/A2**
Mei Ling Sreet **132/B1**
Membina, Jalan **134/B4**
Membina Barat, Jalan **134/B3**
Merbau Road **135/E2**
Merchant Loop **135/F2-136/A2**
Merchant Road **135/F2-136/A2**
Mergui Road **130/C1**
Middle Road **130/C5**
Middlesex Road **128/B4**
Miller Street **131/D6**
Minden Road **128/A4**
Minto Road **131/F5**
Minyak, Jalan **135/D3**
Mistri Road **135/F6-136/A6**
Mohamed Ali Lane **135/F4-136/A4**
Mohamed Sultan Road **135/E2**
Moh Guan Terrace **134/C4**
Monk's Hill Road **129/F3-130/A3**
Monk's Hill Terrace **129/F3-130/A3**
Morse Road **138/B1**
Mosque Street **135/F3-136/A3**
Moulmein Rise **130/B1**
Moulmein Road **130/B1**
Mount Echo Park **133/E1**
Mount Elizabeth **129/E4**
Mount Elizabeth Link **129/E4**
Mount Emily Road **130/B4**
Mount Faber Loop **133/D6-138/C1**
Mount Sophia **130/B5**
Muscat Street **131/E5**
Muthuraman Chetty Road **135/D1**
Mutiara, Jalan **129/D6**

N

Nankin Street **135/F3-136/A3**
Nanson Road **135/E2**
Napier Road **128/B4**
Narayanan Chetty Road **135/D1**
Nassim Road **128/C3-B2-B3**
Nathan Road **128/C5**
Neil Road **135/E4**
New Bridge Road **135/D5-E4**
New Market Road **135/F3-136/A3**
Newton Circus **129/F2**
Newton Road **130/A2**
Nicoll Highway **131/E6**
Nile Road **134/B2**
Niven Road **130/C5**
Norfolk Road **130/B2**
Norris Road **131/D3**
North Boat Quay **136/F2-136/A2-B2**
North Bridge Road **131/D5-136/B2**
North Canal Road **135/F3-136/A3**
Northumberland Road **130/C3**
Nutmeg Road **129/E4**

O

Ocean Drive **139/F5**
Ocean Way **139/F5**
Office Gate Road **128/A3**
Office Ring Road **128/A3**
Oldham Lane **130/B6**
One Tree Hill **128/C5-129/D5**
Ophir Road **131/D5**
Orange Grove Road **128/C3**
Orchard Boulevard **128/C5**
Orchard Link **129/E5**
Orchard Road **129/D4-130/A5**
Orchard Turn **129/E5**
Outram Hill **135/D3**
Outram Park **135/D3-D4**
Outram Road **135/D3-D2-D4**
Owen Road **130/C1**
Oxford Road **130/C2**
Oxley Rise **130/A6**
Oxley Road **130/A6**
Oxley Walk **130/A6-135/E1**

P

Pagoda Street **135/F3-136/A3**
Pahang Street **131/E5**
Palawan Beach Walk (Sentosa) **138/C4**
Palmer Road **135/F6-136/A6**
Palm Valley Road **128/A3**
Park Crescent **135/E3**
Park Road **135/E3**
Parliament Lane **136/B2**
Parliament Place **136/B2**
Parsi Road **135/F5-136/A5**
Pasiran, Jalan **129/F1**
Pasir Panjang Road **132/A6**
Paterson Hill **129/D5**
Paterson Road **129/D5**
Pearl Bank **135/E4**
Pearl's Hill Road **135/E3**
Pearl's Hill Terrace **135/E4**
Peck Hay Road **129/F3**
Peck Seah Street **135/F5-136/A5**
Pekin Street **136/B3**
Penang Lane **130/B6**
Penang Road **130/A5**
Pender Road **133/D6-138/B1**
Peng Nguan Street **134/C4**
Penhas Road **131/F3**
Perak Road **131/D4**
Percival Road **130/B6**
Perumal Road **131/D2**
Petain Road **131/D2**
Petaling Road **131/E1**
Phillip Street **136/B3**
Pickering Street **136/A3**
Pinang, Jalan **131/E5**
Pisang, Jalan **131/E5**
Pitt Street **131/D4**
Plumer Road **131/E3**
Portsdown Avenue **132/A2**
Prince Charles Crescent **133/E2**
Prince Charles Square **133/E1**
Prince Edward Link **136/B6**
Prince Edward Road **135/F5-136/A5**
Prince Philip Avenue **133/E2**
Prinsep Link **130/C5**
Prinsep Street **130/C6-C5**
Pukat Street **135/D1**
Purvis Street **131/D6**

Q

Queens Close **132/A1**
Queen Street **130/C6-131/D5**
Queensway **132/A1**

R

Race Course Lane **130/C3**
Race Course Road **130/C3-131/D3**
Raeburn Park **134/C6**
Raffles Avenue **136/C2**
Raffles Boulevard **136/C1**
Raffles Link **136/C2**
Raffles Place **136/B3**
Raffles Quay **136/B4**
Rain Tree Drive **128/A2**
Rangoon Lane **131/D1**
Rangoon Road **130/C1**
Rappa Terrace **130/C3**
Read Crescent **135/F2-136/A2**
Read Street **135/F2-136/A2**
Redhill Close **133/E3**

STREET INDEX

Redhill Lane **133/E2**
Redhill Road **133/D2**
Republic Avenue **131/F6**
Ridley Park **128/A5**
River Valley Close **135/D1**
River Valley Green **135/D1**
River Valley Grove **129/E6**
River Valley Road **129/D6-130/A6-134/B1-135/D1**
Road J **139/F1**
Road K **139/F1**
Road M **139/E1**
Road N **139/D2**
Roberts Lane **131/D3**
Robertson Quay **135/D2**
Robin Close **128/C1**
Robin Drive **129/D1**
Robin Lane **129/D1**
Robin Road **129/D2**
Robin Walk **128/C1**
Robinson Road **136/B5**
Rochalie Drive **128/B5**
Rochor Canal Road **130/C4-131/D4**
Rochor Road **131/D5**
Rodyk Street **135/D2**
Rowell Road **131/D3**
Rutland Road **130/B3**

S

Sago Lane **135/F4-136/A4**
Sago Street **135/F4-136/A4**
Saiboo Street **135/D2**
Saint Andrew's Road **136/B2**
Saint Gregory's Place **136/B1**
Saint Martin's Drive **128/C4**
Saint Thomas Walk **129/F6**
Sam Leong Road **131/D3**
Sarkies Road **129/F2**
Saunders Road **129/F5**
Scotts Road **129/E4**
Seah Im Road **138/C2**
Seah Street **131/D6**
Second Hospital Avenue **135/D5**
Selegie Road **130/C5**
Seng Poh Lane **134/C3**
Seng Poh Road **134/C3**
Sentosa Cove Avenue (Sentosa) **139/F5**
Sentosa Gateway **138/C3**
Serangoon Road **130/C4-131/E2**
Serapong Course Road (Sentosa) **139/E4**
Serapong Hill Road (Sentosa) **139/E4**
Seton Close **128/C4**
Seton Walk **128/C4**
Shanghai Road **129/D6-134/B1**
Sheares Avenue **137/D5**
Shenton Way **135/F6-136/A6**
Sherwood Road **128/B5-A4**
Short Street **130/C5**
Shrewsbury Road **130/B1**
Silat Avenue **134/C5**
Silat Lane **134/C5**
Silat Walk **134/C5**
Siloso Beach Walk (Sentosa) **138/A3**
Siloso Road **138/B3**

Sing Avenue **131/D2**
Sing Joo Walk **131/D2**
Sit Wah Road **134/C4**
Smith Street **135/E4**
Solomon Street **135/E2**
Somerset Road **129/F5**
Somme Road **131/E3**
Sophia Road **130/B4**
South Bridge Road **135/F4-136/A4**
South Canal Road **136/B3**
Spooner Road **134/C5**
Spottiswoode Park Road **135/D5-D6**
Stamford Road **136/B1**
Stanley Street **136/B4**
Starlight Road **131/D2**
Starlight Terrace **131/D2**
Stevens Close **128/C2**
Stevens Drive **128/C1-129/D1**
Stevens Road **128/C1-C2-129/E3**
Strathmore Road **133/D1**
Street 6 **139/F1**
Street 7 **139/E1**
Street 8 **139/F3**
Street 9 **139/F3**
Street 10 **139/F3**
Sturdee Road **131/E2**
Suffolk Road **130/B2**
Sultan, Jalan **131/E4**
Sultan Gate **131/E5**
Sungei Road **130/C4-131/D4**
Surrey Road **130/A2**
Swiss Cottage Estate **129/D1**
Syed Alwi Road **131/D3**
Synagogue Street **136/B3**

T

Taman Ho Swee **134/C3**
Taman Serasi **128/B4**
Tanglin Gate Road **128/A3**
Tanglin Hill **128/A5**
Tanglin Rise **128/B5**
Tanglin Road **128/C4-133/E1**
Tanglin Walk **128/A5**
Tanjong Beach Walk (Sentosa) **139/D5**
Tanjong Pager Road **135/F6-136/A6**
Tank Road **135/F1-136/A1**
Tan Quee Lan Street **131/D6**
Tan Tock Seng, Jalan **130/C1**
Tan Tye Place **135/F2-136/A2**
Teck Lim Road **135/E4**
Telegraph Street **136/B4**
Telok, Lorong **136/B3**
Telok Ayer Street **135/F5-136/A5**
Telok Blangah Crescent **133/E5**
Telok Blangah Drive **132/C6**
Telok Blangah Green **133/D4**
Telok Blangah Heights **132/C5**
Telok Blangah Rise **133/E5**
Telok Blangah Road **132/B6**
Telok Blangah Way **133/E5**
Temasek Avenue **137/D1**
Temasek Boulevard **137/D1**
Temenggong Road **138/C1**
Temple Street **135/F3-136/A3**
Teo Hong Road **135/E4**

Tessensohn Road **131/D2**
Tew Chew Street **135/F2-136/A2**
Third Hospital Avenue **135/D4**
Tiong, Jalan **133/D2**
Tiong Bahru Road **133/E2-134/B3**
Tiong Boon Road **134/C3**
Tiong Poh Avenue **134/C4**
Tiong Poh Road **134/C4**
Tiverton Lane **129/F6**
Tomlinson Road **128/C4**
Tong Watt Road **135/E1**
Townshend Road **131/E4**
Tras Street **135/F5-136/A5**
Treasure Island **139/F5**
Trengganu Street **135/F4-136/A4**
Tronoh Road **131/E2**
Truro Road **130/C2**
Tupai, Jalan **129/D5**
Tyersall Avenue **128/A4**
Tyersall Road **128/A2**
Tyrwhitt Road **131/E3**

U

Unity Street **135/E1**
Upper Circular Road **136/B2**
Upper Cross Street **135/E2-E3**
Upper Dickson Road **130/C4**
Upper Hokien Street **135/F3-136/A3**
Upper Pickering Street **135/F3-136/A3**
Upper Ring Road **128/A3**
Upper Weld Road **131/D4**
Upper Wilkie Road **130/B4**

V

Veerasamy Road **131/D4**
Verdun Road **131/D3**
Victoria Street **131/D5-136/B1**

W

Wallich Street **135/F5-136/A5**
Walshe Road **129/D2**
Warwick Road **132/A3**
Waterloo Street **130/C6**
Wee Nam Road **130/A2**
Weld Road **131/D4**
West Coast Highway **138/A1-139/D1**
Whitchurch Road **132/A1**
White House Park **128/B2-C1**
White House Road **128/C1**
Wikie Terrace **130/C5**
Wilkie Road **130/B4**
Winstedt Drive **130/A3**
Winstedt Road **129/F3-130/A3**
Woodwich Road (Sentosa) **139/E5**
Worcester Road **130/C2**

Y

Yan Kit Road **135/E6**
Yong Siak Street **134/C4**
York Hill **135/D3**

Z

Zion Close **134/C1**
Zion Road **134/C1-C2**

143

KEY TO STREET ATLAS

Motorway / Autobahn		Autoroute / Autosnelweg
Road with four lanes / Vierspurige Straße		Route à quatre voies / Weg met vier rijstroken
Federal road or trunk road / Bundes- oder Fernstraße		Route nationale ou à grande circulation / Rijksweg of weg voor interlokaal verkeer
Main Road / Hauptstraße		Route principale / Hoofdweg
Other Roads / Sonstige Straßen		Autres routes / Overige wegen
Information / Information		Information / Informatie
One way road / Einbahnstraße		Rue à sens unique / Straat met éénrichtingsverkeer
Pedestrian zone / Fußgängerzone		Zone piétonne / Voetgangerszone
Main railway with station / Hauptbahn mit Bahnhof		Chemin de fer principal avec gare / Belangrijke spoorweg met station
Other railways / Sonstige Bahnen		Autres lignes / Overige spoorwegen
Aerial cableway / Kabinenschwebebahn		Téléphérique / Kabelbaan met cabine
Underground / U-Bahn		Métro / Ondergrondse spoorweg
Ferry line - Landing stage / Fährlinie - Anlegestelle		Ligne de bac - Embarcadère / Veerdienst - Aanlegplaats
Church - Church of interest / Kirche - Sehenswerte Kirche		Église - Église remarquable / Kerk - Bezienswaardige kerk
Synagogue - Mosque / Synagoge - Moschee		Synagogue - Mosquée / Synagoge - Moskee
Temple - Temple of interest / Tempel - Sehenswerter Tempel		Temple - Temple remarquable / Tempel - Bezienswaardige tempel
Police station - Post office / Polizeistation - Postamt		Poste de police - Bureau de poste / Politiebureau - Postkantoor
Parking - Monument / Parkplatz - Denkmal		Parking - Monument / Parkeerplaats - Monument
Hospital / Krankenhaus		Hôpital / Ziekenhuis
Youth hostel - Camping site / Jugendherberge - Campingplatz		Auberge de jeunesse - Terrain de camping / Jeugdherberg - Kampeerterrein
Built-up area - Public building / Bebaute Fläche - Öffentliches Gebäude		Zone bâtie - Bâtiment public / Bebouwing - Openbaar gebouw
Industrial area / Industriegelände		Zone industrielle / Industrieterrein
Park, forest / Park, Wald		Parc, bois / Park, bos
Beach / Strand		Plage / Strand
Restricted traffic zone / Zone mit Verkehrsbeschränkungen		Circulation réglementée par de péages / Zone met Verkeersbeperkingen
MARCO POLO Discovery Tour 1 / MARCO POLO Erlebnistour 1		MARCO POLO Tour d'aventure 1 / MARCO POLO Avontuurlijke Route 1
MARCO POLO Discovery Tours / MARCO POLO Erlebnistouren		MARCO POLO Tours d'aventure / MARCO POLO Avontuurlijke Routes
MARCO POLO Highlight		MARCO POLO Highlight

144

FOR YOUR NEXT TRIP...

MARCO POLO TRAVEL GUIDES

Algarve
Amsterdam
Andalucia
Athens
Australia
Austria
Bali & Lombok
Bangkok
Barcelona
Berlin
Brazil
Bruges
Brussels
Budapest
Bulgaria
California
Cambodia
Canada East
Canada West / Rockies & Vancouver
Cape Town & Garden Route
Cape Verde
Channel Islands
Chicago & The Lakes
China
Cologne
Copenhagen
Corfu
Costa Blanca & Valencia
Costa Brava
Costa del Sol & Granada
Costa Rica
Crete
Cuba
Cyprus (North and South)
Devon & Cornwall
Dresden
Dubai
Dublin
Dubrovnik & Dalmatian Coast
Edinburgh
Egypt
Egypt Red Sea Resorts
Finland
Florence
Florida
French Atlantic Coast
French Riviera (Nice, Cannes & Monaco)
Fuerteventura
Gran Canaria
Greece
Hamburg
Hong Kong & Macau
Ibiza
Iceland
India
India South
Ireland
Israel
Istanbul
Italy
Japan
Jordan
Kos
Krakow
Lake District
Lake Garda
Lanzarote
Las Vegas
Lisbon
London
Los Angeles
Madeira & Porto Santo
Madrid
Maldives
Mallorca
Malta & Gozo
Mauritius
Menorca
Milan
Montenegro
Morocco
Munich
Naples & Amalfi Coast
New York
New Zealand
Norway
Oslo
Oxford
Paris
Peru & Bolivia
Phuket
Portugal
Prague
Rhodes
Rome
Salzburg
San Francisco
Santorini
Sardinia
Scotland
Seychelles
Shanghai
Sicily
Singapore
South Africa
Sri Lanka
Stockholm
Switzerland
Tenerife
Thailand
Tokyo
Turkey
Turkey South Coast
Tuscany
United Arab Emirates
USA Southwest (Las Vegas, Colorado, New Mexico, Arizona & Utah)
Venice
Vienna
Vietnam
Zakynthos & Ithaca, Kefalonia, Lefkas

Travel with **Insider Tips**

INDEX

This index lists all sights, destinations and beaches, plus the names of important streets, places, names and key words featured in this guide.
Numbers in bold indicate a main entry

313@Somerset (Mall) 36, **75**
Action Theatre 89
Alkaff Mansion 108
Arab Street 24, 27, 49, 50, **51**, 125
Armenian Church 30
Art Science Museum 40
Arts House (Old Parliament) 31
Art Stage 23
Asian Civilisations Museum 26, **32**, 106
Bay South 41
Beaches (Sentosa) 57
Biennale 23
Boat Quay 24, 71, 83
Boon Lay 28
Botanic Gardens 23, 55, **58**, 88, 99, 114
Buddha Tooth Relic Temple 46
Bukit Pasoh 84
Capitol Building 32
Cathay (Mall) 36, **75**, 88
Cavenagh Bridge 101, 106
Central Business District 26, 28, 36
Changi Beach Park 55
Chay Yan Street 111
Chijmes **32**, 84
Chinatown 15, 18, 20, 24, 26, 27, **44**, 64, 65, 76, 78, 79, 80, 88, 93, 95, 96, 97, 101, 117, 125
Chinatown Heritage Centre 46
Chinatown Visitor Centre **47**, 125
Chinese Street Opera 88
Civil Defense Museum 114
Clarke Quay 46, 84, 93
Colonial Quarter **30**, 105, 115
Crane Dance 56
Dempsey Hill (Tanglin Village) **59**, 84
East Coast 55, 69
East Coast Park **60**, 96
East Coast Road 102
Elgin Bridge 105
Eng Hoon Street 113
Esplanade Theatres on the Bay 29, **40**, 65, 72, 88, 101, 106
Faber Peak Singapore 54, 109
Far East Square 47
Feng shui **21**, 25, 49
Former Ford Factory 60
Formula 1 **44**, 61, 82, 116, 117
Fort Canning Park **33**, 89
Fountain of Wealth 24, 39
Fuk Tak Ch'i Museum 47
Fullerton Complex 43
Fullerton Hotel 26, **34**
Fullerton, Sir Robert 34, 43
Gambling 25
Gardens by the Bay 23, 28, 39, **41**, 68, 108
Geylang Serai 58
Gillman Barracks 23, 29, **78**, 108
Guan Chuan Street 112
Haji Lane **51**, **77**
Hajjah Fatimah Mosque 51

Harbourfront 53
Hawker centres 15, 20, 62, **65**, 71
Helix Bridge 44
Henderson Waves 57, 108
Holland Village 58
Hort Park 57, 108
Indian Heritage Centre 51
Ion Orchard (Mall) 35, 72, **75**, 100
Istana 34
Jacob Ballas Children's Garden 114
Joo Chiat Road 103
Jurong Bird Park 60
Kampong Glam **49**, 50, 51, 84, 95, 97
Katong Antique House 102
Katong (Peranakan district) 71, 96, **102**
Keong Saik Road 46
Kidzania (entertainment centre) 114
Koon Seng Road 103
Kusu Island 57
Kwan Im Tong Hood Che Temple **34**, 38
Little India 15, 20, 24, 26, 27, **49**, 71, 77, 81, 84, 94, 101, 117, 125
Little India Arcade 81
MacRitchie Reserve 115
Malay Heritage Centre 50, **52**
Malls 24
Marang Trail 109
Marina Barrage 42, 125
Marina Bay 17, 26, 28, **39**, 75, 117, 125
Marina Bay City Gallery 42
Marina Bay Cruise Centre 42
Marina Bay Sands 21, 25, 26, 28, **43**, 65, 72, **75**, 101
Marina Bay Sands Hotel 39, 43, 90, **94**
Marina South Pier 42
Marine Life Park 56
Maritime Experiential Museum 56
Merlion 17
Merlion Park 43
Mount Faber **54**, 109
Mount Faber Scenic Park 54
Mount Imbiah 55
Mount Imbiah Lookout 55
Mustafa (department store) 80
National Design Centre **34**, 77, **78**
National Gallery Singapore 29, **34**
National Library 34
National Museum of Singapore 35
Ngee Ann City (Mall) 36, **76**
Night Safari (zoo) 61
Observation wheel (Singapore Flyer) 39, **44**
Old Parliament (Arts House) 31
Onan Road 104
One Fullerton 43
Orchard Road 13, 20, 24, 28, 29, **35**, 36, 72, 87, 100

Palawan Beach 57
Paragon (Mall) 36, 115
Park Connector 55
Pasir Ris 28
People's Park (cloth market) 80
Peranakan cuisine 62, 69
Peranakan culture 32, 102
Peranakan district (Katong) 71, 96, **102**
Peranakan Museum (Asian Civilisations Museum) 32
Pinnacle@Duxton 32
Qi-Tian-Gong-Tempel 112
Queen Elizabeth Walk 106
Raffles City 91
Raffles Hotel **36**, 84, **92**, 101
Raffles Monument 26, 105
Raffles Place 36
Raffles, Sir Thomas Stamford 16, 26, 27, 30, 33, 36, 58, 86, 105
Red Dot Design Museum 44
Religions 17
Resort World Sentosa 25, 54, **55**
River Safari (zoo) 61
Robertson Quay 84
Scotts Road 35
Sembawang 28
Seng Poh Road 112
Sentosa 17, 28, **53**, 67, 71, 95
Sentosa Boardwalk 54
Serangoon Road 28, 101
Shophouses 24
Siloso Beach 57
Singapore Art Museum 36
Singapore Chinese Cultural Centre (SCCC) 47
Singapore City Gallery (URA) 48
Singapore Flyer (observation wheel) 39, **44**, 125
Singapore Management University 37
Singapore Maritime Gallery 43
Singapore Repertory Theatre 89
Singapore Science Centre 114
Singapore Zoo 61
Singlish 24
Sino-English Catholic School 37
Skypark 43
Smith Street 65
Snow City 114
Southern Ridges **56**, 108
Sports Hub Singapore 61
Sri Krishnan Temple 38
Sri Mariamman Temple **48**, 101, 117
Sri Senpaga Vinayagar Temple 105
Sri Srinivasa Perumal Temple 116
Sri Thendayuthapani Temple 116
St Andrew's Cathedral 39
St John's Island 57
Sultan Mosque 51
Suntec City 24, 39
Takashimaya (department store) 36, 72, **76**, 100

146

CREDITS

Tan Si Chong Su Temple 49
Tanglin Village (Dempsey Hill) **59**, 84
Tanjong Beach 57
Telok Blangah Hill Top Park 108

Thian Hock Keng Temple 28, **49**
Tiong Bahru 63, **110**
Tiong Bahru Market 113
Universal Studios 14, 55
Victoria Theatre and Concert Hall 30, **39**, 88

Vivo City 53, **57**, 65, 68, 73, 87, 110, 115
Wave House 57
Wet markets 29, 125
Yong Siak Street 111
Zoo 61

WRITE TO US

e-mail: info@marcopologuides.co.uk

Did you have a great holiday?
Is there something on your mind?
Whatever it is, let us know!
Whether you want to praise, alert us to errors or give us a personal tip –
MARCO POLO would be pleased to hear from you.
We do everything we can to provide the very latest information for your trip.

Nevertheless, despite all of our authors' thorough research, errors can creep in. MARCO POLO does not accept any liability for this. Please contact us by e-mail or post.

MARCO POLO Travel Publishing Ltd
Pinewood, Chineham Business Park
Crockford Lane, Chineham
Basingstoke, Hampshire RG24 8AL
United Kingdom

PICTURE CREDITS
Cover photograph: Skyline with Sands Hotel and Gardens by the Bay (Getty Images: L. Mckie)
Photos: Corbis/Reuters: E. Su (68); R. Freyer (7, 11, 25, 26/27, 33, 48/49, 59, 60, 70 left, 72/73, 84, 90/91, 97, 98/99); Getty Images: L. Mckie (1 top); R. M. Gill (9, 30, 114/115); huber-images: M. Borchi (47), M. Rellini (4 bottom, 5, 12/13, 42), Scatà (92), Schmid (flap left, flap right, 4 top, 10, 20/21, 37, 40, 52, 54, 56/57, 70 right, 118 top), R. Schmid (2, 14/15, 62/63, 82/83); M. Kirchgessner (114); mauritius images/Alamy (3, 6, 8, 22, 35, 38, 44, 51, 64, 67, 79, 80, 87, 104, 110, 113, 118 bottom, 119, 130/131), B. Bachmann (19 top), R. Handley (76), T. Zaw Wai (19 bottom); mauritius images/Alamy/Art Kowalsky (18 bottom); mauritius images/Alamy/Stockimo: E. Tang (18 centre); mauritius images/foodcollection (18 top); mauritius images/ib: Stengert (17); mauritius images/John Warburton-Lee (95); mauritius images/Prisma (74); A. M. Mosler (89, 115); White Star: Reichelt (116, 116/117, 117)

3rd Edition 2020
fully revised and updated
Worldwide Distribution: Marco Polo Travel Publishing Ltd, Pinewood, Chineham Business Park, Crockford Lane, Basingstoke, Hampshire RG24 8AL, United Kingdom. E-mail: sales@marcopolouk.com
© MAIRDUMONT GmbH & Co. KG, Ostfildern
Chief editor: Stefanie Penck
Authors: Sabine and Dr. Christoph Hein; editor: Christina Sothmann
Programme supervision: Lucas Forst-Gill, Susanne Heimburger, Johanna Jiranek, Nikolai Michaelis, Kristin Wittemann, Tim Wohlbold
Picture editor: Gabriele Forst
What's hot: Sabine and Dr. Christoph Hein
Cartography street atlas & pull-out map: © MAIRDUMONT, Ostfildern
Design front cover, page 1, pull-out map cover: Karl Anders – Studio für Brand Profiling, Hamburg; design inside: milchhof : atelier, Berlin; design page 2/3, Discovery Tours: Susan Chaaban, Dipl.-Des. (FH)
Translated from German by Robert Scott McInnes, Jane Riester; Tom Ashforth; editor of the English edition: Sarah Trenker, Marlis von Hessert-Fraatz, Lizzie Gilbert
Prepress: Nazire Ergün, Cologne
All rights reserved. No part of this book may be reproduced, stored in a retrieval system or transmitted in any form or by any means (electronic, mechanical, photocopying, recording or otherwise) without prior written permission from the publisher.
Printed in China

MIX
Paper from responsible sources
FSC® C124385

DOS & DON'TS

A few things you should bear in mind in Singapore

DON'T BRING DRUGS

Do not even think about it: there are draconian punishments for even the smallest amount of drugs (e.g. designer drugs, hashish, cocaine, etc.) in Singapore, including the death penalty – and they also apply to foreigners. Merely being in possession is enough to get you into trouble.

DON'T SMOKE OR EAT CHEWING GUM

Smoking in air-conditioned restaurants, public buildings and lifts is forbidden – and the fine can amount to 1,000 S$. The famous ban on chewing gum was eased after twelve years: you can now buy two kinds of chewing gum 'for medicinal purposes' in chemist's shops – for example, as a substitute for nicotine for those trying to give up smoking. But you are naturally still not allowed to spit it out on the street.

DON'T GET TAKEN IN BY RIP-OFF ARTISTS AND TOUTS

Be careful of 'special' offers that initially appear to be extremely reasonable. They often turn out to be a rip-off. This can apply to tailors or the 'English student's' free tour of the city. It is the same with the touts who talk to you on the street 'Copy watch? T-shirts? Girls?' The *Official Singapore Guide,* which you can get free of charge at the airport, lists all those shops with the so-called *Singapore Gold Circle* guaranteeing their trustworthiness and quality.

DON'T UNDERESTIMATE THE SUN AND HEAT

Singapore is on the equator. The sun is scorching even when the sky is cloudy. You should also not forget that you will sweat a great deal – in spite of the high humidity. Drink a lot and often – at least three litres is recommended. Use sun creams with a high protection factor. You can buy them in all chemist's shops in Singapore – and usually cheaper than at home.

DON'T GO ON AN EXCURSION AT THE WEEKEND

From Saturday at noon to Sunday evening, hundreds of thousands of Singaporeans flock to all of the excursion destinations you also want to visit. If at all possible, try to visit them during the week from Monday to Friday.

DON'T TOUCH!

Some women try to blackmail foreign men by claiming that they have been sexually harrassed. You could be faced with legal proceedings and high fines. Just brushing against someone in the underground or disco can be enough. Keep your distance!